D1263242

LONE PARENTS, EMPLOYMENT AND SOCIAL POLICY

Cross-national comparisons

Edited by Jane Millar and Karen Rowlingson

DEMOGRAPHY LIBRARY
POPULATION STUDIES CTR.
UNIV. OF PENNSYLVANIA
403 MCNEIL/6298

First published in Great Britain in November 2001 by

The Policy Press
34 Tyndall's Park Road
Bristol BS8 1PY
UK

Tel +44 (0)117 954 6800
Fax +44 (0)117 973 7308
e-mail tpp@bristol.ac.uk
www.policypress.org.uk

Design and production of text and cover © The Policy Press 2001

Text © Jane Millar and Karen Rowlingson

British Library Cataloguing in Publication Data

A catalogue record for this book is available from the British Library

ISBN 1 86134 320 5 paperback

A hardcover version of this book is also available

Jane Millar is Professor of Social Policy and **Karen Rowlingson** is Lecturer in Social Research, both at the University of Bath, UK.

Cover design by Qube Design Associates, Bristol.

Front cover: photographs supplied by kind permission of Format Photographers, London.

The right of Jane Millar and Karen Rowlingson to be identified as editors of this work has been asserted by them in accordance with the 1988 Copyright, Designs and Patents Act.

All rights reserved: no part of this publication may be reproduced, stored in a retrieval system, or transmitted in any form or by any means, electronic, mechanical, photocopying, recording, or otherwise without the prior permission of The Policy Press.

The statements and opinions contained within this publication are solely those of the editor and contributors and not of The University of Bristol or The Policy Press. The University of Bristol and The Policy Press disclaim responsibility for any injury to persons or property resulting from any material published in this publication.

The Policy Press works to counter discrimination on grounds of gender, race, disability, age and sexuality.

Printed and bound in Great Britain by Hobbs the Printers Ltd, Southampton.

Contents

List of tables and figures

Tables

Figures

Acknowledgements

Thanks to our contributors for their speed, efficiency and willingness to deal with all our queries at short notice. Thanks also to Camilla Lucas at the University of Bath for her help in preparing the manuscript. Dawn Rushen at the Policy Press was the most helpful of the editors, and we greatly appreciate her patience and competence. The Department for Work and Pensions sponsored the seminar at which these papers were first presented and we are also grateful for their support. Jane Millar would also like to thank colleagues in the Political Science Program at the Australian National University, where she spent some time as a visitor while working on this book.

Jane Millar
Karen Rowlingson
Centre for the Analysis of Social Policy,
University of Bath
October 2001

Notes on contributors

Jonathan Bradshaw is Professor of Social Policy at the University of York and Associate Director of the Social Policy Research Unit. His main research interests are in poverty, living standards, family change and comparative social policy. His two most recent books are *Poverty: The outcomes for children* (Family Policy Studies Centre, 2001) and *Absent fathers?* (Routledge, 1999). He is current President of the Foundation for International Studies in Social Security (FISS).

Christine Chambaz works in the Directorate of Research, Statistical Studies and Evaluation (DREES) in the French Ministry of Employment and Solidarity. Her main activity consists of studying the impact of social transfers on living standard inequalities and poverty, by microsimulating the French social and fiscal system and by drawing analysis from large surveys, such as the European Community Household Panel.

Sandra K. Danziger is Associate Professor of Social Work and Director, Program on Poverty and Social Welfare Policy, University of Michigan. Her research examines family well-being and welfare policy implementation. She recently co-authored 'Human capital, physical health, and mental health of welfare recipients: correlates and consequences', *Journal of Social Issues* (2000).

Sheldon Danziger is Henry J. Meyer Collegiate Professor of Social Work and Public Policy and Director of the Center on Poverty, Risk and Mental Health at the University of Michigan. He is the co-author of *America unequal* (Harvard University Press and Russell Sage Foundation, 1995) and *Detroit divided* (Russell Sage Foundation, 2000), co-editor of *Confronting poverty* (Harvard University Press and Russell Sage Foundation, 1994) and *Securing the future* (Russell Sage Foundation, 2000) and author of numerous articles and book chapters.

Majella Kilkey is Lecturer in Social Policy at the School of Comparative and Applied Social Sciences, University of Hull. She is a co-author of *The employment of lone parents: A comparison of policy in 20 countries* (Family Policy Studies Centre, 1996), and author of *Lone mothers between paid work and care. The policy regime in twenty countries* (Ashgate, 2000).

Trudie Knijn is Associate Professor at the Faculty of Social Sciences, Department of Cross-Cultural Studies, University of Utrecht. She has published articles on care (services) and welfare states, gender and citizenship, and welfare policies for lone mothers. She is the co-author of 'Careful or lenient: welfare reform for lone parents in the Netherlands', *Journal of European Social Policy* (2001).

Hilary Land is Professor of Family Policy and Child Welfare at the University of Bristol. She has a long-standing interest in family policies from comparative and historical perspectives. Recent publications include (with Kathleen Kiernan and Jane Lewis), *Lone motherhood in twentieth century Britain* (Open University Press, 1999) and 'New Labour, new families?' in *Social Policy Review 11*, edited by Hartley Dean (1999).

Jane Lewis is Barnett Professor of Social Policy at the University of Oxford. She is the editor of *Lone mothers in European welfare regimes* (Jessica Kingsley, 1997) and the author of *The end of marriage? Individualism in intimate relationships* (Edward Elgar, 2001).

Ruth Lister is Professor of Social Policy at Loughborough University. Her research interests include poverty and social security, citizenship and gender. Her most recent book is *Citizenship: Feminist perspectives* (Macmillan, 1997).

Alan Marsh is Professor of Social Policy at the University of Westminster and Deputy Director of the Policy Studies Institute (PSI). At PSI he carries out a programme of research into social change and social security policy focused on low-income families, lone parents, and disabled people. He has recently published *Low-income families in Britain: Work, welfare and social security in 1999* (DSS, 2001).

Claude Martin is a Sociologist, Research Fellow at the Centre national de la recherche scientifique (CNRS) and Professor in the Institut d'études politiques in Rennes (France). He is also Director of the Laboratoire d'analyse des politiques sociales et sanitaires (National School of Public Health). His research interests are the welfare state, social and family policies reforms in Europe. Recent publications include *l'Après divorce* (Presses Universitaires de Rennes, 1997) and, with J. Commaille, *Les enjeux politiques de la famille* (Bayard éditions, 1998).

Jane Millar is Professor of Social Policy and Director of the Centre for the Analysis of Social Policy at the University of Bath. Her main research interests are social security and family policy, especially lone parenthood, poverty, and support for children. Recent publications include *Private lives, public responses: Lone parenthood and future policy* (PSI, 1998, co-editor with Reuben Ford); and the chapter on the UK in *Benefits for children: A four country study* (edited by K. Battle and M. Mendelson, Caledon Institute, Canada, 2001).

Karen Rowlingson is a Lecturer in Social Research at the University of Bath. She has previously worked at the PSI where she carried out research into lone parenthood and family finances. She has published *Social security in Britain* (Macmillan, 1999) and *The growth of lone parenthood* (PSI, 1998) both with Stephen McKay.

Kristin S. Seefeldt is a Senior Research Associate in the University of Michigan's School of Social Work. Her research focuses on implementation analysis and field research of welfare and employment and training policies and programmes. With Sandra Danziger, she is the author of 'Ending welfare through work first' (*Families in Society*, 2000).

Anne Skevik is a researcher at NOVA (Norwegian Social Research). Her main research interests are lone parenthood; comparative family policy; and child maintenance arrangements. Recent publications include the doctorate thesis, *Family ideology and social policy: Policies toward lone parents in Norway and the UK* (NOVA, Oslo, 2001).

Frits van Wel is Assistant Professor at the Faculty of Social Sciences, Department of Cross-Cultural Studies, University of Utrecht. He has published articles on (lone) motherhood in the Netherlands, social intervention, and youth cultures. He is co-author of 'The labor market orientation of single mothers on welfare in the Netherlands', *Journal of the Marriage and the Family* (2001).

Jane Waldfogel is Associate Professor of Social Work and Public Affairs at Columbia University School of Social Work, and Research Associate at the Centre for Analysis of Social Exclusion at the London School of Economics and Political Science. She studies family leave, childcare, welfare, and child welfare. She is the author of *The future of child protection* (Harvard,

1998) and co-editor (with Sheldon Danziger) of *Securing the future* (Russell Sage, 2000).

Peter Whiteford is Principal Administrator (Social Policies), Non-Member Economies and International Migration Division of the Organization for Economic Co-operation and Development (OECD). He has worked in the Australian Department of Family and Community Services, and at the University of York, UK and the University of New South Wales, Australia. His recent research has concentrated on international comparisons of systems of social protection and of poverty and income distribution.

Foreword: Lone parents: the UK policy context

This foreword sketches the broader policy context within which policies towards lone parents and employment are being developed in the UK. In some ways, policies towards lone parents are emblematic of New Labour's welfare reform project, the dominant theme of which can be summed up in the two mantras: 'reforming welfare around the work ethic' and a third way in welfare 'that believes in empowerment not dependency'. Policies to encourage lone parents off social assistance and into paid work are a key plank in delivering the project.

Lone parents have also been at the centre of controversy over benefit levels. When New Labour came to power it gave notice that it rejected a status quo supported by those who "believe that poverty is relieved exclusively by cash handouts" (DSS, 1998, p 19). Improving benefit levels for those not in work was regarded as 'old Labour' and therefore not on the agenda. Furthermore, within a few months of coming to power, the government implemented a Conservative plan to abolish the modest additional benefits paid to lone parents, both in and out of work, which followed a period of vilification of lone mothers by Conservative politicians and the media. They were cast as "a drain on public expenditure and as a threat to the stability and order associated with the traditional two-parent family" (Kiernan et al, 1998, p 2). This discourse of lone mothers as a threat overlaid a longer standing discourse of lone mothers as a problem.

The decision to go ahead with the abolition of lone parent benefits created an outcry, which took the government aback. It created an enormous amount of ill-feeling and contributed to a widespread perception that the welfare reform agenda was a cuts agenda. However, partly as a result of the anger generated, there was something of a rethink on the benefits front in the 1998 Budget a few months later. Improvements in benefits for children in families both in and out of work were announced. A year later the Prime Minister committed the government to the eradication of child poverty in two decades and one of its policy tools is proving to be further improvements in children's benefits.

These two themes – an active welfare state focused on work not welfare (New Labour) and the eradication of child poverty (old Labour) – are explored briefly. This is followed by discussion of a rather less well articulated theme, described as the crossing of the Rubicon from "the left bank of welfare-for-all to the right bank of means-testing" (*The Economist*, 6 March 1999).

An active welfare state

The 1998 Green Paper on welfare reform established the central principle of welfare reform as: "work for those who can, security for those who cannot". It held out a vision of "a new welfare contract" in which the first two duties of the individual are to "seek training or work where able to do so" and to "take up the opportunity to be independent if able to do so". The first duties on government are to "provide people with the assistance they need to find work" and to "make work pay" (DSS, 1998, p 80). This encapsulates the central concerns to promote responsibility and opportunity, primarily through paid work (see Lister, 2002: forthcoming).

Welfare-to-work

The vehicle for exercising these responsibilities and seizing these opportunities is a series of New Deal 'welfare-to-work' programmes (see Chapter Two) together with a new integrated 'working age agency'. The aim of the new agency, the Prime Minister announced, is "to accelerate the move from a welfare system that primarily provides passive support to one that provides active support to help people become independent" through paid work. He emphasised that it will promote a 'new culture' of independence and responsibilities and will develop the "partnership approach to working with local authorities and the private and voluntary sectors" in delivering welfare-to-work policies (Blair, 2000).

The introduction of the working age agency is linked to that of a new requirement that virtually all claimants of working age will have to attend interviews with a personal adviser to discuss the prospects of finding work. Although there is no work obligation as such on lone parents and others not actually classified as unemployed, attendance at the interviews will be a pre-condition of an initial claim and of subsequent entitlement to full benefit. This new requirement was announced in 'tough' language typical of New Labour when it wants to impress Middle England. The Social Security Secretary, for instance, made clear that there were to be "no apologies" for "our tough benefits regime" (*The Independent*, 10 February 1999).

Typical of this 'tough benefits regime' is increasingly punitive sanctions for unemployed people who fail to comply with the New Deal, as well as a series of drives against 'fraudsters', aimed particularly at those believed to be working 'on the side' while claiming benefit. The view is that, with unemployment at its lowest overall level for years and with the assistance that the government is now providing, there is no excuse for people not to take full-time jobs in the formal labour market. In other words, with opportunities come responsibilities.

However, critics argue that there are still parts of the country, in which the groups covered by the New Deal tend to be concentrated, where the jobs are not available. There is also a growing concern that such strict and inflexible social security rules are discouraging people from volunteering and contributing to their communities, in other words from exercising responsibility in ways other than through a job. This links in with arguments, put particularly in relation to lone parents, about the need to value the work of care as a form of citizenship responsibility.

The government's responsibility agenda, although focused primarily on paid work, is not confined to it. It is using the benefit system more generally explicitly to promote responsible behaviour in ways which are novel in the modern UK benefits system. Similarly, its reforms of the child maintenance system emphasise the financial responsibilities of non-resident parents.

Making work pay

The other piece in the active welfare state jigsaw is the raft of policies designed to 'make work pay' – the carrots to sweeten the sticks. These are of two kinds, aimed at increasing in-work incomes and at easing the transition into paid work. Policies to increase in-work incomes include:

- the introduction of a statutory minimum wage for the very first time in the UK; despite its low level, it is of particular importance to female workers;
- a real increase in child benefit – especially for the first/oldest child;
- the introduction of new tax credits administered by the Inland Revenue, in place of less generous means-tested benefits.

Payment of the credits through the wage packet is supposed to signal more clearly that 'work pays' and to be less stigmatising than the cash benefits they replace. This remains to be proven. In fact, in face of criticism that payment of the Working Families' Tax Credit (WFTC) through the wage packet would mean a shift in resources from mothers to fathers, to the detriment of children, the government compromised and agreed that one-earner couples could have a choice as to payee. Subsequently, it accepted the argument completely. It now proposes, from 2003, to replace the WFTC with a new Integrated Child Credit (ICC) paid to the caring parent, alongside an Employment Tax Credit (ETC) for low-income working adults, whether or not they have children.

A number of small but useful changes are being introduced to ease the transition into paid work and to cushion people if they fall back onto benefit after a short period. In addition, there are also a number of limited 'family-friendly' employment measures, mainly the result of European directives, and a national childcare strategy (see Chapter Twelve).

Eradication of child poverty

Most of these initiatives also contribute to the goal of the eradication of child poverty, the level of which is one of the highest in the industrialised world. There are, in addition, further measures more specifically targeted on this goal, involving both benefits and services.

Benefits

Of particular significance has been a phased 80% real increase (by October 2001) in the income support rates paid for children aged under 11 and a smaller real increase for older children. This is a very welcome move but the government is reluctant to trumpet it, so as not to alienate 'Middle England' tax payers. The result is that many people seem unaware of it and continue to criticise the government for doing nothing for families not in work.

Despite these improvements (and also some improvements to certain benefits for severely disabled people, pensioners and carers), the government has resisted calls for a comprehensive review of the adequacy of benefits. There has been no public official review of benefit levels since they were first set after the Second World War.

There have also been some improvements to maternity benefits, including a trebling of the lump sum maternity grant paid to poorer mothers (with a further £200 increase promised in 2002). More in tune with the New Labour philosophy, the increase was 'in return for parents meeting their responsibilities', that is, the grant will be conditional on attendance at child health check-ups, which is a new departure in UK social security policy but is a long-established practice in France.

Services

The maternity grant has been incorporated into a new Sure Start programme, inspired by practice in the US. Sure Start works with children aged under three and their parents to promote children's physical, social and emotional development. There is also to be a new Children's Fund. The bulk of it will be devoted to local preventive work with children primarily in the 5-13 age group, in partnership with local authorities and the voluntary sector.

Although these services are not part of the welfare reform programme as such, they do exemplify how that programme is part of a wider strategy for tackling poverty and social exclusion. They also illustrate how that wider strategy places particular emphasis on area-based interventions and partnership between the statutory and other sectors.

The initial pledge to abolish child poverty in two decades has been supplemented with a further pledge to halve it in one and also to publish annual monitoring reports. In 2000, the government estimated that it will have lifted 1.2 million children out of poverty by the end of its first Parliament. This is broadly in line with independent analysis. Overall, it is an impressive start, but there is still a long way to go, given that there are over four million children in poverty.

Across the means-testing Rubicon

The final theme can be discerned in a number of policy measures, which together are strengthening the means-tested side of the social security system relative to its universal and contributory elements. This is not an explicit strategy and indeed there are some counter examples. Nevertheless, a growing number of commentators are suggesting that we are witnessing the slow death of National Insurance (NI) and movement towards a two-tier system in which the majority are expected to look to private sources of insurance and the poor have to rely on means-tested support. Those expressing concern about the demise of NI include the government's Social Security Advisory Committee and the House of Commons Social Security Select Committee. The latter has expressed 'unease' that the NI system "is disappearing by default, without proper acknowledgement or debate" (2000, para 1).

Ministers themselves are disinclined to debate the issue of the balance between different kinds of benefit. They prefer a pragmatic 'what works' approach, although some argue that means-tested benefits do not work very well and could undermine other goals such as promoting personal responsibility.

At the same time, although there has been a real increase in the value of child benefit, means-tested support for children is being increased by significantly more and the proposed ETC can be seen as an extension of means-tested subsidies for low pay. Moreover, it and the proposed ICC have been described by the Treasury as "a further important step towards tax and benefit integration" (HM Treasury, 2000a, para 2.29), the implication being the further extension of means-testing. This, the Chancellor of the Exchequer has made clear, will mean cementing the couple rather than the individual as the basic benefit unit, with possible implications for independent taxation.

Conclusion

The government is clear in its objectives to create a social security system focused on promoting paid work and to end child poverty. Beyond that, the direction of welfare reform is not always obvious, especially when the reality and the rhetoric are at odds with each other – sometimes with a more progressive reality than rhetoric (Lister, 2000b).

In terms of the underlying structure of social security, that is, the balance between contributory, categorical and means-tested benefits, there is no explicit strategy at all. Instead, there are a number of pragmatic steps, made in the name of 'targeting' and of 'what works', which could result in a rather different welfare mix to that traditionally associated with the UK: one which shifts us further towards a liberal residual model of welfare, albeit of a uniquely British variety (Glennerster, 1999).

Ruth Lister
Loughborough, 2001

Comparing employment policies for lone parents cross-nationally: an introduction

Jane Millar and Karen Rowlingson

Policy towards lone parents in the UK has undergone significant changes since 1997. In particular, for the first time in the post-war period, the government is offering positive support for lone parents to enter the labour market. A target has now been set to reach a lone-parent employment rate of 70% within 10 years (DfEE, 2001a). This is being implemented through policies that are intended to support and encourage lone parents to take up employment, including in-work benefits and improved support for childcare. Lone parents receiving Income Support will have to take part in compulsory work-focused interviews but benefit support will continue to be available to those who do not choose to enter paid work. However, in some other countries more radical measures have been introduced, with lone parents being required to seek work, to take up training, or to participate in work or work-based employment programmes, as a condition of benefit receipt.

The aim of this book is to explore the nature of the policy changes affecting lone parents, the rationale for these, the way in which they are being implemented, and the outcomes for lone parents and their children. The approach is both country specific and thematic. Part 1 includes six country-based chapters that provide a detailed and contextualised examination of national policy goals, how these have been implemented, and their outcomes. Part 2 includes five chapters that explore particular aspects of policy through comparative cross-national analysis, and a concluding chapter that reviews future policy options. This chapter provides an introduction to the collection through a discussion of three topics: the aims of the book; the choice of the countries included and the topics covered for each; and the five thematic issues addressed.

Before turning to the specifics of the issues to be addressed in the book, however, it is worth pausing to note the wider importance of these policy trends. As Ruth Lister points out in the foreword, the government is committed to the creation of an 'active welfare state', in which the main role of policy is to enable people to support themselves through paid employment. Including lone parents in this goal – even on a voluntary basis – represents a break with the past, and a shift away from the assumptions about the role of mothers that have shaped UK policy for many years. It places paid work at the centre of the relationship between citizen and the state, with active participation in society defined in terms of active participation in employment (Levitas, 1998; Lister, 2000a). This raises questions about the nature and extent of the social rights of those who provide unpaid care work in the family, as most women continue to do. What happens to 'rights to give and receive care' (Knijn and Kremer, 1997) if all working-age adults are expected and required to engage in paid labour? This tension between requirements to work and obligations to care is particularly visible in respect of lone mothers, as is clear from the policy debates and recent policy changes that are discussed in this book.

Examining policy and understanding implementation

The government has cited cross-national comparisons of employment rates for lone parents to argue that it is possible to achieve higher employment rates in the UK. For example, in the Treasury's pre-Budget report in November 2000:

> Employment rates of lone parents in the UK are low, both in comparison to lone parents in other countries and compared to mothers in couples in the UK.... More recently, the proportion of lone parents in work in the UK has begun to rise ... although the UK still lags substantially behind other industrialised countries. In the US, around 70 per cent of lone parents are in work, and in France over 80 per cent. The reasons for these differences are complex but may include the demographic characteristics of lone parents, health and education, the area in which they live, the availability and cost of childcare, work requirements and, historically, the gains to work. Yet the characteristics of lone parents in both France and, particularly, the US are broadly similar to those of lone parents in the UK. (HM Treasury, 2000b, Box 4.2)

A number of previous cross-national studies have sought to explain these variations in employment rates, most comprehensively the study by Jonathan Bradshaw and his colleagues in the mid-1990s (Bradshaw et al, 1996), and from a more socio-cultural perspective in the work of Simon Duncan and Rosalind Edwards (Duncan and Edwards, 1997b). Our aim in making cross-national comparisons is, however, rather different. We did not set out to explain cross-national variations in employment rates, but to explore the policy measures behind these and specifically to examine how other countries were putting work-based systems for lone parents into practice, and with what results. To do this it was necessary to place these policy measures in their national context, in order to explain the nature and form of these.

This was the agenda addressed in the policy-oriented seminar that provided the starting point for this book. The seminar was held at the University of Bath in the autumn of 2000, funded by the Department of Social Security[1] and attended by representatives from several other government departments involved in making and implementing policy for lone parents. The focus on policy implementation and policy outcomes was intended to help policy makers consider, evaluate and develop different policy options. We wanted to explore the potential advantages and disadvantages of these policy shifts to employment-based systems, to examine how policy goals were being translated into practical measures, and to analyse how success (or failure) was being defined and measured.

The countries and topics

The countries included were chosen to represent a variety of approaches to the issue of lone parents and employment, but also to include countries which have made policy changes in the same sort of direction as the UK. Three are European countries: France, the Netherlands and Norway. The other two are English-speaking and non-European: Australia and the US. There is also a chapter exploring the same issues in the UK itself. The authors were asked to address (as far as possible) a set of common issues which included: describing the demographic profile of lone parenthood; the labour market participation rates of lone and married mothers; attitudes to employment; the rules regarding employment obligations and whether, how and why these had changed; the operation of labour market programmes; the nature and level of other measures to support employment, especially 'make work pay' and childcare policies; and the way in which outcomes were being defined and measured. In addition to this wealth of information, the authors were also asked to place this in context, to provide a rounded picture that would help the reader understand the genesis of policy change, and how policy towards lone parents related to the wider social and economic policy agenda within each country.

Many countries could have been included but, as in all cross-national research, it was necessary to select and focus on particular cases. We chose these pragmatically rather than theoretically. In each case there was some aspect of policy and/or practice that we thought particularly interesting and potentially illuminating to UK policy debates. The US was an obvious choice in this respect, with US policy and evidence already playing a significant role in policy debates in the UK. In 1996, the US introduced the Personal Responsibility and Work Opportunity Reconciliation Act, which, among other measures, made it compulsory to participate in employment or employment-related activities as a condition of receiving welfare, even for lone mothers with very young children. It also gave the individual states a great deal of autonomy in how they applied the new system, making state variation even more substantial and thus providing a range of examples of policy and practice innovation. State support for childcare has increased substantially and so have the federal programmes to 'make work pay', especially the Earned Income Tax Credit.

Australia was chosen because of the apparent similarities between the New Deal for Lone Parents and their main labour market programme for lone parents, the Jobs, Education and Training (JET) programme introduced in 1989. This is a voluntary programme, in which participants are assessed by a JET adviser, who can then refer them for education, fund a pre-vocational course, or refer them for assistance with looking for work. Australia is also interesting because lone and married mothers are not treated as separate categories for benefit purposes, with the Parenting Payment (Single) for lone parents and the Parenting Payment (Partnered) for partners (usually wives) of income support recipients with dependent children. And Australia is currently introducing some of the same sorts of policies as the UK, including compulsory work-focused interviews for lone parents with primary school age children.

Of the European countries, Norway and the Netherlands were chosen because both have recently introduced new activity requirements for lone parents. In Norway lone parents used to be eligible for the 'transitional allowance' without a work test until the youngest child was aged 10. Since 1998, receipt of this benefit has been limited to three years (five if the parent is in education) and only those with children aged under eight are eligible. Lone parents with children aged over three are required either to seek work, take a part-time job, or take part in education and training as a condition of receiving benefit. In the Netherlands there is no special lone-parent benefit, but lone parents receiving social assistance were not required to seek work if they had dependent children under the age of 18. From 1996, lone parents with a youngest child aged over five may be required to be available for full-time or part-time work, at the discretion of the local social assistance office. There are now proposals to extend some activity requirements to all lone parents, regardless of the age of the child. By contrast, France was chosen as a country where there has been no recent policy change and which has apparently already achieved what many of the other countries are seeking: relatively high employment rates for lone parents, alongside relatively generous lone-parent benefits.

The countries thus represent a range of different approaches to employment-related policies for lone parents: compulsory or voluntary; with different definitions of the group covered; treating lone parents as a separate group or within the general system; combining national and local or federal and state systems; and with varying degrees of discretion in administration.

The countries also vary in terms of the context within which lone parenthood exists. The US has the highest rate of lone parenthood in the developed world, followed some way behind by the UK and Norway. Australia has a slightly lower rate of lone parenthood, with the Netherlands a further step away. France has the lowest rate of lone parenthood of all the countries covered in this book. In the US and UK, teenage lone parenthood and single motherhood are much more common than in the other countries.

There are also differences in terms of the employment rates of lone parents in these countries. France has the highest rate of employment for lone mothers in all these countries, followed by Norway and the US in a second tier, then by Australia, the UK and the Netherlands. There are also variations in the relative generosity of benefit rates for lone parents, and these do not seem to be linked to employment rates. Benefit rates for 'inactive' lone parents in the US (where they are allowed to qualify for such benefits) are very meagre. The UK's system of support for non-employed lone parents is also not generous, although there have been recent changes that have substantially increased benefit levels for children in families receiving Income Support. In Australia the parenting benefits are set at 25% of average male earnings. The most generous levels of support for non-employed lone parents are in France, the Netherlands and Norway.

In terms of the relationship between poverty and lone parenthood, the US and then the UK have the highest rates of poverty among lone parents, and these have increased in recent years. Poverty rates are also relatively high in Australia but have fallen since the 1980s. Lone parents in France, Norway and the Netherlands have low rates of lone-parent poverty.

There are thus both similarities and differences across these countries. Our national and thematic approach allows us to compare policies within these various contexts to see how they work (or do not work) in practice.

The themes

Part 2 of the book explores a number of more general themes. These chapters are partly based on the national chapters, making comparisons across these six countries. But the thematic chapters also take a wider view, first by placing these six countries in the context of other countries and their policies; and second, by placing policy for lone parents in the context of social policy more generally. This includes, for example, policies intended to help parents reconcile work and family life, policies aimed at tackling poverty among poor families, and welfare-to-work policies as they affect unemployed people and other benefit recipients.

The first chapter in Part 2 starts with wider issues and discusses how changing assumptions about the gendered division of labour within the family are influencing policy in many countries. This includes a critical assessment of both the extent to which this is justified by actual changes in the work/care practices of women and men, and the extent to which care work is adequately addressed by policy makers and governments. The second chapter is also contextual, but in a different way. This chapter summarises cross-national evidence on demographic trends in lone parenthood, how these vary across countries, and how far they explain differences in the labour market participation rates.

These two chapters provide the context for the three following chapters, which return to specific policy areas. These chapters examine in turn the three main types of policies and programmes that have been introduced with the aim of helping lone parents enter, and stay in, paid work. These are measures to *make work possible* (labour market programmes); to *make work pay* (financial support for employment); and to *make work feasible* (measures to help reconcile work and family life). Each of these encompasses a range of different possible policy instruments, and the chapters describe these, assess the sort of impact they have had in different contexts, and consider whether there are any lessons or implications for UK policy. The final chapter also considers implications for the UK. It first of all considers what lessons can be drawn about specific policy measures, and then discusses broader issues that affect whether or not policies to encourage lone parents to get and keep paid work will be successful.

Overall, the book gives a comprehensive account of existing and emerging employment-based policies for lone parents; their origins, objectives and implementation.

Note

[1] We are grateful to the Department of Social Security (now the Department for Work and Pensions) for funding the seminar.

Part 1: Policies within specific countries

TWO

Helping British lone parents get and keep paid work[1]

Alan Marsh

Introduction

By most international comparisons British lone parents have low rates of labour market participation. Fewer than four out of 10 work full time, which in Britain is 16 hours a week or more, when they qualify for in-work benefits. Britain also has more lone parents than most other countries. About one in four of Britain's seven million families with dependent children are headed by a lone parent, which is a threefold increase in 25 years. This means that 1.7 million lone-parent families are caring for about three million children. More than nine out of 10 of them are women. Six out of 10 rely on out-of-work benefits, often for long periods, and more than half live in social accommodation. They are prone to hardship and form the largest group in Britain among people of working age who live on household incomes below half the national average. This chapter sets out the development of policy in this area. It next provides a profile of lone parents' demographic and employment patterns in Britain. The chapter then discusses the incentives and barriers to work before speculating about the future direction of policy.

The development of policy

It is beyond debate that Britain's lone-parent families need more income and it would be hard to argue that increased labour market participation, where possible, should not provide part of this increase. To this end, British 'welfare-to-work' policy has four main strands:

- wage supplementation, including cash payments through Working Families' Tax Credit (WFTC) and a National Minimum Wage, to 'make work pay';
- active case management;
- child support payments;
- a national childcare strategy, including cash additions to wage supplements.

Making work pay

Since 1971, successive British administrations have relied on direct wage subsidies to try to ensure that parents have an incentive to work greater than the value of their benefits when out of work. This is especially important for lone parents because unlike couples with children, they are not required to seek work until their youngest child is 16 or 18 years old and in full-time education.

From 1971, Family Income Supplement (FIS) provided limited cash payments to parents working more than 30 hours a week. Family Income Supplement had a poor record, reaching only about 200,000 families and leaving some worse off in work. Family Credit replaced FIS in April 1988, lowering the qualifying hours of work to 24 per week and based on a net income formula. No one could now become worse off by earning more, though withdrawal rates of benefit entitlement against new income remained high, typically between 70 and 80%, creating what Field and Piachaud (1971) have called 'the poverty trap'.

In 1991, 350,000 families received Family Credit, 38% of them lone parents. In 1992, the qualifying hours were further reduced to 16 per week, which particularly assisted lone parents. Other reforms included useful bridging payments of Housing Benefit to ease the transition to work, introduced in October 1996. By 1999 the caseload had risen to 800,000 families and half were lone parents.

Thus, a policy emerged that relied on a system of 'in-work benefits' to supplement the wages of low-paid workers with children, led by Family Credit and backed up by Housing Benefit and Council Tax Benefit for those with high housing costs, high local taxes and small wages. The policy drew criticism from those who felt that extending means testing for people in work was unfair and attracted stigma. The proportion with 'withdrawal rates' of over 80% had increased and compared unfavourably with the much-reduced tax regime for better-off families. People could become discouraged and get stuck in low-paid jobs when they might be striving for better terms. A dependency on out-of-work benefits was replaced, it was said, by a dependency in work.

It is hard to know whether remaining in low-paid work is being 'stuck' or just a sensible strategy that balances demanding home care with undemanding or short working hours (Bryson et al, 1997). The gains for lone parents were marked since the adult component of their Family Credit was the same as for couples. As for renewed dependency in work, research indicated that families who could move on from Family Credit did so unhesitatingly (Bryson and Marsh, 1996). There was, anyway, an awareness that their Family Credit would no longer be available when children grew up and the disincentive of high withdrawal rates were cushioned by the six-month duration of the awards.

In October 1999, Family Credit was replaced by Working Families' Tax Credit. This is not a tax credit in the full sense, since it is not worked out annually at the same time as tax codes are worked out, but separately every six months. Many recipients also qualify for other health and welfare benefits[2]. Working Families' Tax Credit offered several improvements over Family Credit. The rates of payment were increased and the withdrawal rate against new income was reduced from 70 to 55%, which eased the poverty trap[3]. Help with childcare was altered so that even those with the smallest wages would now benefit. Whereas Family Credit allowed recipients to keep £15 a week in Child Support, all such payments are now ignored when working out WFTC.

As a result of these changes, lone parents who work, claim WFTC and receive child support payments, can now expect a standard of living similar to those of many single-earner couples with children. Potentially, this is a major improvement. The difficulty is that only a minority of lone parents will receive all three elements of this income package. However, as from April 2001, the new system delivers a guaranteed *minimum* income of £214 a week to any family with two children receiving WFTC, and typically they will have more. This compares with an equivalised average income after housing costs of £108 a week for lone parents who were out of work in 1999 (Marsh et al, 2001, Table 5.1). The loss of other benefits, on the other hand, typically the loss of help with housing costs and local taxes from in-work incomes, reduces the difference between these two figures. And those getting extra help with childcare still have to find 30% of their outlay, which from small wages can be a drain on final income.

The new system has been underpinned by three other measures:

- the introduction in April 1999 of a National Minimum Wage, now £3.70 (€6.00) an hour, which effectively prevents too much of the wage subsidy from ending up in employers' pockets;
- adjustments to National Insurance payments that removed the lowest paid from liability but protected their benefits, a problem which had previously undermined the position of low-paid female workers;
- the introduction of higher tax thresholds and a 10p in the pound tax rate for the lowest paid.

As a policy, all this amounts to a deep commitment to low-wage subsidy.

Active case management

The Labour government came to office in 1997 with a manifesto commitment to introduce a range of New Deal programmes for both the unemployed and the *non*-employed. The first was a New Deal for Lone Parents (NDLP) whose design had taken on board lessons from the evaluation of the Australian Jobs, Education and Training (JET) scheme and the Greater Avenues for Independence (GAIN) programme in California. Lone parents whose youngest child was older than five years and three months were invited to attend voluntarily a meeting with a personal adviser. This meeting considered the whole range of their circumstances influencing their preparation for work.

Evaluation of the early stages of the NDLP was positive. Although the majority of those invited declined to attend, quite large numbers of unexpected volunteers from among those with children younger than five turned up looking for advice. Obviously, personal advisers had the luxury of dealing with clients who were, to varying degrees, keen to work. Their advice was well received. Half the programme participants got work and 28% of these credited their personal adviser with a significant part in their success. Others said that their search was made easier by the help they received. Compared to similar areas, the eight areas chosen to pilot NDLP achieved a 3.3% improvement in the rate of return to work (Hales et al, 2000). The scheme began nationally in 1998.

Two recent developments have set aside the voluntary nature of coming into the office to hear advice from a personal adviser:

- *The ONE⁴ experiment* is aimed at the in-flow to benefit. New benefit claimants, including lone parents, will be required to meet a personal adviser as a condition of their claim being processed.

• *The work-focused interview* (the personal adviser meeting) will be aimed more at the stock of benefit claimants, starting with those whose youngest child is 13 to 15 years old. From April 2001 onwards these interviews are compulsory for lone parents with older children.

Child support

The introduction of the Child Support Agency (CSA) in 1995 removed from the courts the responsibility for recovering from non-resident parents a proportion of their income for the financial support of their children. It was not explicitly a pro-employment policy for lone parents. Had it been more successful in boosting the proportion achieving payments, however, an increase in the proportion working would probably have resulted. Given its new simplified formula for calculating liability and new lease of life, it may yet do so. It was known that lone parents who worked were more likely to receive child support payments (Bradshaw and Millar, 1991). But this was thought to be one more among other advantages that better educated women had, including the ability in their own right to return to work when they needed to. Subsequent research showed that when educationally disadvantaged lone parents receive maintenance it helps them get work (Finlayson and Marsh, 1998). It provides an income they can rely on in work, which under the new rules for WFTC leaves their cash subsidy untouched.

The national childcare strategy

The Department for Education and Employment is supporting a national strategy aimed to improve the availability of good quality childcare for children up to the age of 14. It has concentrated on starting children in full-time education at the age of four rather than five and on the provision of after-school clubs and holiday schemes, effectively lengthening the school day nearer to their parents' working hours. This measure is aimed at the most often cited problem of bridging the gap between three and six o'clock each afternoon.

Demographic and employment patterns

A social profile of Britain's lone parents

Demographics

Table 2.1 provides a summary of the main social characteristics of Britain's lone parents in 1999, and compares these distributions with similar surveys carried out over the past 10 years.

As their numbers grew, so the social composition of lone parents changed. In the early 1970s, a fifth of Britain's 600,000 lone parents were widows. Now only 4% are widows. Growth in the late 1970s and early 1980s was first associated with a surge in separations from marriage and divorce. Later, new growth came from a sharp increase in the proportion who had never married or cohabited (Rowlingson and McKay, 1998). By the 1990s these trends stabilised, though by then barely more than half were entering lone parenthood from legal marriage. The rest were divided evenly between those who had never lived as a couple since a year before the birth of their eldest child, and those who had cohabited.

The rest of the pattern shown in Table 2.1 is a fairly stable one over the 1990s. Lone parents remained overwhelmingly women, for example, and more than half continued to rely on social housing. Most are white, but the proportion that is non-white is higher than among the general population of a similar age (about 9% rather than 6%). But there are some interesting trends. The proportion with pre-school aged children fell from 47 to 37% in eight years, which together with some improvement in their educational qualifications, will encourage those hoping to improve lone parents' rates of labour market participation. Their children were two years older in 1999 compared to 1991, on average. This was part of an ageing trend. Lone parents' average age increased three years in 10 – from 32 to 35 – and the proportion aged under 25 fell from 23 to 12%.

The age trend also reflects slow outflow from the lone parent population: the average length of spells in lone parenthood increased steadily in successive samples. The 1991 sample reported in Table 2.1 was re-interviewed in 1993, 1994, 1995, 1996 and 1998 – this data will be referred to from now on as 'the 1991 cohort'. After eight years, half the 1991 cohort were still lone parents looking after dependent children and more were alone with their non-dependent children. Less than a third (32%) had re-partnered.

Table 2.1: Characteristics of lone-parent families (excluding the bereaved)

	1989	1991	1993	1994	1999
		Column % (except means and medians)			
Marital status					
Divorced	45	36	35	36	27
Separated from marriage	18	18	22	19	21
Separated from cohabitation	}37	22	25	24	28
Never lived as a couple		24	18	21	24
Sex					
Female	95	95	94	96	95
Male	5	5	6	4	5
Age					
Under 25 years	23	18	15	14	12
25-29 years	20	22	20	19	17
30-34 years	20	21	24	21	22
35-39 years	15	18	20	21	20
40 years+	22	21	22	24	29
Mean age (all)	32 yrs	33 yrs	33 yrs	34 yrs	35 yrs
Divorced	36 yrs	37 yrs	37 yrs	38 yrs	39 yrs
Separated from marriage	33 yrs	34 yrs	36 yrs	35 yrs	36 yrs
Separated from cohabitation	}26 yrs	31 yrs	30 yrs	31 yrs	32 yrs
Never lived as a couple		27 yrs	27 yrs	28 yrs	28 yrs
Median age (all)	31 yrs	32 yrs	33 yrs	34 yrs	34 yrs
Number of dependent children					
1	54	46	49	48	50
2	31	34	35	36	33
3	10	15	11	11	12
4+	4	5	5	5	5
Age of youngest child					
0-4 years	–	47	43	39	37
5-10 years	–	31	33	35	35
11-15 years	–	18	18	22	22
16 or 17/18 years and in FTE	–	3	6	3	6
Median age of youngest child	–	5 yrs	7 yrs	7 yrs	7 yrs
Median age of oldest child	8 yrs	9 yrs	10 yrs	10 yrs	11 yrs
Household size					
2	36	38	37	38	39
3	36	34	37	37	37
4	16	19	17	17	15
5+	12	9	10	8	8
Left school at age					
Before 16 years	–	29	28	27	20
16 years	–	49	47	49	53
17-18 years	–	15	18	19	18
19 years+	–	7	6	5	9

Note: Some percentages do not total to 100 because of rounding.

Table 2.1: contd.../

	1989	1991	1993	1994	1999
		Column % (except means and medians)			
Highest qualification					
None	50	41	38	39	26
Below O-level	12	21	16	14	15
GCE O, City & Guilds	23	22	25	28	34
GCE A or similar	5	6	9	8	10
Above A-level	9	10	12	11	14
Housing tenure					
Owner	24	27	30	25	26
Social tenant	55	56	53	55	54
Private tenant	6	10	7	9	11
Other tenure	13	7	11	11	9
Ethnic group					
White	89	91	93	94	91
Black – Caribbean	4	3	3	3	3
Black – African	1	1	*	1	2
Indian	*	1	1	*	1
Other	4	2	1	*	3
Refused/not answered	1	3	2	1	*
Time spent as a lone parent: current spell					
Mean	–	4y 9m	4y 7m	5y 3m	5y 6m
Median	–	3y 7m	3y 5m	4y 3m	4y 5m
Number of respondents	*1,342*	*938*	*849*	*833*	*2,402~*

Notes:
* >0.00 but <0.5
~ Number of lone parents, not including those known to be bereaved.
Source: 1989 data from Bradshaw and Millar's survey quoted in Ford et al (1995)
1991/93/94 data from PSI Programme of Research into Low-Income Families surveys quoted in Marsh et al (1997)
1999 data from the Survey of Low-Income Families (Marsh et al, 2001) which also included a large sample of low-income couples not shown here

Employment patterns: work and entry to work

Thirty-eight per cent of lone parents work 16 hours a week or more, which is the point at which they qualify for WFTC (Table 2.2). A further 6% work less than 16 hours a week, even though earnings above £15 a week are surrendered pound-for-pound against their Income Support, which is their main out-of-work social security benefit. Five per cent are unemployed and seeking work in the official sense, so a total of 49% can be said to be economically active. Most of the rest (41% overall) say

Table 2.2: Lone parents' economic activity status in 1999 (%)

Working 16+ hours	38
Working <16 hours	6
Unemployed and seeking work	5
On a training scheme	*
Full-time education	2
Sick/disabled (<6 months)	1
Sick/disabled (6+ months)	4
Looking after home or family	41
Caring for a sick, elderly or disabled person	1
Retired	*
Other	1
Base	2,494

* <0.5%.

Source: 1999 data from the Survey of Low-Income Families (Marsh et al, 2001)

they are at home looking after their families, while the remainder are mostly sick or disabled. Only tiny numbers are in full-time education.

The proportion in work had risen from the 27% in 'full-time' work in 1991, which was then defined as 24 hours a week or more. Subsequent changes in the benefit rules make this comparison difficult.

Among those not working, only 15% have any record of paid work of 16 or more hours a week in the previous two years, 36% have not worked in the past five years and 16% have never had a paid job. In contrast, workers had often held their jobs for a long time. Those earning above Family Credit levels had been in work for six and a half years – longer on average than they had been lone parents.

In the 1999 sample, the majority of the workers were workers when they became lone parents. Looking at the previous two years, only 6% of those entering lone parenthood out of work had entered work six months later. Of those entering as Family Credit recipients (which they had claimed as a couple) three quarters remained on Family Credit. Of those entering as better-paid workers, eight out of 10 remained in work, though a third moved onto Family Credit.

Being in work was associated with being a homeowner rather than a social tenant, having better educational qualifications, having been married, avoiding family ill-health and receiving child support payments. This emphasises the initial gulf in advantage and disadvantage between workers and non-workers: they are socially and economically different populations, so migration from one to another is quite difficult.

This also means that static comparisons between workers and non-workers among lone parents are not always very helpful in estimating what factors might help them into work *during the time that they are lone parents.*

In the 1991 cohort, movement into work was slow in the following seven years. Among those interviewed in 1998, the proportion in work had risen from 29% in 1991 to exactly half, an increase of just three percentage points a year. A multivariate model of the *rate* of entry to work showed that meeting a new partner was associated with entry to work[5]. But having young children, especially new babies, having sick children, and beginning lone parenthood in hardship, were powerful and independent factors in preventing entry to work. Young children and hardship were incremental factors too: having two young children rather than one was independently significant, so was being in severe hardship rather than moderate hardship. And time was also an independent factor: the longer they remained out of work from 1991 onwards, the smaller grew their chances of entry into work, all else considered.

The subtext of the cohort survey findings seemed clear. Bringing up small children in difficult circumstances causes out-of-work lone parents to centre on that task. The more difficult that task, the more intensely they centre on it. However much the financial advantages of work may beckon, coping with the domestic task isolates them into a non-work identity. This also explains why the decision to go to work, when it comes, seems to come so suddenly. They seem to 'flip' between identities.

Employment patterns: work and benefits

Many who stay in work, and most who manage to enter work from Income Support, relied on continued support from means-tested benefits such as Family Credit and Housing Benefit, and will now rely on WFTC. In-work benefits make up some of the income lost by the absence of the children's father, though not all non-resident fathers were current workers. It is the bridge British lone parents cross as they move slowly from Income Support to work. Among those in the 1999 cross-section survey who had *entered* work in the previous two years, seven out of 10 had claimed Family Credit on entry and another one in 10 claimed within two months of starting work. Similarly, three quarters of the 1991 cohort who entered work by 1998 claimed Family Credit as they did so.

Lone parents' position in the labour market was so dependent on Family Credit, and now on WFTC, that it is usually sensible to condition any analysis of their labour market participation in relation to it. Table 2.3 shows the position in 1999.

In fact, only 12% of all lone parents have jobs that pay enough to lift them clear of the scope of Family Credit and about a quarter of these had claimed the benefit in the past. At the introduction of WFTC, the proportion left clear of in-work cash assistance will be about 7 to 8%.

If we take this combined work and benefit status and divide it by the four most important individual measures associated with working and not working, we obtain a kind of 'core profile' that describes the main problems that beset lone parents in relation to the labour market (Table 2.4). The role played by Family Credit and now by WFTC is clear, since recipients were more like the out-of-work lone parents than they were like the higher earners.

Family Credit, and WFTC, also paid a 'bonus' of what is now just over £11 a week if recipients managed to work 30 hours a week or more. Figure 2.1 shows how entry to work and the choice of shorter or longer working hours (divided at 30 hours) is related to the transition of their children first to primary school and then to secondary school.

Only when the youngest child passes into the secondary stage at age 11 or 12 does a longer working week predominate, and even then about

Table 2.3: Work and benefit status in 1999 (%)

• *Non-working*	Not working 16 or more hours per week, although some working fewer hours	62
• *Self-employed*	Self-employed and working 16 or more hours per week	3
• *Family Credit claimant*	Employed, working 16 or more hours per week and receiving Family Credit	18
• *Eligible non-claimant (ENC)*	Employed, working 16 or more hours per week, and eligible for, but *not* receiving, Family Credit	5
• *Moderate income*	Employed, working 16 or more hours per week, and income exceeds Family Credit limit by up to 35%	6
• *High income*	Working 16 or more hours per week, and income exceeds Family Credit limit by more than 35%	6
Base:		2,494

Source: 1999 data from the Survey of Low-Income Families (Marsh et al, 2001)

Table 2.4: Core profile of lone parents' position in the labour market (%)

	Non-work	FC claimant	ENCs	Self-employed	Moderate income	High income	(all)
Social tenants	66	49	31	21	14	10	(53)
With no qualifications	44	34	22	29	17	5	(37)
With long-standing illness	35	23	20	23	22	14	(30)
With pre-school child	44	29	16	15	13	14	(35)
Base	1,551	441	131	71	147	153	(2,494)

Note: FC = Family Credit; ENC = eligible non-claimant
Source: 1999 data from the Survey of Low-Income Families (Marsh et al, 2001)

Figure 2.1: Lone parents and work

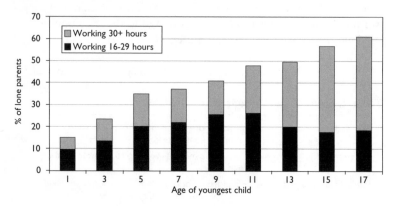

Source: 1999 data from the Survey of Low-Income Families (Marsh et al, 2001)

a quarter still work fewer than 30 hours. It is particularly worth noting that more than half of British lone parents with only teenage children are in work. Add to the total working all those unemployed and seeking work and their economic activity rates approach 70% at the point when their youngest child is leaving education, typically in their own mid-40s. By comparison, British *men* aged 45-64 have economic activity rates of 78% (ONS, 1998). We will hardly ask more of lone parents.

Is it worth working?

Given the kind of barriers faced by so many out-of-work lone parents, the rewards must be substantial to justify the effort needed to overcome them. The theory of incentives was outlined earlier. What is the evidence? There are three questions we can ask: do lone parents think work is worthwhile? Do they get enough extra cash for their efforts? Do their material living standards improve?

Attitudes

Those in the higher income brackets could hardly question their gains from work compared to out-of-work benefit levels. Those earning less and claiming Family Credit also felt in little doubt. Those among them who had earlier claimed Income Support were overwhelmingly sure that Family Credit was better: 82% of them said they preferred Family Credit and only 12% had any remaining preference for being out of work and on Income Support. By comparison, about a third of those on Income Support who had once had the experience of working and claiming Family Credit said they preferred their life on Income Support.

Incomes

In cash terms, Family Credit recipients were £57 a week better off than they would be on their equivalent out-of-work incomes[6]. This figure fell to £40 a week if average childcare and travel costs were factored into the estimate, however, the new rules under WFTC will widen this gap considerably.

Hardship

In terms of material well-being, the 1999 survey used a complex measure of hardship to detect the relative difference in living standards between families with differing work and benefit positions. The scale adds up a large number of items of everyday expenditure such as food, clothing, durables and simple social participation that respondents say they cannot have because they cannot afford them. To these are added reports of problem debts, poor housing conditions, overcrowding, and financial anxieties[7].

Families who exceeded the threshold on one or two of these dimensions were said to be in 'moderate hardship', while those exceeding three or

23

more were in 'severe hardship'. Table 2.5 shows the effects of work on these hardship scores.

The 12% of the 1999 sample who had earnings above the Family Credit levels were experiencing relatively little hardship, even among those who worked shorter hours, because many of these had child support payments too. The contrast between these and the large group relying solely on Income Support could hardly be more complete. Those on benefit were six times more likely to be in hardship. Those working and claiming Family Credit were better placed, but by no means clear of hardship. Some were recent entrants from Income Support and it can take a long time to recover material living standards after years of hardship. The small group working part time also saw improvements – it is amazing what a difference just £15 a week[8] can make in abating the rate of severe hardship. In fact the average difference in family incomes between all those in severe hardship and those experiencing none was just £34 a week.

Barriers to work

This section reviews briefly some of the well-known barriers to work faced by out-of-work lone parents and looks at the new and sometimes

Table 2.5: Lone parents' hardship by work and benefit status in 1999 (%)

	Not in hardship	Moderate hardship	Severe hardship	Base
Combining work and benefits				
Working 30+ hours and claiming FC	33	51	16	*114*
Working 30+ hours not claiming FC	66	28	6	*352*
Working 16-29 hours and claiming FC	33	46	21	*354*
Working 16-29 hours not claiming FC	59	33	8	*123*
Working <16 hours and claiming IS	24	48	28	*107*
Not working and claiming IS	15	42	43	*1,192*

Note: FC = Family Credit, IS = Income Support
Source: 1999 data from the Survey of Low-Income Families (Marsh et al, 2001)

quite surprising evidence for their height and difficulty as lone parents themselves experience them.

Intentions

By 1994, it was quite easy to describe British lone parents' orientation to the labour market: out of every 10 lone parents:

- three worked 16 hours a week or more;
- three were ready to work, one of them looking actively and a few trying part-time work of less than 16 hours a week;
- three would look for work one day, but not yet;
- one believed they might never work.

In 1999, intentions had moved somewhat (Table 2.6):

- four worked 16 hours a week or more (38%);
- two were ready to work, either looking actively (10%) or working less than 16 hours a week (5%) or ready to look soon (6%);
- three will look for work one day, but not yet (32%);
- one would (probably) not look for work (4% did not know when they might look and 5% thought they never would).

Only 5% in 1999 appeared to rule out work altogether, usually because of illness. But the proportion holding back from work has not changed.

Table 2.6: Lone parents looking for work in 1999 (%)

	Non-working lone parents	All lone parents
Working 16+ hours per week	–	38
Currently looking for work	17	10
Not currently looking for work, and...		
Working less than 16 hours	7	5
Expects to look in the next few weeks/months	9	6
Expects to look sometime in the future	52	32
Does not know when he or she will look	7	4
Does not expect to look for work in the future	7	5
Base	*1,537*	*2,494*

Source: 1999 data from the Survey of Low-Income Families (Marsh et al, 2001)

The increase in workers came from a faster take-up into work from among those who were ready to go to work. This is an interesting finding because it suggests that improvements in labour demand, together with fewer lone parents with pre-school children, account for the improvement in work participation rates, rather than anything that is happening among lone parents themselves.

Parenthood, work and choice

The majority of lone parents were until recently wives, husbands (though rarely) or partners sharing the care of young children. Traditionally, at least, the balance of advice to them, from family, friends and even professionals, will not have favoured an early re-entry to work. These values can be deeply held and are not easily thrust aside just because the children's father or mother is gone. More than a third still have pre-school children. The judgement that there are times when a parent's best choice is to remain with the children, typically following a difficult separation from their other parent, is not one to be challenged carelessly on the grounds that work is always better.

Choice features quite strongly in their answers to the question "is there anything in particular that is stopping you looking for a job of 16+ hours per week?" (Table 2.7). At least a third of those open to the idea of working but not yet ready to seek work actively, said simply that their place was with their children and they did not want to spend any more time away from them. About half this group also complained about the lack of childcare or its likely cost, while those not considering work were far more likely to cite their own or their child's illness or disability.

Among lone parents, having a new baby is one of the more effective barriers to work. In the 1991 cohort, a quarter had had new babies or were pregnant by 1998. Half of them also had new partners.

Few thought that jobs might not be available – though few had probably thought things through that far – while a minority still persisted in the belief that they would be better off not working.

The following sections look at some of these reasons for not working.

Hardship, morale and health

Many out-of-work lone parents experience a malign spiral of hardship, poor health and low morale. There is something about this experience that builds up its own barriers to work. Using a scale of morale that

Table 2.7: Lone parents' reasons for not working 16+ hours per week in 1999 (multiple response percentages)

Is there anything in particular that is stopping you looking for a job of 16+ hours per week?	Looking for work		Not looking for work			All
	Working <16 hours	Expects to look over next few months	Expects to look some-time in future	Does not know when will next look	Does not expect to look in future	
Nothing, already looking	38	0	0	0	0	0	7
Cannot afford childcare	20	19	26	28	13	5	23
No childcare available	12	26	22	19	8	1	16
Don't want to spend more time away from children	4	37	27	34	22	10	27
Own illness/disability	6	5	11	13	35	50	16
Child's illness/disability	1	6	4	9	9	6	7
Other family illness	<1	1	1	3	3	2	2
No work available	4	1	4	2	4	2	2
Don't have the skills	5	5	10	6	5	11	6
Studying/training scheme	3	0	8	9	2	1	6
Better off not working	6	0	12	12	9	6	10
Would not be able to pay rent or mortgage	4	8	3	2	1	0	3
Pregnant	0	0	0	0	0	10	1
Retired	5	0	6	4	7	10	5
Base: non-working lone parents	255	115	143	801	108	115	1,537

Source: 1999 data from the Survey of Low-Income Families (Marsh et al, 2001)

combined self-reported happiness and self-esteem, we were able to show that those in severe hardship were three to four times more likely to suffer low morale, compared with those not in hardship. It is quite hard to contemplate work if you are that demoralised and hard up.

The links with ill-health are equally strong. Overall, reports of 'a long-standing illness or disability' doubled among out-of-work lone parents between 1991 and 1999, from 17 to 35%[9]. Even among those actively seeking work, 29% had such a problem and the majority of these thought it would restrict their working opportunities. However, this fraction rose to a third among those delaying a search for work until sometime in the future and it was more than half among those doubtful that they would ever start to look.

The experience of the 1991 cohort was particularly interesting in this respect. They started out in 1991 somewhat healthier than other British women of a similar age. Then their health deteriorated until a third were suffering long-term problems by 1998. Part of this deterioration appeared to have its origins in injury sustained during separation from violent partners, and part was connected to poor health behaviour, including high rates of smoking.

Children's and families' health

Among out-of-work lone parents, the same proportion who have long-standing illness or disability themselves, have children who have the same problems (35%), rising to 43% in those who do not expect to seek work in the foreseeable future. One in 10 of all out-of-work lone parents have a child whose illness restricts opportunities to work. The same proportion has someone else in the house for whom they have caring responsibilities, usually their own parent. In the 1991 cohort study, little more than half the whole sample (workers included) reached 1998 without one or other member of the family ill in this way. In 12% of cases, parent and child were both ill.

Qualifications and skills

The profile of British lone parents above noted a lack of marketable qualifications among them, though some improvement had occurred over the past 10 years. Among out-of-work lone parents the problem is worse: 44% have no academic qualifications, 62% have no vocational qualifications, and a third have neither. Those looking for work have more, although 22% of them have none and only one in six have anything better than basic school leaving qualifications. The weaker their attachment to the labour market, the fewer qualifications they have.

Few had received any training recently. Just 3% of out-of-work lone parents on Income Support (though 7% of those actually looking for work) had participated in the New Deal for Lone Parents. Sixteen per cent had attended a training course in the previous two years that did not lead to a qualification. However, almost three quarters of out-of-work lone parents (72%) would consider going on a training course. Twelve per cent had recently applied for a course, 53% said they had just considered it and 35% said they would consider it in the future.

Fewer than half hold that other passport to a job in Britain: a driving licence. Fewer still have access to a car.

Childcare

As you would expect, a great deal of British research on out-of-work lone parents has centred on the issue of childcare. Most research has identified a lack of affordable childcare as a major barrier to work (Holtermann and Clarke, 1992). It seems a simple question: if lone parents work and their younger children are out of school, then self-evidently someone else has to be looking after them. For such an obvious proposition, the research evidence can be surprisingly hard to interpret. One thing we have learned from the Programme of Research into Low-Income Families (PRILIF) (see for example, Ford, 1996) is that the issue is a good deal more complicated than seems reasonable.

In Table 2.7 above, a third of out-of-work lone parents cited a lack of affordable childcare as a barrier to work and only a minority of these said it was the sole barrier. Similarly, lone parents long-established in work rarely cited childcare as a major difficulty that they had to overcome to enter and/or to keep paid work. This was a particular surprise in the 1991 cohort study whose successful workers rarely cited childcare as a major obstacle they had found difficult to overcome. Following these families in their journey from Income Support into work, it seemed clear that arranging childcare was the last hurdle into work in a long row of hurdles. They seemed to seek work that fitted their own view of their childcare needs – that is, the arrangements for care that best fitted what they wanted for themselves and their children – rather than trying to find childcare that suited a particular job. High on their list of childcare needs was the opportunity to spend as much of their own time with their children as possible.

Lone parents' passage into work is a journey marked by a number of changes in attitude and self-definition, and by a resumption of control over their personal circumstances. If that process fails in other ways, typically a failure of family health or lack of other support, then the issue of childcare becomes sidelined. It is really this process that makes the data so hard to read. Childcare needs only come into focus at the threshold of work, not before.

Among British lone parents in work, 68% used some form of childcare, though only about half of these (36%) paid for it at a median cost of £30 a week. Only among the highest paid workers did the majority pay for childcare. Four out of 10 of working lone parents with children under five managed to avoid paying for childcare (mainly through grandparents' help and free nursery school provision), but those who did not paid £50 a week.

What is to be done?

Over the past two years there have been two key policy changes: a further increase in cash incentives to work and the introduction of active case management, which is moving towards a non-voluntary system. Further changes intended to improve the quality and availability of childcare, to improve parents' and children's health, and to increase the flow of child support payments are all coming into play now. This last section briefly reviews these current policy concerns in the light of the evidence above.

Wait and see

For three groups of working lone parents, the effects of the WFTC will be more noticeable than for others:

• those whose earnings entitled them to only little help from Family Credit, or none, will now get more;
• those receiving child support from non-resident parents, who can now keep all they receive;
• those paying for childcare from relatively small earnings, who can now get 70% of their outlay in addition to an award of WFTC up to their maximum entitlement. Previously the childcare component was included in the total up to the maximum.

The main gains will be concentrated among those earning in the mid-range of lone parents' typical wages. Far fewer than previously, though, should now occupy the lower earnings range because they are now supported by the minimum wage. It was not at all uncommon to see applications for Family Credit from lone parents earning less than £2.50 an hour. It is not a coincidence that such a family began receiving their maximum WFTC for working 30 hours a week at £3.60[10] an hour in 1999.

When lone parents report for their ONE interviews, or their work-focused interviews (personal adviser meetings), or see the New Deal adviser, or simply receive good advice from friends (which tends to be their usual source of information), they will hear encouraging news. Few will doubt that *under the right circumstances* there is much to be gained from work. But it remains true that the gains are much larger once lone parents' wages rise above the National Minimum Wage levels to, say, £5 an hour. Then they are better able to withstand travel costs and residual childcare expenses, which are still 30% of the total cost of childcare. There are many parts of Britain where women with few qualifications, or none, would find it difficult to get this rate. Thus the main beneficiaries will be concentrated in London and the South East, though they also face the highest housing and travel costs.

Nevertheless, British lone parents have, for the first time, a reasonable chance of obtaining through work a standard of living that most other families would recognise as acceptable among single-earner two-parent families. An income package made up of wages and WFTC is still a relatively modest living compared with the majority of British families. Improved help with childcare will make work possible in some cases where it was not before. This should increase lone parents' work incentives and, for those able to respond, it should also improve their standard of living.

When the effects of all these changes are known, new policy initiatives might be useful. But so much has been done, further changes ought to be limited to improvement in the new policy lines established, as the remainder of this chapter suggests.

Continue to improve childcare

Childcare is the last barrier to work that lone parents overcome. It allows a decision to work to be enacted; it neither allows the decision itself nor creates the working opportunity. However, it is still important and additional provision at the right time will help ease more people into work more quickly. Many lone parents are uncertain whether their younger children will tolerate childcare and often have to road test various forms of childcare before even considering getting a job. The opportunity to do this will greatly assist lone parents to become more 'work ready', and will build their confidence. In the end though, lone parents look for a job that suits their childcare needs. This judgement includes the amount of time they themselves can spend with their children.

Probably the most effective measure in Britain recently has been the *de facto* lowering of the school entry age to four. The National Childcare Strategy is building a system of after-school clubs, which are so effective in the US and Canada, and out-of-school childcare services. The Department for Education and Skills is supporting a strong recruitment programme for jobs in childcare, some of it targeting unemployed young men.

Improve health and reduce hardship

If ever there was a case for joined-up government, improving lone parents' access to work by improving their health has to be one. The Sure Start programme provides £540 million to all families in disadvantaged areas, offering help to families whose children have emotional and behavioural difficulties, or problems with learning or simply poor health. It includes all-round advice on infant feeding and childcare. It is in some respects a striking revival of post-war paternalism and, since Sure Start intervention is direct and practical, it is all the more welcome[11]. Among lone-parent families, improving the health of very young children is probably one of the most important first steps in improving their parents' health. And the evidence is clear that it will help more lone parents enter work.

The evidence for failing health among lone parents themselves must be taken seriously. An effective welfare-to-work plan for many lone parents, especially the relatively young single lone parents and recently separated lone parents, will begin long before they focus on the problems of looking for jobs and childcare. Initiatives through Health Action areas and outreach programmes to reduce smoking and improve diet are welcome from an employment point of view, as well as for their own sake.

However, the first step in restoring the optimism and the sense of well-being essential to turn the view of even the most disadvantaged lone parent outward towards work, is to improve the present standard of living. Hardship reduces morale and allows little room for the kind of optimism and forward planning that personal advisers and work-focused interviews hope to encourage. The increases in the Income Support rates for younger children will assist. However, now that the incentives to work have been increased, there is room to add further to Income Support rates.

Increase the flow of child support payments

It is not clear at the moment what proportion of lone parents receive child support payments. In the early 1990s, the figure overall was stuck at 30%. The 1999 survey found 25% receiving payments directly and an unknown proportion, perhaps another 10 to 15%, having payments collected by the (then) Department of Social Security.

The new and simpler rules for assessment given to the CSA, together with other measures, are intended to raise compliance to 75%. If this is achieved, it will have a striking effect on lone parents' standards of living and their opportunities to work. The new disregard of £10 a week for those on Income Support is an important departure in policy. The average payment to out-of-work lone parents is now £52 a week, among those cases for whom we have information. If these amounts are carried into work they would be added to earned income, untouched by entitlements to WFTC. Altogether, this will raise the cash incentive to work to a figure of typically more than £100 a week. This leaves a wide margin to increase the Income Support disregard for those out of work, without significantly damaging incentives.

It is true that absent parents have lower incomes and higher rates of unemployment than other parents (Bradshaw et al, 1999). But this is not a discouragement to ensuring that orders for child support payments are put in place promptly. They are unlikely to remain unemployed for the next 10 or 15 years.

Accept what is happening

Lone parenthood will continue. About four out of 10 newborn British children will spend a significant part of their childhood with only one of their parents. The present government has set a target of removing all Britain's children from poverty in 20 years. If this project is to be kept on track, huge numbers of lone parents will have to move from sole support on public assistance into much greater income self-sufficiency. The evidence shows that it is no use waiting for them all to find new partners. While they remain alone, each will require an income package that mixes benefits, earnings, WFTC, support for childcare, sometimes in-work support for housing, and preferably child support payments too. Policy will have to accept that many lone parents will go the distance and spend more than a decade alone with their children.

It should be clear by now that the 'British problem' is that there are so many severely disadvantaged lone parents who begin lone parenthood both disadvantaged and out of work. In Britain, the term 'social exclusion' is not used lightly. We have severe problems in social geography. British lone parents have been caught in the maw of 25 years of rapidly widening social and economic inequality. The gap in real living standards between the lower and higher income brackets has widened faster in Britain than any other Organisation of Economic Co-operation and Development (OECD) country, except New Zealand. Almost every trend has moved against lone parents' interests, particularly against those of the majority who *entered* lone parenthood out of work. Too many remain stranded in shrinking islands of social accommodation, in places without the right kind of jobs, with meagre stocks of human capital between them, with young children, uncertain health and not enough optimism.

On the positive side, current policy now addresses the full range of these difficulties, to the extent that it has not in the past. A combination of increased cash incentives (public and private), active case management, better childcare and better healthcare really ought to have a positive impact. Much will depend on the continued positive health of the labour market itself. The most vulnerable workers are usually the first to fall out in a slump, though lone parents, once in work, have shown surprising resilience in the past.

Employment trends are also favourable, as the British economy expands its service sector and generates more jobs with flexible hours that fit well with lone parents' required work patterns, underwritten by wage supplements. Lone parents do not go to work until they are ready. But when they are ready they do go to work, and they stay there. Increased incentives and case management ought to help more get ready sooner. Flows into work will increase and the proportion relying on Income Support will fall.

But it will not fall to zero. There will continue to be a group of lone parents, some traumatised by violent separation or others, mothers with new-born babies for example, who will need transitional assistance, care, good housing and other help. The better the quality of that assistance, the sooner they will be in good enough shape to contemplate the task of working in a paid job and bringing up children alone. There is no sensible reason why they should be asked to prepare for this task in poverty. Perhaps the simplest guide to policy is to ask whether as a society we should expect any more from lone parents than we expect from married or cohabiting parents.

Notes

[1] This paper is based on a programme of research into Britain's low-income families, carried out at Policy Studies Institute (PSI) since 1991. Alan Marsh and Stephen McKay began the programme. Later, important contributions were made by Reuben Ford, now of the Social Research and Demonstration Corporation, Vancouver, and Louise Finlayson, now of the Scottish Executive, and Richard Dorsett at PSI. Currently, the Social Security Research Team at PSI is continuing the work, consisting of Alan Marsh, Stephen McKay, Alison Smith and Augusta Stephenson. Nearly all of the research findings used in this paper are the work of this team. The Analytical Services Division of the British Department of Work and Pensions funds the work. The usual disclaimer applies: opinions, conclusions and errors are all my own.

[2] Those with awards of £70 a week or more.

[3] Even when claimed with other benefits, combined withdrawal rates cannot now exceed 69%.

[4] ONE is not an acronym. It is a contraction of 'One Stop Shop' – whereby all the advice needed to claim benefits, seek work and otherwise return to financial self-sufficiency is delivered in one place by one adviser.

[5] We were unable to establish which was more important: whether meeting a partner allowed lone parents to get a job more easily or whether they got a job and found a partner there.

[6] This is partly a hypothetical estimate which calculates the likely entitlement if they were to stop work and claim Income Support and other benefits. It cannot make allowance for likely behavioural changes, such as the outcome of renewing the pursuit of child support payments that would be triggered by the Income Support claim.

[7] The nine indicators for the 1999 hardship measure are:
- reports two or more problems with quality of accommodation;
- lives in overcrowded accommodation;
- cannot afford to keep home warm;
- worries about money almost all the time and runs out of money most weeks;
- has no savings and two or more debts;
- has a relative material hardship score on food items in the highest 20%;

- has a relative material hardship score on clothes items in the highest 20%;
- has a relative material hardship score on leisure and entertainment items in the highest 20%;
- has a relative material hardship score on consumer durables in the highest 20%.

[8] British lone parents can now keep £20 a week of their earnings from work of less than 16 hours a week, compared with £15 before April 2001, but any more is deducted pound-for-pound from their Income Support. They can also keep £10 of any child support payments, which previously they lost altogether.

[9] There is insufficient space to discuss some of the obvious problems that accompany self-reported health in surveys. A good discussion is available in Cohen et al (1995). For a review of lone parents' health, see Popay and Jones (1991).

[10] This was the National Minimum Wage on introduction in 1999. It is now £3.70 per hour.

[11] The author was born in 1945 and has memories of free orange juice, vitamin supplements and what seemed to be weekly visits to child health clinics.

THREE

Welfare reform and lone mothers' employment in the US[1]

Jane Waldfogel, Sandra K. Danziger, Sheldon Danziger and Kristin S. Seefeldt

Introduction

An increasing share of children in the US are living with lone mothers. In 1998, 23% of children under the age of 18 lived with a lone mother, up from 18% in 1980 and 8% in 1960 (see Table 3.1). Although there are differences in the extent of lone parenthood across racial and ethnic groups, the share of children living with lone mothers has risen in all groups: from 1980 to 1998, the share of children living with a lone mother rose from 14 to 18% for whites, from 44 to 51% for African-Americans, and from 20 to 27% for Hispanics (see Table 3.2)[2]. In the US, the term 'single mother' is typically used to describe women who have children and who are not currently married. It is important to note that a substantial number of these women may be cohabiting; this has not traditionally been tracked in US data. In this chapter, the authors use the terms 'single mother' and 'lone mother' interchangeably.

The share of children whose mothers have never been married has grown more rapidly (see Tables 3.1 and 3.2). In 1998, 9% of all children lived with never-married mothers, three times the 2.9% rate in 1980 and more than twenty times the 0.4% rate in 1960. Between 1980 and 1998, the share of children living with never-married mothers rose from 1 to 5% among whites, from 13 to 32% among African-Americans, and from 4 to 12% among Hispanics. By 1998, 39% of children living with lone mothers were living with never-married mothers.

Historically, lone mothers have had a higher labour force participation rate than married mothers (Burtless, 2000). However, their participation

Table 3.1: Living arrangements of children under the age of 18 (1960-98)

Year	% living with lone mother	% living with never-married mother
1960	8.0	0.4
1970	10.8	0.8
1980	18.0	2.9
1990	21.6	7.6
1998	23.0	9.0

Source: US House of Representatives (1998, Appendix G)

Table 3.2: Living arrangements of children by 'racial'/ethnic group (1980-98)

Year	% living with lone mother	% living with never-married mother
White		
1980	14	1
1990	16	3
1998	18	5
African-American		
1980	44	13
1990	51	27
1998	51	32
Hispanic		
1980	20	4
1990	27	8
1998	27	12

Source: US Bureau of the Census (1999, Table 83)

rate has varied by marital status (see Figure 3.1). Until recently, never-married mothers' participation rate was lower than that of previously married mothers (and lower than that of married mothers). Figure 3.1 shows an increase in the participation rate of lone mothers in the late 1990s, with a particularly sharp rise for never-married mothers after the mid-1990s; their participation rate now slightly exceeds that of married mothers.

Lone-mother families have high poverty rates. In 1999, the rate for children living in lone-mother families was 42%, as compared to 17% for all families with children (US Bureau of the Census, 2000). These high child poverty rates are often attributed to the US social welfare system,

Figure 3.1: Labour force participation rates of women with children (1960-98)

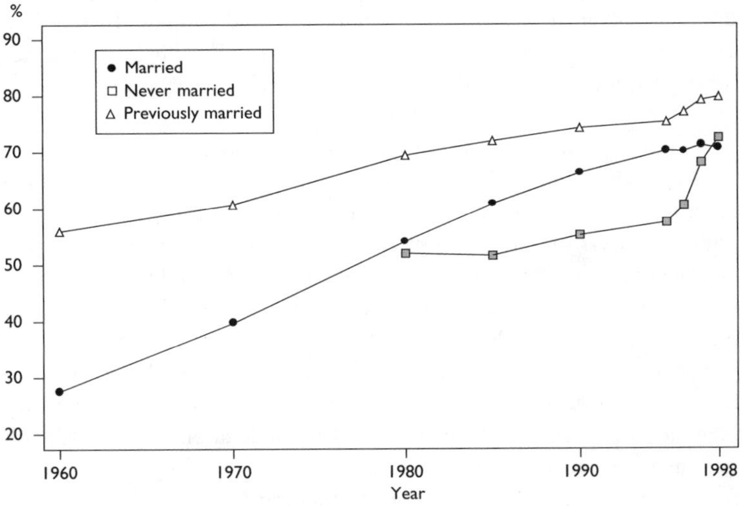

Source: US Bureau of the Census (1999, Table 659)

which provides a more limited range of benefits than other Western industrialised nations and relies to a larger extent on means-tested and targeted, rather than universal, benefits (Katz, 1996, p x). For instance, the US has no universal child benefit or allowance, no universal public health insurance and no benefit for non-disabled individuals who are out of work, unless they have sufficient recent work experience.

Three federal entitlement programmes have been particularly important for the economic well-being of lone-mother families. The first, Aid to Families with Dependent Children (AFDC), was designed for lone-mother families (but later extended to two-parent families with an unemployed breadwinner). Until 1996, AFDC was an entitlement programme, available to any family meeting the eligibility criteria, which consisted of having low income and assets (until recently, no work or work-related activity was required). Payment levels, set by states, have varied widely by state and over time, but have tended to be low; in no state and year have AFDC benefits been sufficient to raise family incomes above the poverty line. The second federal entitlement programme, Food Stamps, provides coupons for purchasing food to low-income individuals and families. Single-mother families receiving AFDC are automatically eligible for

Food Stamps. In states with low AFDC benefit levels, Food Stamps play an important role in raising family incomes, although still not above the poverty line. The third federal entitlement, Medicaid, provides health insurance coverage to low-income individuals and families. In addition, there are a few smaller entitlement programmes in which some lone-mother families participate (for instance, the Supplemental Security Income programme for disabled individuals).

A number of discretionary programmes also provide support to some lone-mother families. The Women, Infants, and Children programme provides food coupons for low-income pregnant women and women with infants; various housing assistance programmes provide rent subsidies or places in public housing for low-income families; and the Head Start programme, discussed below, provides pre-school education to children from low-income families.

The 1990s saw major changes in US welfare policies. At the national level, the 1996 Personal Responsibility and Work Opportunity Reconciliation Act (PRWORA) ended the federal entitlement to cash assistance and replaced the previously open-ended funding for the AFDC programme with capped block grant funding for a new time-limited cash assistance programme, called Temporary Assistance to Needy Families (TANF). The PRWORA sought to reduce welfare dependency by mandating work or employment-related activities as a condition of receiving welfare, even for lone mothers with small children. It gave states the autonomy to change programme rules, including reforms that make combining welfare and work more attractive, and greatly expanded funding for childcare for women engaging in employment-related activities, combining welfare with work, or leaving welfare for work (for a review of the PRWORA provisions, see Pavetti, 2000).

As federal welfare reform was being implemented, other federal reforms designed to make work more attractive for low-income single mothers were passed. The Earned Income Tax Credit (EITC), greatly expanded in 1993, is an important source of income for women leaving welfare for work. The federal minimum wage was raised in 1993, and health insurance benefits were extended to more children from low-income families through the 1997 Children's Health Insurance Program (CHIP). By the late 1990s, in most states, a lone mother would be financially better off working than remaining a non-working welfare recipient – the welfare trap had been sprung.

Welfare reforms at the state level have been even more far-reaching. The impetus for federal reform came from state experiments that followed a previous welfare reform, the 1988 Family Support Act. A 'waiver' process allowed states to seek permission to make fundamental programme changes, such as imposing time limits and requiring work. Waivers began under the Bush administration and accelerated during the Clinton administration. By 1996, 46 states had been granted waivers.

After the PRWORA passed, states took advantage of the new flexibility in TANF. For instance, while the federal law sets a five-year time limit for receipt of cash assistance, states may set shorter time limits. Most adopted the federal lifetime limit, but practices vary widely. For example, Tennessee maintains a five-year cap; it also terminates benefits after 18 months of receipt and does not allow families to reapply for assistance until another three months have passed. Another 16 states set time limits shorter than 60 months, ranging from 21 months in Connecticut to 48 months in Florida and Georgia. Less than 10 states plan to provide assistance beyond federal limits, although nearly all states have extension and exemption policies to the time limit (Gallagher et al, 1998). Likewise, while the federal law requires recipients to work within two years of welfare receipt, 20 states (plus the District of Columbia) require engagement in work or a work-related activity at the time they apply for assistance or within the first three months of receipt (National Governors' Association Center for Best Practices, 1999).

States must impose financial penalties – 'sanctions' – for recipients who do not comply with the work requirements. These penalties range from immediate withdrawal of the family's full benefits (used by 16 states), to withdrawal of a portion of the family's benefits (12 states plus the District of Columbia), to gradual withdrawal of benefits (22 states) (US General Accounting Office, 2000). Seven states impose 'lifetime' sanctions when recipients are in continued 'non-compliance'; such sanctions function like the time limits, but with recipients' benefits potentially terminated sooner. Sanctions may be affecting more families than the time limits.

These reforms were designed to move lone mothers into work – by mandating work, making work pay and helping with childcare – and the evidence suggests that they did just that. Between 1994 and 1999, the national welfare caseload was reduced by half, from five million cases to just 2.5 million, and recipients as a percentage of the US population fell from 5.5 to 2.3% (US Department of Health and Human Services, 2000). Over the same period, the labour force participation of all lone mothers increased by 10 percentage points; the participation of never-married mothers (the group of lone mothers most likely to have been on welfare) increased more than 15 points (from under 50% in 1990 to 65% by 1998).

By 1997, the participation rate of never-married mothers with pre-school age children exceeded that of married mothers with pre-school age children for the first time in the thirty-plus years that such statistics have been published; and the participation rate of all lone mothers exceeded that of married mothers for the first time since 1987 (Burtless, 2000).

Although the strong economy played a role, analysts agree that welfare reform was responsible for a substantial part of this increased employment (see Danziger, 1999). McKernan et al (2000) tested the impact of 10 state welfare policies on the employment rate of lone mothers and found that eight policies – raising hours of work requirements, reducing days of assistance before work requirement, reducing maximum months of benefits, increasing percentage of benefits lost on first sanction, increasing months of transitional childcare benefits, excluding the value of a vehicle from asset limits, raising the total asset limit, and changing the way housing assistance was treated – significantly increased lone-mothers' employment but had no effect on the employment of single women without children (a group that should not have been affected by welfare reforms).

This evidence suggests that state-level reforms contributed to the increased lone-mothers' employment in the 1990s, although the increases would have been smaller if unemployment rates had been higher and if the minimum wage and EITC had not been increased. Therefore, we now examine some key state-level reforms, using evidence from selected states to illustrate the three major types of policies that have been used in the US to move lone mothers from welfare to work: mandating work (Michigan); making work pay (Michigan and Minnesota); and helping families with childcare (Illinois).

These kinds of policies are complementary. A strategy to move women from welfare to work and out of poverty will be most effective if it combines elements from all three. We consider them separately because states treat these as distinct policy areas and because this framework facilitates comparison with different policies in other countries. Although our focus is on the impact of welfare reform on lone-mothers' employment, these policies may also affect child and family well-being. We briefly consider those issues as well.

Mandating work

Prior to the 1996 reform in the PRWORA, there were many exemptions from participation in work and training activities. Now, nearly all recipients must engage in 'work activities' within two years of receiving assistance.

Furthermore, states must meet work participation requirements – each year, an increasingly larger share of the caseload must work. 'Work' is defined as subsidised or unsubsidised employment, community service, on-the-job training, participation in job search or job search readiness activities (limited to six weeks in a year and no more than four weeks consecutively per participant), or participation in short-term vocational training[3].

States have also adopted policies to make work more attractive to recipients. Prior to the PRWORA, after four months of work, recipients could expect nearly a dollar reduction in benefits for every dollar earned. Now states can set their own policies. A number have expanded this 'earned income disregard', allowing recipients to keep some of their benefits as earnings increase. (We return to this issue in the section 'Making work pay'.)

Overall, states now have more discretion in designing TANF programmes than they did under AFDC. This flexibility is constrained to some extent by federal work requirements and by bureaucratic inertia. Most states have adopted a Work First approach to move recipients into the labour force. Such programmes assume that finding a job and developing work skills through direct experience, rather than participating in education and training, is the best strategy for finding work.

Some states have intensified efforts to divert applicants from receiving cash welfare and entering the welfare rolls. This practice, called diversion, may be accomplished through: (1) providing one-time financial assistance; (2) requiring mandatory job search as a condition of eligibility; and/or (3) linking applicants to other services or resources. Three fifths of states use diversion activities, with lump sum payments and/or mandatory upfront job search being the most common (Maloy et al, 1998). An applicant accepting a lump sum payment is ineligible to receive TANF for some specified period. Mandatory job search prior to eligibility determination seeks to direct job-ready applicants into work. Referring applicants to other services in lieu of cash benefits is driven by beliefs that cash assistance should be a last resort and that services provide a better way of promoting work.

The importance of implementation

The policies enumerated thus far are written into state law or policy manuals. How policies are implemented is determined by decisions made by those carrying out the day-to-day work. The increased state flexibility, coupled with the emphasis on work, has transformed the role of the welfare office and the functions of staff from providing benefits to supporting work. Welfare office staff now have greater discretion than prior to 1996. How that discretion is used has an enormous effect on clients. In some states, the probability of being sanctioned varies significantly by local office (Fein and Wang, 1999). The definition of 'non-compliance' may also matter. For example, in Michigan, a client not cooperating with the Work First programme may have her grant reduced. If that same client is working and quits working, her grant may be terminated. In Wisconsin, for each hour a client does not participate in an assigned activity, her cheque is reduced by the hourly minimum wage. If she does not participate at all, she may receive no grant. In states requiring job search as part of the application process, the amount of assistance given to applicants could affect entry into the system; if applicants are provided little or no guidance during their search, they may give up and never become eligible for cash assistance.

The trend toward contracting out for services has accelerated since the PRWORA. Many states have privatised parts of the welfare system, particularly the job search and placement functions. Greater privatisation could have far-reaching consequences for clients. Concerns about accountability, withholding services (due to profit motive, for example), and dissimilar services across providers are amplified when a private agency is involved.

Recipient process in Michigan

In Michigan, families apply for TANF, called the Family Independence Program (FIP), at one of more than 100 Family Independence Agency (FIA) offices across the state. Most offices take applications on a walk-in basis in the morning hours. The applicant, typically a lone mother, receives a combined application form (for Food Stamps, medical assistance, childcare and cash benefits) and must show documentation for sources of income, employment, citizenship and birth certificates, school registration and local address. She must cooperate with child support requirements and help identify the father of her children. The applicant is usually seen by the Family Independence Specialist (FIS) worker who goes over eligibility information, discusses policies and rules, and focuses on the requirements of the Work First programme.

Within two weeks, she must attend a Work First orientation session run jointly by the welfare agency and Work First programme staff, where programme rules and work requirements are detailed. Availability of childcare and employment and training options are mentioned during orientation. Attendance at orientation is part of the application process; if she does not attend, she will not receive cash assistance. If she attends orientation and the first day of Work First activities and is financially eligible, the FIS opens her case.

The client and her FIS also develop a Personal Responsibility Plan and Family Contract, outlining her goals and responsibilities and what the programme will provide to help meet those goals. The plan may include goals such as finding employment through Work First, or returning to school for further training. This plan is initiated within the first two months of her receiving assistance and may be modified, particularly when the client meets with her worker.

State policy requires that FIS workers make quarterly home visits. If the recipient falls into sanction status (for non-compliance), home visits are on a monthly basis. The home call is designated to build a trusting relationship between the client and the worker so that the client will discuss family concerns. The workers rely on informal interaction and client self-disclosure to uncover any employment barriers. Formal diagnostic or structured assessment tools are not used.

Unless the client is already employed for at least 20 hours a week at the minimum wage (or more, depending on the ages of her children and her marital status), she must attend a Work First programme. She will be exempt from the work requirement *only* if she has a disabling health problem or cares for a family member with a health problem, has a newborn less than three months of age, is a teen parent attending school, or is aged over 65. During 1997, about 20% of the caseload was deferred from work requirements and between 36 and 56% of recipients reported earnings from work, while the remainder (between one half and one quarter) of cases expected to be searching for work. By 1999, the proportion of the caseload deferred averaged 42%, growing each month. This is due to continued declines in the caseload[4]. The proportion of cases with earnings averaged around 33%.

Once in Work First, the types of assistance and the sequencing of services she would receive vary, depending on the programme model chosen by the local provider. In 1998, for the most part, Michigan's 83 Work First programmes conformed to one of four different approaches that vary along a continuum of formal services[5].

At one end of the spectrum are 20 programmes in which the client participates for approximately one week in structured 'job search readiness' activities, such as résumé and letter preparation and mock interviews. She would also attend workshops on topics relevant for job retention and life skills, such as anger management and budgeting. At the same time or during the next week, she would search for work. To assist her job search, she has access to free telephones to call employers, newspaper advertisements, and lists of job openings culled from the state employment agency. Additionally, programme staff may call employers on her behalf, supply her with leads on jobs, bring employers to the Work First site for interviews, and/or take her for interviews with potential employers.

The largest group of Work First programmes, three eighths, provide either formal job search workshops or specialised direction and support in job search, but not both. Ten programmes offer workshops on a variety of topics, covering job seeking, retention and life skills, but provide less staff assistance during the direct job search phase. The other 21 offer workshops related to job search skills or provide workshop activities only to clients who do not find a job within the first week or two of being in the programme. However, in these programmes, the agency provides a full array of specialised job search services, linking directly clients with employers.

Another one quarter of the providers primarily offer instruction on job search techniques in the workshops. The agency supplies job postings and access to job listings, but clients are responsible for making direct contacts with employers and arrangements for interviews.

Finally, five of the 83 programmes offer few structured services. They assist clients with résumé preparation and provide listings of open jobs, but group workshops are rare, and job search efforts are primarily the client's responsibility. These programmes are in rural areas, so group activities may not be feasible.

These latter two types of Work First programmes reflect a belief that it is best for clients to find a job on their own. Two reasons are cited: clients may be more likely to stay in jobs they found for themselves, as opposed to ones 'given' to them by staff, and clients need to learn the skills of job search, so that they can conduct future searches. The other programme models, in which staff assist clients during the job search, assume that clients have certain disadvantages (in their ability to conduct a job search and/or their qualifications), compared to other job seekers and therefore need more assistance in securing employment[6].

Clients unable to find work within four weeks may still be required to search for work or may be placed in a work experience position or a vocational training class. If, however, a woman drops out of the programme or is otherwise determined non-compliant, her case will be sent back to the FIA for review. If the caseworker finds that she does not have a legitimate reason for not cooperating, her benefits will be reduced by 25%. After four months, if she continues to be out of compliance, her case will be closed. If she is a new applicant, she must demonstrate compliance within the first 60 days of her case opening, or she can be dropped from the rolls immediately.

If this client gets a job, Work First will check at 30-day intervals to see if she remains employed, up to the 90th day on the job or for as long as the client remains on assistance. If she loses her job and is still on cash assistance, she will be re-referred by her case worker to Work First and start the process of job search again.

Assessment of Work First

Michigan's Work First programme is similar to that of many of the states. Local administrators in Michigan generally express support for the mandatory labour force attachment model (Danziger and Seefeldt, 2000), but they raise concerns about how well this programme model works for some recipients. Work First managers identify both structural and personal impediments to success. However, few programmes systematically evaluate recipients for depression, domestic violence, or other personal problems, much less provide referrals or access to service providers to treat the problems (for a review of barriers to work, see Danziger et al, 2000). Some problems which managers cite as impediments to employment that are also common among recipients – transportation needs, childcare problems, low sense of personal mastery and lack of job skills – are sometimes targeted for services. Most programmes provide childcare subsidies, along with vouchers for public transportation or vans. Lack of work experience, self-esteem and 'soft' skills (those that pertain to personality, attitude and ability to get along with customers, co-workers and supervisors) are the target of some workshops and job search strategies. In contrast, health and mental health problems are not usually assessed or treated, and educational pursuits are not generally supported as alternatives to or substitutes for employment. As welfare rolls continue to decline, it is likely that the proportion of the caseload with these problems will increase.

Given the needs of welfare recipients and the current programme design, in what directions might the Work First model be improved? First, applicants would be assessed and referred for services for health and mental health problems and perhaps would receive treatment prior to job search. Because managers realise that such problems make people hard to employ, some recipients might be allowed to fulfil their work requirement by participating in treatment[7]. In at least two states, Oregon and Utah, welfare-to-work programmes are staffed with mental health professionals who provide counselling services and referrals to treatment programmes (Johnson and Meckstroth, 1998).

Second, clients with few work skills, little prior work experience, and educational deficiencies might be referred for more intensive training. While long-term investments in education and training are not allowable under the PRWORA, participation in short-term job training is allowed. In Michigan, the Work First programme now allows clients to participate in 'condensed vocational training', no longer than six months in duration, or to combine work with training or participation in high school equivalency (General Educational Development test [GED]) preparation. However, GED preparation does not count towards work participation rates (except in the case of teenage recipients).

Programmes could also provide financial assistance for clients' car purchases and repairs. A new federal programme, Access to Jobs and Reverse Commute Program operated through the US Department of Transportation, has the goal of improving transportation options for welfare recipients.

Mandating work and job search, in the context of the economic boom of the 1990s, moved many recipients into the work force. However, many have moved into low-skill, low-paying jobs. The reforms to the mandated work approach suggested here would, if successful, do a better job in promoting the broader goals of job retention, job growth, and increased family well-being.

Making work pay

In late 2000, the entitlement to cash assistance had ended and welfare rolls had declined more than most analysts had predicted when the reform was passed. The PRWORA did not, however, transform the cash-based safety net of AFDC into an effective work-based safety net – there is no guarantee that a lone mother who seeks work but cannot find a job will receive any cash assistance or any opportunity to work in return for assistance.

As mentioned above, however, the PRWORA gave states great latitude in setting welfare rules related to how the earnings of welfare recipients affect their cash assistance payments. As a result, more than 40 states have changed their rules to do more to 'make work pay'. Most have eliminated the 'welfare trap' that previously existed – that is between 1981 and 1996, most single mothers experienced a decline in net income if they went from being a non-working welfare recipient to a part-time worker at the minimum wage.

This disincentive resulted from the fact that once a welfare recipient worked for four months, benefits were reduced by one dollar for every dollar earned. And many women lost Medicaid when they went to work. Thus, single mothers were faced with the choice of receiving welfare or working, and many 'chose' welfare, both because it allowed them to stay at home with their children and because work did not pay.

The PRWORA's strict work requirements no longer allow a single mother to choose to stay at home with her children, but the law no longer prevents a state from supplementing her low earnings with cash assistance. For example, in Michigan, a woman must work once her youngest child is three months or take part in work-related activities for at least 20 hours per week – she cannot choose to stay at home with her baby. However, Michigan now allows her to keep her first $200 in monthly earnings and 20% of the remainder; California has a $225 disregard and allows her to keep 50% of the remainder; Illinois disregards 67% of her earnings (Gallagher et al, 1998). In Michigan, a single mother of two children who does not work can receive a maximum cash benefit of $489 per month. If she works 30 hours per week at the minimum wage ($5.15 per hour), she will earn about $670 per month. Under the new earnings disregard she will receive $113 per month in cash assistance in addition to her earnings[8].

In addition to welfare reform, there has been a major change outside of welfare that also increases the financial rewards of work. The EITC, enacted in 1975, provides all working poor families with a refundable income tax credit (ie the family receives a payment from the Internal Revenue Service if the credit due exceeds the income tax owed). The EITC raises the effective wage of low-income families, is available to both one- and two-parent families, and does not require them to apply for welfare. The maximum annual EITC for a poor family was $953 in 1990. After several legislative increases, the maximum EITC for families with two or more children was $3,756 in 1998; it was $2,272 for families with one child. A single mother with two children earning $670 per month would receive an EITC of about $3,000 per year. The payment is usually received once a year, as a lump sum payment.

In addition, in 1986 a woman leaving welfare for work and her children would have lost medical coverage, but by 1997, her children would remain eligible for government paid health insurance because of a post-PRWORA programme, the Children's Health Insurance Program.

Danziger et al (2001) document that it pays to move from welfare to work in Michigan. The authors analysed data from a sample of about 700 women who received welfare in February 1997 and were interviewed in Autumn 1997 and 1998. Respondents reported, for the month before the interview, work hours, earnings, welfare receipt and income from a variety of sources. Respondents were also asked about work-related childcare and transportation expenses. In addition to the reported income sources, the study imputed the value of federal and state income taxes, the EITC and the employee's share of Social Security taxes.

The authors classified the women by their work/welfare status: wage-reliant women were those who reported earnings, but no cash welfare income (43.6% of the sample at the second wave, 1998); combiners were those who reported both earnings and cash welfare in the interview month (27.1% of the sample); welfare-reliant mothers were those who received welfare but no earnings (20.4%); the final category included those who were neither working nor receiving cash welfare (8.9%).

When Danziger et al took all these income sources and the EITC into account and subtracted taxes, work-related childcare and transportation expenses, they found that the average net monthly income was $1,677 for wage-reliant mothers, $1,449 for combiners, $1,027 for welfare-reliant mothers and $1,178 for those not working and not receiving welfare. Working mothers have, on average, higher incomes than welfare mothers. Wage-reliant mothers had an average net income 63% higher than that of welfare-reliant mothers, and women combining work and welfare had a net income 41% higher than that of the welfare-reliant. Thus, in Michigan it does now pay to move from welfare to work.

Nonetheless, poverty remains high for these single mothers after welfare reform – the monthly poverty rate for all respondents was 53.5% (the official US 1998 federal poverty threshold for a household of the woman's size is divided by 12); 38.4% of wage-reliant mothers, 53% of combiners, 83.3% of welfare-reliant mothers and 68% of those who were neither working or receiving welfare were poor. The good news is that poverty is much lower for workers than for non-workers. The bad news is that poverty remains very high for workers, and the annual poverty rate would be even higher than these numbers indicate because most wage-reliant women do not work, and hence do not earn this much, every month.

Similar results are evident from the Minnesota Family Investment Program (MFIP), which was evaluated in a randomised demonstration by the Manpower Demonstration Research Corporation (MDRC) (this summary is based on Berlin, 2000). For long-term welfare recipients, MFIP increased the welfare benefit by 20% for those who took a job and allowed recipients to keep 38% of every dollar earned. It also required long-term recipients who were not working at least 30 hours per week to participate in job search or other work requirements. Thus, MFIP anticipated the kind of welfare reform that has evolved in most states after 1996 – increased work requirements to boost work effort and increased work incentives to make work pay.

According to the MDRC evaluation (Knox et al, 2000), the percentage of single-parent long-term programme participants who worked in an average quarter (in the first nine quarters after the programme began) was about 50%, compared to 37% of the controls. The poverty rate was about 75% for the treatment group, but 85% for the controls. Unlike the data from the Michigan sample, these data do not include income from other household earners, an estimated value of taxes and the EITC, or a measure of work-related expenses. But the results are similar – welfare reforms that increase work requirements and work incentives improve the financial situation of welfare recipients when they move into work, but more must be done if poverty is to be reduced.

Thus, in a booming economy, most welfare recipients can find some work but many do not escape poverty. The economic incentives now in place are in accord with the goals of policy planners – on average, wage-reliant mothers and those combining work and welfare are economically better off than welfare-reliant mothers. These results also suggest that more attention should be paid to factors that prevent those remaining welfare-reliant from going to work. The new economic incentives and the increased pressure to leave welfare make it unlikely that many lone mothers are rejecting work and choosing to stay on welfare. Rather, many of them have problems, such as poor physical and/or mental health or lack of job skills, which prevent them from getting and keeping jobs even when unemployment rates are low (Danziger et al, 2000).

In the aftermath of welfare reform, many welfare-reliant mothers are at high risk of losing cash assistance benefits due to sanctions and/or impending time limits. And, in many states, mothers combining work and welfare are also at risk of losing benefits due to time limits. Now that it is economically beneficial to move from welfare to work, there remains a need for additional policies to make work pay enough so that a greater percentage of working mothers can escape poverty and for enhanced policies to help welfare-reliant mothers move into regular jobs or into subsidised employment.

The law now requires lone parents who have no serious impairments to take personal responsibility and look for work. However, the PRWORA absolves the state of any responsibility; even if a woman diligently searches for work without finding a job, her cash assistance can be terminated. At a minimum, lone mothers should be offered an opportunity to perform community service in return for continued cash assistance. A more costly option, but one that would have a greater anti-poverty impact, would be to provide low-wage public service jobs as a last resort. Welfare recipients who were willing to work could then combine wages with the EITC and support their families even when there was little employer demand for their skills.

If we are to reduce poverty as well as the welfare caseload, we must demonstrate a greater willingness to spend public funds to complete the task of turning a cash-based safety net into a work-oriented safety net. For recipients with the most extensive personal problems as mentioned in the previous section, this requires an expansion of social service and treatment programmes, but also merits experimentation with supported work programmes, where participants work in closely supervised settings.

Helping families with childcare

The federal government and states have greatly expanded their investment in childcare since the PRWORA was enacted. The Act consolidated federal funding into a Child Care and Development Block Grant (CCDBG); 20 billion dollars were allocated for the period 1997 to 2002, reflecting a 25% increase (an additional four billion dollars) over the spending provided under prior legislation (US House of Representatives, Committee on Ways and Means, 1998). States can increase spending further by shifting federal funds out of their TANF block grants. Additionally, states were given new flexibility in designing subsidy systems.

As a result, state childcare systems are now more varied than ever before. In this section, we use data from Illinois to illustrate one state's policies. Illinois is a large state that has greatly increased childcare spending since the PRWORA, but still faces challenges in meeting the childcare needs of lone mothers. Illinois is not representative of other states. As we shall see below, it is one of few states to guarantee childcare assistance to low-income families; it has made a somewhat higher level of investment in childcare than other states; and it is one of few states that contract directly with childcare providers. Illinois thus provides a good example of expanding childcare provision. (For an overview of childcare developments in all states, see Blank and Poersch, 2000.)

Policies that help families find and pay for adequate non-parental childcare can facilitate the employment of lone mothers. All else equal, mothers facing lower childcare costs are more likely to be employed, particularly low-income or single mothers (Han and Waldfogel, 2000). Low-income single mothers also report being more likely to work when care is more available (Mason and Kuhlthau, 1992) and when they are more satisfied with the quality of care (Meyers, 1993). Problems with childcare can lead lone mothers to leave jobs and can also adversely affect attendance, work hours and career advancement.

In addition, the quality of childcare may influence child outcomes. When childcare is of a high quality, children gain cognitively and socio-emotionally (National Institute of Child Health and Human Development [NICHD] Early Child Care Research Network, 1999, 2000). However, the quality of care in most settings in the US is only poor to fair, with children from low-income or single-mother families the least likely to attend high-quality day care centres, unless they are fortunate enough to get a subsidised space in a private day care centre or in an especially good Head Start centre (Head Start is the federal government's early education programme for three- and four-year-olds from low-income families) (Galinsky et al, 1994). Thus, it is important to consider both how to make childcare more affordable and accessible and how to improve its quality.

Policies to make childcare affordable and accessible include: providing subsidies; giving families choices to use the subsidies; expanding the supply of care, so that care is available at the hours families need it; and integrating welfare and non-welfare subsidies, so that families do not lose their subsidy when they leave welfare for work. There are also ways to enhance the quality of care. We consider these aspects of childcare policy in Illinois.

Providing subsidies

Every state sets its own policies for childcare subsidies. Typically, states set eligibility criteria (including a family income cut-off expressed as an amount in dollars, or a percentage of the poverty line, or of the state's median income, and a requirement that the parent be working or participating in education or training) and then provide subsidies to a subset of eligible families, depending on the availability of funds. Prior to the PRWORA, welfare recipients or former welfare recipients had priority, but this is no longer required under federal law (although it is still often the case in practice).

Illinois had this kind of policy until 1997. Now, any family whose income falls below 50% of the state's median income (and who meets the other eligibility criteria) is guaranteed a childcare subsidy. To make the guarantee feasible, Illinois dropped its family income cut-off, from $26,230 to $21,819 for a family of three (Adams and Schulman, 1998), and thus has a relatively low income cut-off (50% of state median income and roughly 155% of the 1999 federal poverty line) compared to other states (whose cut-offs range from 50 to 85% of the state median income and from 125 to 255% of the poverty line) (State Policy Documentation Project, 1999). Illinois recently implicitly raised its cut-off by disregarding the first 10% of a family's earnings in computing income eligibility.

Illinois is one of only five states that guarantee a subsidy to low-income families. The others are Iowa, whose cut-off is 155% of the federal poverty line; Kansas, at 185%; Rhode Island, at 225%; and Wisconsin, at 165% (State Policy Documentation Project, 1999).

The guarantee provides a powerful message to low-income women with children – "There are no waiting lists. All families who fall within the income categories for their family size are eligible" (Illinois DHS, 2000a, p1). As the public becomes more aware of this guarantee, the share of eligible families using subsidies, many of whom will never have received welfare, is likely to increase.

Unfortunately, only limited information on subsidy use is currently available. A study of welfare leavers interviewed in late 1998, found that 36% received a childcare subsidy, but that 31% reported problems paying for childcare (Julnes and Halter, 1999). We do not know what share of other low-income women are receiving subsidies or how the rates of subsidy receipt have changed over time. Evidence from other states suggests that rates of subsidy use have been surprisingly low, possibly because women are not receiving information about subsidies or think that they are not eligible, find applying too difficult, or perceive that waiting lists are too long (Meyers and Heintze, 1999; US Department of Health and Human Services, Child Care Bureau, 1999).

In addition to eligibility criteria, the rate at which providers are reimbursed affects the use of subsidies. If a provider accepts a state-subsidised client, it must accept this price for its services (although if its regular rate is higher, it may in some states ask the parent to make up the difference). Illinois now pays up to the 75th percentile of the 'market rate', similar to most other states. In the fiscal year 1999, 81% of childcare providers in Illinois said that they would accept a subsidised client, up from 60% the previous year (Ramsburg and Montanelli, 2000) when its rate had been as low as the 43rd percentile of the market rate in some communities (Adams and Schulman, 1998).

States also set co-payment policies. Consistent with standard practice, Illinois requires a family to make a small co-payment, which varies according to the family's income. Co-payments for one child range from $1 per week for the poorest families to $31 per week for those with incomes close to the income cut-off for eligibility. Co-payments do not vary according to the cost of the care. Child advocates consider this important, as it does not create incentives for families to choose lower cost forms of care.

As welfare caseloads have fallen and as more single mothers have gone to work, Illinois' spending on childcare and the numbers of children served have grown dramatically. Total spending on childcare grew from $187 million in the fiscal year 1995 to a projected $656 million in the fiscal year 2001, while the numbers of children served each month grew from 65,000 to a projected 218,000 over the same time period (see Table 3.3). Although data on the share of children in low-income lone-mother families being served are not available, the increase must be large as well.

Table 3.3: Childcare spending and numbers of children served in Illinois (1995-2001)

Year	Annual spending (in $ millions)	Children served (per month)
1995	187	65,000
1996	226	82,000
1997	263	92,000
1998	307	115,000
1999	448	154,000
2000	591	195,000
2001	656	218,000

Source: 'DHS child care', DHS Division of Transitional Services (www.state.il.us/agency/dhs.budget/overview/transsvc.pdf)

Giving families choices

Illinois, like other states, reimburses childcare arranged by families, as well as care delivered by contracted providers. Most subsidised families select a provider and then work with a local Child Care Resource and Referral Agency (a non-profit organisation that helps families locate childcare and that in Illinois also administers the subsidy) to set up the reimbursement. Parents can choose any type of care – a childcare centre, family day care home, or care provided in their own home or in a relative's home – and any specific provider, so long as space is available and the provider meets licensing requirements. Providers bill the state once a month, and payments are issued about three weeks later. About one in six subsidised families use care delivered by providers (typically, large day care centres) that have contracts with the state to provide a certain number of slots at an agreed rate. (Illinois is unusual in this regard, as states have tended to move away from contracts to voucher type systems.)

Illinois notes, "This dual system provides families with the freedom to choose from a variety of childcare settings to best meet the needs of both parents and children" (Illinois DHS, 2000b, p 3). However, choices are constrained by the supply of care available. If there are shortages of care of particular types or for children of particular ages or at particular hours, allowing parents to choose may not ensure that parents' and children's needs are met. There may also be shortages in particular neighbourhoods or communities (Julnes and Halter, 1999).

Expanding supply

Illinois, like most states, has historically had a limited supply of certain types of care (Adams and Schulman, 1998), especially care for infants and toddlers, and care during night and weekend hours. Demand for these types of care has grown since welfare reform. For instance, the number of families seeking toddler care doubled from 1997 to 1999, while the number of families requesting weekend care increased by more than 50% (Ramsburg and Montanelli, 2000). To address supply shortfalls, the state now offers incentives to providers. For instance, licensed providers who make 25% of their slots available to children under two, and who reserve half of those slots for subsidised children, are reimbursed at a 10% higher rate for the children they serve under the age of two. Incentives are also offered to licensed providers who agree to stay open at nights and on weekends.

Integrating welfare and non-welfare services

There is a tension in childcare policy between targeting services to welfare recipients and making services more universally available, so that families are not denied benefits simply because they leave welfare or did not receive welfare in the first place. Prior to the PRWORA, federal policy required states to guarantee childcare to working recipients; other families could be served only to the extent that funds remained. The PRWORA gave states the flexibility to design their own policies. Many states continue to give current and former welfare recipients priority, thus setting up competition between them and low-income families who have not been welfare recipients. Illinois, as noted above, guarantees a subsidy to any family whose income falls below 50% of the state's median income, without regard to welfare receipt. And because the subsidies are administered by childcare resource and referral agencies or contracted providers, applicants need not have any contact with the welfare department. Indeed, non-welfare families now make up the majority of subsidy recipients – their share increased from 46 to 57% from 1998 to 1999 (Ramsburg and Montanelli, 2000).

Quality enhancements

Although the quality of care in many settings is poor or mediocre (Galinsky et al, 1994; Helburn, 1995; NICHD Early Child Care Research Network, 1999), little is known about the quality of care being used by the children of women leaving welfare. Few studies of welfare leavers have measured childcare quality (Fuller and Kagan, 2000). With regard to the type of care, women leaving welfare for work are more likely to use informal care (such as care by a friend or relative) than formal care (such as care in a day care centre or licensed day care home); and women who do not have a subsidy are the least likely to use centre-based care. However, we do not know whether this reflects the fact that they could not afford centre-based care, or that they preferred to use a friend or relative.

Data on the quality and type of care being used in Illinois is sparse as well. Most subsidy recipients make their own arrangements, with only about one sixth using contracted centres. About two thirds of subsidy recipients use informal types of care, with 41% using relatives and 25% using in-home care (Piecyk et al, 1999).

Illinois is attempting to improve childcare quality through increased funding. In the fiscal year 2000, Illinois spent $27 million on quality enhancement efforts, up from $7 million two years earlier (Illinois DHS, 2000b). A major quality enhancement effort involves making Head Start more accessible to the children of employed mothers. Head Start has long provided fairly high-quality care for children of low-income lone mothers. However, because Head Start programmes are typically part-day programmes and are not open year-round, using them has been a problem for employed mothers. Illinois is spending nearly $8 million each year to enable selected Head Start programmes to open all day and all year and to focus on the children of employed mothers. Illinois is also spending about $1.5 million in the fiscal year 2001 on a programme to monitor the childcare delivered by relatives or provided in-home (this kind of care, which is exempt from licensing, serves about two thirds of the children funded by subsidies). Illinois will also spend $2.4 million in the fiscal year 2001 (up from $1.4 million the previous year) on the TEACH (Teacher Education and Compensation Helps) programme (imported from North Carolina), which offers family or centre-based childcare providers funding to attend college, and financial incentives to stay on as providers after they complete the programme.

Assessing Illinois' experience with childcare

Illinois' experience suggests that a state can develop a more coherent policy and play a more active role in the childcare market. Illinois has greatly increased spending to lower costs, to make more care available, and to improve the quality of care. It is one of only a few states that guarantee a childcare subsidy to low-income families. To support this policy, Illinois has greatly increased state funding for childcare, but it has also targeted its funding to families below a relatively low-income cut-off.

Unfortunately, we do not know as much as we would like about how effective these efforts are. Lone-mothers' employment has increased rapidly in Illinois and in other states, but we do not know how important childcare has been in driving that increase. Few studies have examined the impact of childcare policies on employment after welfare reform, and they have not examined specific childcare policies or the impact on child outcomes. Bainbridge et al (2000) found that increased government expenditure on childcare subsidies accounts for only a small share of the increase in lone-mothers' weekly employment post welfare reform.

Lessons from the US experience

Welfare reform has been more successful than most policy analysts anticipated when the 1996 PRWORA was signed. Bolstered by a strong economy and a surge of federal funding to the states, welfare reform has contributed to large declines in the welfare rolls and increased work among lone mothers, and has been modestly successful in raising incomes for those who work. We illustrate what selected states have done in three key areas – mandating work, making work pay, and helping with childcare – that contribute to these successes to date.

However, many lone mothers, who are not able to find and keep jobs, are worse off financially as a result of the reforms. Many others are no better off financially – they have simply moved from the ranks of the welfare poor to the working poor. In many states, a single mother with a pre-school age child is expected to work at least 30 hours per week, at a minimum wage job with only a modest amount of childcare subsidy and EITC, and health insurance only for her children.

Thus, the picture from the states is mixed. Welfare-to-work programmes, programmes to make work pay, and childcare subsidies have contributed to the increased employment of lone mothers. However, lone mothers and their children remain at high risk of poverty and hardship.

These results suggest that countries that are willing to end the entitlement to cash assistance, and accept some increases in hardship, can look to the US as a model for increasing the employment of lone mothers. Other countries, however, might derive a different lesson and choose to both increase employment and reduce financial hardship. Following this path requires a range of policies and services not yet available in the US, which would more completely transform a cash-based safety net into a work-based safety net. For the most part, even though the US has, since the PRWORA, done a better job at making work pay and helping families with childcare, it has not done enough to provide work opportunities and social services for those who have been unable to find steady work in the best labour market in three decades.

Notes

[1] This research was supported in part by grants from the Ford Foundation and the Joyce Foundation. We are grateful to Elizabeth Inez Johnson for help gathering data on state welfare and childcare programmes, to Gina Adams for helpful conversations about childcare policies, and to Maria Cancian and Jane Millar for

helpful comments on an earlier draft. We are also grateful to the Centre for Analysis of Social Exclusion (CASE) at the London School of Economics where Waldfogel and the Danzigers were visitors when this paper was prepared. A version of this paper was published by CASE as a CASE paper.

[2] In the US, a child is a person below the age of 18, and a lone mother is a mother whose marital status is either never married or previously married (ie divorced, separated or widowed). Thus, included in the count of lone mothers are women who may be cohabiting.

[3] No more than 20% of the caseload can participate in vocational training and count towards the work participation rate.

[4] The number of deferred cases has remained around 32,000, while the total caseload declined from approximately 155,000 at the beginning of 1997 to about 77,000 at the end of 1999.

[5] Two programmes could not be categorised using this scheme.

[6] Due to the manner in which data is kept in Michigan (regionally, rather than by the Work First agency), we are unable to determine if one of the four Work First programme models is more effective at moving clients into jobs.

[7] While these activities do not count towards the federal work participation requirement, states are not precluded from assigning clients to non-work activities.

[8] All amounts are given in US dollars. As of September 2001, one US dollar was equal to £0.68 British pounds.

FOUR

Lone parents and employment in Australia[1]

Peter Whiteford

Introduction

Over the last 30 years, the number of lone-parent families[2] in Australia has trebled from 7.1% of families with children in 1969 to 21.4% in 1999 (ABS, various years). The level of lone parenthood in Australia is thus somewhat lower than in other English-speaking countries or some Nordic countries, but higher than in many countries of continental Europe.

Rates of growth of lone parenthood were particularly rapid in the 1970s (10.5% per year on average), slowed in the 1980s (3.4% per year), but increased again in the 1990s (6.5% per year, and from a much higher base). Table 4.1 summarises trends in family formation and dissolution related to the growth in lone-parent families. Over the past 30 years fertility rates have declined, as has the crude marriage rate. The divorce rate was very low (under one per 1,000 population) until the 1975 Family Law Act, which provided for no fault divorce after 12 months separation. The divorce rate rose sharply in 1976 to more than 4.5 per 1,000 of population. This largely reflected the formal recognition of a backlog of longstanding marriage breakdowns. After 1976, the divorce rate dropped back to fluctuate between 2.5 and 2.9 per 1,000 of population. This is equivalent to between 10 and 12 per 1,000 married persons. The proportion of divorces involving children fell from around 60% in 1986 to around 53% in 1998.

Births outside marriage have increased significantly, from less than 10% in the 1960s to around 29% in 1998. However, the proportion of all births where the father has his name on the birth certificate has increased from under half in the 1970s to more than 85% by the late 1990s. It can

Table 4.1: Selected family trends, Australia (1966-99)

	1966	1971	1976	1981	1986	1989	1992	1995	1998	1999
All lone parents (000s)	–	124.6	203.3	282.2	319.9	330.3	412.1	463.8	548.8	545.4
% of families with children	–	7.1	10.1	13.2	14.6	14.6	17.1	19.0	21.5	21.4
Lone parents on benefits	–	44.0	116.6	194.5	250.9	248.9	287.2	324.9	372.3	384.8
Coverage rate (%)	–	35.3	57.4	68.9	78.4	72.5	69.7	70.1	67.8	70.6
Total fertility rate	2.88	2.87	2.06	1.94	1.87	1.84	1.89	1.82	1.76	
Crude marriage rate (per 1,000 population)	8.3	9.2	7.9	7.6	7.2	–	6.6	6.1	5.9	
Crude divorce rate (per 1,000 population)	0.8	1.0	4.5	2.8	2.5	2.5	2.6	2.8	2.7	
% of divorces involving children	64.5	67.6	67.6	60.5	59.7	55.3	52.9	–	53.4	
Births outside marriage (% of all births)	5.1	7.4	9.3	10.1	16.8	20.2	24.0	26.6	28.7	
Births acknowledged by father (%)	–	–	46.9	60.4	70.6	75.9	81.0	83.3	87.1	
Teenage birth rates per 1,000 females aged 15-17	–	–	–	–		10.7	10.6	10.6	–	
De facto couples (% of all couples) (% with children)	–	–	–	–	5.7	–	8.5 (39)	–	–	
Living arrangements of children				(1982)					(1997)	
With natural parents (%)				–			83		74	
With one step-parent (%)				–			4		8	
Registered married (%)				86			81		76	
Cohabiting (%)				3			5		6	
All couples (%)				89			86		82	
Mother only (%)				10			13		16	
Father only (%)				1			1		2	

Source: ABS (1998, Cat No 4102.0); De Vaus and Wolcott (1997)

be calculated that 4.9% of persons born in 1976 did not have their father officially identified, but in 1998 this was around 3.7%. Teenage birth rates have fallen very significantly from 48.9 per 1,000 female teenagers in 1966 to around 20 per 1,000 female teenagers in the late 1990s. This was mostly related to a sharp fall in the early 1970s, and a more gradual decline thereafter, with rough stability since the late 1980s. Cohabitation has become more common, although it is still only a small proportion of couples who live together. However, the proportion of cohabiting couples who have children has increased from 39 to 46% over the 1990s.

Lone parenthood in Australia is most commonly the consequence of separation or divorce (63% of lone parents in 1997)[3] and is also concentrated among persons over the age of 35 (61.4% of lone parents). Since the 1970s, age-specific rates of lone parenthood have fallen for teenagers, but because births to teenagers fell even more, lone mothers have increased as a proportion of all teenage mothers.

Table 4.2 provides a profile of lone-parent families in 1999. Most lone parents are women – 89% in 1999 and nearly 95% of those with a youngest child under five years. Overall, about one third of lone parents have a youngest child under five years of age (and nearly 40% if those whose youngest child is a dependent student aged 15 to 24 years are excluded). Female lone parents are more likely to have younger children than males, and are themselves younger. Half of all lone parents have only one dependent child.

Indigenous families have much higher levels of lone parenthood than those from other backgrounds, with around one third of indigenous families having lone parents, but indigenous families comprise only a very small percentage of the total Australian population. Women born overseas in other English-speaking countries tend to have rates of lone parenthood that are higher than the overall average, while most of those born in non-English-speaking countries tend to have lower rates of lone parenthood. The major exception is among families from Indo-China, who have had very high rates of lone parenthood, probably as a consequence of being refugees.

The benefit system

Levels of receipt of income-tested benefits among lone-parent families are among the highest in the Organization of Economic Co-operation and Development (OECD). Around 70% of Australian lone parents receive government income support payments[4], an increase from around 50% in

Table 4.2: Characteristics of lone-parent families with dependent children, Australia (June 1999)

	Females		Males		Persons	
	000s	%	000s	%	000s	%
All lone-parent families	485.6	100.0	59.7	100.0	545.4	100.0
Youngest child dependent						
0-4	160.9	33.1	9.3	15.6	170.2	31.2
5-9	137.1	28.2	11.9	19.9	149.0	27.3
10-14	119.7	24.7	19.1	32.0	138.8	25.4
15-24	67.9	14.0	19.4	32.5	87.3	16.0
Number of dependants						
1	237.3	48.9	38.2	64.0	275.5	50.5
2	164.4	33.9	16.7	28.0	181.2	33.2
3+	83.8	17.3	4.8	6.0	88.7	16.3
Employed						
Full-time	109.0	22.4	31.4	52.6	140.4	25.7
Part-time	119.3	24.6	6.4	10.7	125.7	23.0
Unemployed	42.3	8.7	5.5	9.2	47.7	8.7
Not in labour force	215.0	44.3	16.5	27.6	231.5	42.4
Age						
15-19	7.5	1.5	–	–	7.6	1.4
20-24	44.0	9.1	1.3	2.2	45.3	8.3
25-34	147.4	30.4	9.2	15.4	156.7	28.7
35-44	195.8	40.3	26.9	45.1	222.7	40.8
45-54	81.7	16.8	18.1	30.3	99.8	18.3
55+	8.1	1.7	4.5	7.5	12.7	2.3
Marital status (1997)						
Never married	143.8	32.1	12.3	17.9	156.1	30.2
Separated/ divorced	274.0	61.1	49.6	72.3	323.6	62.6
Widowed	29.7	6.6	6.4	9.3	36.1	7.0
Total	**448.2**	**100.0**	**68.6**	**100.0**	**516.8**	**100.0**

Source: ABS (June 1999, Cat No 6244.0); ABS (1997)

the 1970s, but a decline from levels approaching 80% in the early 1980s. In 1999, a further 10% of lone-parent families in low paid work received 'higher rates of family assistance' to supplement their earnings.

The Commonwealth introduced a national scheme of income support for lone parents in 1942. This assisted women with dependent children whose husband had either died or deserted them 'through no fault of their own', and who were unable to secure maintenance. Women who had lived in long-standing relationships were supported if their husbands died, but not if they were deserted. The basic concept underlying this support was of the loss of the breadwinner and consequent poverty (Jordan, 1980). Over time the scope of these provisions was widened. A major step was taken in 1973 with the introduction of Supporting Mothers Benefit, which made unmarried mothers and deserting wives eligible for Commonwealth assistance six months after the qualifying event. In 1977 support was extended to fathers. In 1980 the six-month waiting period was abolished. Since then virtually all lone parents have been eligible for the same form and level of assistance, irrespective of the reason for their lone parenthood[5].

Up until 1987, eligibility included those whose youngest dependent child was below 24 years of age and a full-time dependent student. It was then restricted to those with a youngest dependent under 16 years of age. In 1993 the system was liberalised by the removal of the maintenance income test applied on pensions and its application only to payments for children. In 1998 the Sole Parent Pension was renamed Parenting Payment (Single), with the other part of this programme – Parenting Payment (Partnered) – being paid to the partners (usually wives) of income support recipients with dependent children. In July 2000 as part of the compensation package accompanying the introduction of a Goods and Services Tax (VAT), rates of assistance were increased, the withdrawal rate on payments was reduced, and there were extensive changes to the system of assistance for families with children (Whiteford, 2000).

In summary, the main thrust of successive policy changes has been to extend uniform levels of assistance to virtually all lone parents, irrespective of the causes of their lone parenthood, and more recently to emphasise the parenting role provided by lone parents, and to equate this to the parenting role of mothers with partners.

The primary income support benefit for lone parents is the Parenting Payment (Single) (PPS). This is currently around A\$387 per fortnight[6]. Payments are indexed twice a year to the Consumer Price Index, and annually to Male Total Average Weekly Earnings (MTAWE) to ensure that payments do not fall below 25% of MTAWE. To be eligible for PPS, a lone parent must have responsibility for a qualifying child under 16 years of age, or an older child (with a disability) for whom the Carers Allowance is paid, and must have been an Australian resident continuously for two years, or must have become a lone parent while already resident in Australia. The PPS is available on an indefinite basis, so long as the parent has a qualifying child, and is not living in a 'marriage-like' relationship. Those receiving PPS are not required to actively look for work, although in the 2001 Budget it was announced that those with a youngest child aged six to 12 will be required to attend annual interviews and those with a youngest child of 13 years plus will be required to participate in around six hours of work–related activities per week.

The maximum PPS is paid until private incomes reach A$130.60 per fortnight for one child (plus an additional A$24.60 per fortnight for each additional child). Above this level of private income, payments are reduced by 40 cents for each dollar of gross taxable income. The point where the PPS is no longer payable for a parent with one child is nearly A$1,100 per fortnight. Child support payments are exempted from the income test for PPS and only reduce payments for children.

Lone parents are eligible for additional assistance for each child, with higher rates of assistance (Family Tax Benefit Part A) payable to persons receiving PPS or in low-paid work. Since July 2000 there has also been a non–means-tested payment for all single income families with children – including lone parents – that is paid at a higher rate for families with a youngest child under five years of age (Family Tax Benefit Part B). Both payments are refundable tax credits, although those receiving the PPS must receive these in the form of direct fortnightly deposits to bank or building society accounts. Lone parents on PPS also receive a small payment to assist with the costs of pharmaceutical drugs. They may be eligible for further assistance depending on their circumstances (whether renting publicly or privately, whether they have a telephone, whether they live in a remote area, whether they are caring for a child with a disability, or whether they are studying).

There are two main forms of assistance with rental costs, but none with mortgage costs. Income support recipients and low–income working families with children may be eligible for Rent Assistance (RA). Rent Assistance is available to those in the private rental market who pay rent above specified levels, varying by numbers of children. Around 35% of all lone parents rent privately. Public rental housing rebates are available to those with incomes below specified thresholds. Around 20% of lone parents live in public housing. While arrangements differ across states, most households pay between 20 and 25% of their gross income in rent. Generally speaking, the subsidies received by those in public housing are far more valuable than RA, and there are waiting lists to get into public housing.

The total package of benefits for a lone parent with one child under five years is around 45% of MTAWE, with the basic PPS being 25% of MTAWE. A lone parent would not lose entitlement to PPS until private income – not including child support – is roughly 70% of MTAWE. Because of the high cut-out points and because there are no 'hours rules' for benefit receipt, income support recipients can combine extensive part-time work and receipt of benefits. Around 27% of lone parents on PPS also have earnings. Around 30% of the lone parent population are completely reliant on benefits.

A central policy objective over the past 25 years has been to improve the cash incomes of lone parents, primarily through extension of coverage of income support and then through increases in levels of income support. This strategy has not been given equal emphasis in all periods, but still remains the dominant long-term characteristic of policy towards lone parents. From 1987 there was an explicit package to end child poverty, including increases in real rates of child allowances for income support recipients and low-income working families, and price indexation of these payments for the first time. Considerable effort was made to increase take-up of these allowances. Another reform was the introduction of the Child Support Scheme, which involved the administrative collection of child maintenance obligations (Millar and Whiteford, 1993). In 1997-98, there was around A$530 million in child support collected through the Child Support Agency and A$636 million paid through private agreements registered with the Child Support Agency. These payments benefited half a million families with roughly three quarters of a million children. At June 1998, 44.1% of PPS recipients were declaring child support, compared with 26% in 1988.

The most recent estimate of trends in child poverty by Harding and Szukalska (1999, 2000) uses differing poverty lines (the Henderson poverty line, plus a range of poverty lines set at either 50% of mean or median equivalent family income), and differing equivalence scales. Using the Henderson poverty line they estimated that child poverty rose from 20 to 24% of children between 1982 and 1996. However, using all other measures, poverty is estimated to have fallen by roughly 30 to 40%, to between 8 to 12.5% of children. A study by the OECD (Oxley et al, 2001) produces similar results. The OECD estimated that between 1984 and 1993-94 poverty was nearly halved among non-working lone parents and reduced by 80% among non-working couples with children, with the overall child poverty rate falling from 15.5 to 10.9%.

Analysis of trends in the incomes of lone-parent families shows that the real mean income of lone parents has increased by around 40% since

1973, compared to 21% for couples with children and 8% for the population as a whole (not adjusted for changing family size). As a consequence the average income of lone parents has increased from 54% of the population average to 70%, and from 37 to 44% of that of couples with children. Nevertheless, roughly 60% of lone parents receive government benefits as their principal source of income, and around 40% receive more than 40% of their income from cash benefits.

In summary, policy changes have been effective at reducing income poverty among families with children, even if child poverty has not 'ended'. However, lone parents remain concentrated among lower-income groups and are significantly more likely to be reliant on social security benefits than are other working-age population groups.

Employment patterns and trends

Around 47% of lone mothers were employed in 1999 and 63% of lone fathers. Roughly 9% of both lone mothers and lone fathers are unemployed. Just under half of those lone mothers with jobs are employed full time, compared to more than 80% of lone fathers with jobs. It is worth noting that the definition of full-time work is 35 hours a week or more. Table 4.3 shows a detailed disaggregation of labour force status and hours of work of parents. More than half of all lone mothers were not employed in June 1999, compared to 40.1% of partnered mothers. The proportion of lone mothers working less than 15 hours per week was slightly less than for partnered mothers (10.9 versus 13.1%), and the proportion working 35 hours per week or more was also only slightly different (22.3 versus 25.6%). The gap is widest for those working between 15 and 34 hours. Nevertheless, lone mothers who work have higher average hours than partnered mothers, because a slightly higher proportion of those who work do so full time.

Table 4.4 shows trends in the labour force status of lone and partnered mothers by the age of their youngest child. For both lone and partnered mothers, employment levels are strongly related to the age of the youngest child. From the early 1990s onwards, there appears to be a more marked increase in participation levels of lone mothers where the youngest child is a dependent student aged 15 to 24 years. Up until the early 1990s, lone mothers were significantly more likely to be employed full time than employed part time. However, full-time employment among lone mothers peaked at around 26% in 1991, and dropped back to around 22% for the rest of the 1990s. Full-time employment among partnered mothers

Table 4.3: Labour force status and hours of work, employed parents, Australia (June 1999) (%)

	Not employed			Part-time		Full-time	Average weekly hours worked		
	Unemployed	Not in labour force	Total not employed	0-14 hours	15-34 hours	35 hours+	Part-time workers	Full-time workers	All employed
All lone parents	8.8	42.4	51.3	10.0	13.0	25.7	16.2	40.3	28.9
Male lone parents	9.1	27.6	36.0	3.2	7.3	52.8	15.9	43.6	39.0
Female lone parents	8.8	44.3	53.1	10.9	13.7	22.3	16.3	39.3	27.2
Partnered mothers	3.0	37.1	40.1	13.1	21.2	25.6	16.8	38.9	26.2
Partnered fathers	4.2	7.2	11.4	1.7	3.7	83.3	19.2	45.0	43.4
All persons	4.4	35.6	40.0	7.2	8.9	44.0	15.9	42.2	35.2

Note: Expressed as a percentage of civilian population aged 15 years and over.

Source: ABS (June 1999)

Table 4.4: Labour force status of lone mothers and partnered mothers by age of youngest dependent child, Australia (1985-99) (%)

	Lone mothers				Partnered mothers			
	FTE	PTE	Unemp.	LFPT	FTE	PTE	Unemp.	LFPT
1985								
0-4	12.0	10.0	6.2	28.3	10.9	19.5	3.0	33.4
5-9	15.7	17.0	5.7	40.9	22.8	30.9	5.0	58.8
10-14	27.7	15.5	5.5	48.7	28.3	29.7	3.8	61.7
15-24	31.4	16.3	–	50.8	30.7	26.0	1.8	58.5
Total	21.0	14.3	5.4	40.8	20.1	27.0	3.4	50.5
1991								
0-4	13.3	15.9	8.2	37.4	14.6	29.5	3.4	47.2
5-9	21.9	24.1	8.9	54.9	27.2	38.4	4.4	69.9
10-14	32.3	21.1	5.3	58.4	35.2	35.4	3.1	73.7
15-24	51.0	15.8	4.3	71.1	37.3	29.3	1.8	68.4
Total	26.1	19.2	7.1	52.3	25.0	32.8	3.4	61.3
1995								
0-4	11.1	14.7	8.3	34.2	15.4	30.6	3.4	49.4
5-9	21.0	30.9	10.3	62.0	25.0	40.0	5.1	70.1
10-14	31.6	20.7	8.7	60.8	37.4	35.0	3.6	76.0
15-24	40.8	23.6	5.5	70.1	39.1	29.6	3.5	72.3
Total	22.4	21.6	8.5	52.6	26.5	34.3	3.8	64.6
1999								
0-4	9.6	15.7	9.9	35.5	15.9	30.2	3.3	49.4
5-9	21.4	31.7	9.2	62.2	27.5	38.8	3.4	69.7
10-14	26.5	28.3	7.9	64.0	33.5	37.8	2.3	73.6
15-24	47.9	24.0	6.6	80.5	38.0	33.3	2.7	74.0
Total	22.4	24.6	8.7	57.5	25.6	34.3	3.0	63.0

Note: FTE = full-time employment, PTE = part-time employment, Unemp. = Unemployed, LFPT = Labour Force Participation.
Source: ABS (various years)

increased only slightly after the early 1990s. From 1995 onwards there was a small gap in the levels of full-time employment among lone and partnered mothers (around 3 to 4 percentage points), and a more substantial gap in levels of part-time employment (around 9 to 12 percentage points).

Lone mothers have consistently experienced higher unemployment ratios than partnered mothers. In the 1980s the gap was around two percentage points, but has since widened to more than five percentage points. In 1999 lone mothers were nearly three times more likely to be unemployed than corresponding partnered mothers. Lone mothers also have longer durations of unemployment than partnered mothers, with the proportion unemployed for 26 weeks or more being 42% compared to 34% of partnered mothers.

Table 4.5 shows the 'employment gap', the difference between the respective employment to population ratios for lone and partnered mothers with the same characteristics. In 1999, the total employment gap was around 13%, ranging from nearly 21% for those whose youngest child was 0-4 years, to a 'surplus' of 0.6% for lone mothers with a youngest dependant aged 15-24 years. Most of the employment gap is due to differences in part-time employment (9.7% compared to a 3.2% difference in full-time employment), although there are also significant gaps in full-time employment for all except those whose youngest child is aged 15-24 years. The gap in part-time employment is large for those with a youngest child under five years of age. Employment gaps are greater for mothers under the age of 35 years.

A different perspective on the employment patterns of lone parents is offered by the Survey of Employment and Unemployment Patterns (SEUP), a longitudinal survey carried out in 1995 and 1996 (ABS, 1998). The survey covered two groups – the general population and persons classified as *jobseekers*[7] in May 1995. Among the general population, only 38% of lone parents worked for the whole year from September 1995 to September 1996. Another 25% worked part-year. The corresponding proportions for wives (with and without dependants) were 55 and 17%.

Table 4.5: The 'employment gap' for lone and partnered mothers, Australia (June 1999) (%)

	Full-time	**Part-time**	**Total employment**
Youngest child			
0-4	−6.3	−14.5	−20.8
5-9	−6.1	−7.1	−13.2
10-14	−7.0	−9.5	−16.5
15-24	+9.9	−9.3	+0.6
Age of mother			
15-34	−	−	−15.8
35-44	−	−	−12.2
45 and over	−	−	−6.5
Total	−3.2	−9.7	−12.9

Source: Calculated from ABS (1999)

Among working lone parents, three in 10 had more than one job during the year. Nearly a third of lone parents were unemployed and looking for work at some stage during the year, compared to 18% of husbands and 14% of wives. Twenty-five per cent of lone parents were completely absent from the labour force for the whole year and a further 21% were absent for part of the year. Lone parents were more likely to make labour force transitions – in or out of work or between full-time and part-time work – than husbands or wives. Just over a quarter of lone parents had a transition, compared to 19% of wives and only 10% of husbands. The likelihood of not being in work was substantially higher for lone parents with younger children.

Of the jobseeker sample, 41% of lone parents were working at the end of the year (and 9% of these were looking for different jobs). This compares to 48% of husbands and 47% of wives among jobseekers who were in employment at the end of the year. Around one third of lone parents who had been jobseekers at the beginning of the year were still looking for jobs at the end of the year. Among those who found jobs, nearly 60% were working part time, and roughly two thirds of these would have preferred longer hours in the same job.

Longitudinal data emphasise that a static analysis of lone parents' labour force behaviour is limited. For example, in 1995 less than half of all lone parents had a job at a point in time, but nearly two thirds had a job at some point in the year. Again, while about one in 12 lone parents are unemployed at a point in time, about one in three experience a spell of unemployment during a year. Over the course of a year about three quarters of lone parents participate in the labour force. This suggests that many lone parents are very committed to labour force participation. In particular, the unemployment rates show that a much higher proportion of lone mothers actively (if unsuccessfully) look for work than do married mothers, despite the fact that the benefit system gives them the 'option' of withdrawing from the labour force to look after their children.

Orientations to work and changing work requirements

As noted earlier, payments for lone parents are not subject to a work test so long as there is a qualifying child under 16 years of age, or if there is an older child with a disability requiring care. Apart from the UK, this appears to be the most liberal eligibility requirement for lone parents in the OECD. In fact, until 1987 eligibility conditions were even more liberal. Lone parents were entitled to assistance without a work test so long as they had a dependent student child less than 25 years of age.

This policy was originally based on the assumption that in a married couple husbands would normally have been the sole wage earner, so that mothers would have reduced capacity for employment following the death of a husband, or more rarely divorce (Jordan, 1980). Shaver (1990) argues that some of these features were reinforced by the non-contributory nature of the social security system, so that unlike in the US, for example, lone parents were not relegated to a restrictive social assistance scheme. The result was that "the fiscal logic of Australian income security allowed an ideology of maternalism to take direct, material form in pensions supporting widows and lone parents in full-time motherhood" (1990, p 13).

Over time, the logic of this approach has become less relevant to contemporary conditions. The Social Security Review in the second half of the 1980s canvassed lowering the eligibility age for dependent children to encourage labour force participation among lone parents (Raymond, 1987), and the government implemented the change in 1987. A number of subsequent studies assessed what happened to lone parents after the withdrawal of assistance. In fact, 80% of those affected by the change in entitlement age continued to receive some form of income support. Of these around five eighths continued to receive benefits without being work-tested.

In September 1999, the Minister for Family and Community Services announced that a Reference Group would be appointed to guide the development of a Green Paper on welfare reform. The final report on 'Participation Support for a More Equitable Society' was delivered in July 2000. The main conclusion of the report is that Australia's social support system should "activate, enhance and support people's capacities for economic and social participation" (Wilson, S., 2000, p 19). For lone parents, the most relevant proposals involve a new framework of 'mutual obligations'. Parents with pre-school age children should be regarded as fulfilling their obligations through their parenting role. Parents whose youngest child had entered primary school should be required to attend an annual face-to-face interview to discuss future plans and link them to available assistance on a voluntary basis. Parents whose youngest child had started secondary school should be required to attend the annual interview, and to enter a part-time participation plan to undertake job-search, training, education or other preparation for work activities. The measures announced in the 2001 Budget (as outlined above) are not exactly as proposed, but they do place more obligations on parents to seek, or prepare for, paid work.

Labour market programmes for lone parents

The most well-known initiative to encourage labour force participation among lone parents in Australia is the Jobs, Education and Training (JET) programme, which was introduced in 1989. Participation in JET is voluntary and it is open to all lone parents, plus some other groups. JET encourages participation from three groups of lone parents receiving PPS. These include teenagers, those who have received the payment for more than 12 months and whose youngest child is at least six years old, plus those who will lose eligibility for the payment within four years due to their youngest child turning 16 years.

After assessment, the adviser can refer the JET participant to an educational institution, fund a pre-vocational course, or register the person as looking for work and refer them to employment assistance. Participants are encouraged to find their own childcare, but if this is difficult there is specialised assistance available. JET participants, and certain other students who study full or part-time in approved courses, may receive the Pensioner Education Supplement of A$60 per fortnight and an Education Entry Payment of A$200 for each year of study.

At June 1998 there were 109 JET advisers providing a visiting service throughout Australia. Between 1989 and 1998 around 393,000 people were interviewed by JET advisers. By 1996 there were around 50,000 new JET interviews per year, which was roughly 15% of the stock of lone parents on benefits. The most common activity was referral to the Commonwealth Employment Service (CES), the then public sector job placement agency[8]. Around two thirds of those interviewed actually registered with the CES. The number of labour market placements per year was equivalent to about two thirds of CES registrations. The number of persons referred to education was roughly the same as the number of CES registrations. Around a third of those interviewed sought assistance with finding childcare. By 1996, there were around 20,000 employment placements per year, equivalent to roughly 6% of the stock of beneficiaries, and about 40% of the number of new JET interviews.

Indicative data on JET outcomes are available from the 1997 Evaluation Report (DSS et al, 1997). Data for these purposes came from a number of sources, the most important of which were administrative databases, plus a survey of 3,500 JET and non-JET participants undertaken by a private agency. In the absence of experimental data, the approach taken was to compare JET and non-JET participants in matched groups.

In assessing the following results, it can be noted that in terms of personal characteristics, there were few areas where JET participants appeared to differ to any marked extent from those of non-participants in the same groups. Just under half of all participants had been referred to the CES, with little difference across groups. Overall, slightly more participants had actually registered with the CES than had been referred to it. Only 20% of JET participants had been placed in a labour market programme, with placements being particularly low for teenagers. Just over 20% were placed in education, with rates being lower for those with young children, and for older participants. A similar pattern applied to those who received an Education Entry Payment. A quarter of participants had received an Employment Entry Payment. Just under 30% of participants were recorded as having earnings, of whom 7.3% had earnings below the free area (the amount of private income that a benefit recipient is allowed to receive before payments start to be reduced), and 21.2% had earnings above the free area. The proportion of participants with earnings increased with the age of the youngest child, and was higher among those who had been receiving payments for between three and five years. Receipt of earnings also increased with age to peak at around one third of those aged 35 to 49 years, before declining somewhat.

Table 4.6 shows cancellations of payments associated with JET. The

Table 4.6: Cancellation rates* for JET and non-JET participants, by duration of payment (1996) (%)

	JET		Non-JET		JET	
Duration of payment	Total cancellation rate	Of which % for earnings	Total cancellation rate	Of which % for earnings	% of stock	% of cancellations for earnings
1-6 months	–	–	–	–	–	–
6-12 months	25.6	25.3	24.1	15.9	27.5	39.5
1-2 years	19.5	23.4	18.7	14.9	38.6	51.0
3-5 years	15.4	23.1	13.4	15.0	42.8	61.0
5+ years	15.0	29.4	10.8	14.5	40.9	61.4
Total	18.1	23.1	17.3	15.2	39.8	45.8

Note: *Cancellation rates are expressed as a percentage of the sum of the stock plus the cancellations in the year.

Source: Whiteford (1997) (data from the 1996 JET evaluation)

total cancellation rate is slightly higher for JET participants than for non-participants, with the exception of those with durations of five years or more, where the cancellation rate is nearly 50% higher. However, JET participants appear to have been a higher proportion of those cancelled by reason of earnings, which suggests that JET participants are more likely to have moved into work than non-participants.

Table 4.7 compares levels of receipt of earnings among persons who remained on payments at February 1996. For each group, the table shows the proportion of JET and non-JET participants with earnings in 1996. These are compared with the percentage of JET participants with earnings at the time of their initial JET interview, plus the proportion of non-JET participants who did not participate because they already had earnings. This emphasises the fact that choice of a different basis for comparison will lead to different conclusions. For example, if lines two and three are compared then it appears that the differences between JET and non-JET participants are not particularly large in absolute terms – only about 6.3 percentage points higher among those who have been through JET. These

Table 4.7: Receipt of earnings among JET and non-JET participants, by target group (1996) (%)

	Youngest child 6-13	Teenager	Youngest child 14+	Other	Total
1. JET participants with earnings at initial JET interview	19.7	3.3	21.0	12.1	15.1
2. JET participants with earnings in February 1996	33.7	11.5	35.6	24.4	29.3
3. Non-JET with earnings at February 1996	29.8	6.7	31.3	18.7	23.0
4. Non-JET due to employment or education	–	–	–	–	23.4
Difference between 2 and 3	3.9	4.8	4.3	5.7	6.3
Difference between 1 and 2	14.0	8.2	14.6	12.3	14.2
Difference between 3 and 4	–	–	–	–	–0.4

Source: Whiteford (1997) (data from the 1996 JET evaluation)

differences are larger in relative terms, particularly for teenagers, who have much lower levels of earnings. If JET participants are compared to themselves when they had their initial JET interview, the differences are much larger in relative and absolute terms – about 14 percentage points rather than 6 percentage points.

Table 4.8 provides a tentative comparison between the results found for JET and those reported in Mead's (1996) analysis of welfare-to-work programmes in the US. The US studies employed experimental methods to estimate changes in average earnings associated with the various programmes. The Australian figures refer to the differences between the average earned incomes of JET and non-JET participants in each group. These are the product of the differences in the proportion with earnings and the average earnings of those with earnings, averaged across each group. For example, teenagers in JET have average earnings that are 130% higher than teenagers who did not participate in JET. However, this group is small, the proportion with earnings is small, and their average earnings are also small. Nevertheless, across all JET groups average earnings

Table 4.8: Results of main Manpower Development Research Corporation welfare employment evaluations and JET compared (%)

Study	Change
Arkansas 1985	31
Baltimore 1985	17
California GAIN 1994	25
Riverside GAIN 1994	40
Cook county 1987	1
Florida 1995	3
San Diego 1986	23
San Diego SWIM 1989	29
Virginia 1986	11
West Virginia 1984	4
Average*	16
JET target group	**difference**
Child 6-13	18
Child 14+	12
Teenager	130
Other	30
Total JET	32

Note: *Simple average unweighted by number of participants in each study.
Source: Mead (1996, pp 33-4); Whiteford (1997)

are roughly one third higher than average earnings for non-participants. This is a greater difference than the estimated change associated with any of the projects, apart from the Riverside GAIN demonstration.

Assessment of the success or otherwise of JET appears to be split between the official view that it has been very successful, and critics who question its effectiveness. Assessment is complicated by the fact that the evaluations that have been undertaken of JET have not been based on an experimental method, so that none of the evidence can be regarded as definitive. The criticisms are summarised by McHugh and Millar (1997), who point out that it is difficult to say whether any improvements in education, training and employment can actually be attributed to the programme. The basis for measuring savings from the programme is not clear. Given the voluntary nature of JET there is a problem of self-selection in that lone parents who participate are likely to be the most highly motivated. They also quote Jordan (1994) that participation in education and training is taken as a positive outcome when it is no more than a stage that may or may not result in positive employment outcomes. Their final set of arguments is that after the introduction of JET, employment levels of lone parents actually fell, while unemployment rates rose substantially.

All these arguments have considerable force, and are correct as far as they go. Most importantly, because the JET evaluations did not use an experimental design it is simply not possible to say whether JET does or does not work. Having said this, my own view is that the negative appraisal of JET is too strong, and that there are a number of arguments (and evidence) for seeing the programme as quite successful.

The first point relates to the possibility of selection bias because JET is a voluntary programme. Against this it can be noted that the primary reason given by those who chose not to participate in JET is that they already had a job or were in education or training. This implies the existence of a bias in the opposite direction, although whether it is sufficient to offset the other is uncertain. The second argument relates to official claims that JET has saved money, but that the basis for assessing this is unclear. While the basis for assessing the programme's success is unclear, critics may have pitched their criteria too high. In particular, the design features of the Australian income support system means that it is close to impossible to leave the programme. This is simply because the cut-out point for benefits is so high relative to average earnings, and in fact is higher than in any other social assistance scheme in the OECD.

In addition, while JET has a high profile, it is not an expensive programme. There are around 1,500 participants per JET adviser.

Administrative outlays are equivalent to expenditure of between A$300 and A$400 per participant whose earnings are counted as producing savings. For many, 'participation' means no more than having one interview with a JET adviser. Thus, the success of the programme is being measured by outcomes for groups of people receiving vastly different levels of contact and assistance. It is plausible that helping lone parents find employment takes a lot more than the average level of input for JET participants, but correspondingly it is possible that success would be more marked if the target group were to be narrowed in this way.

A further measurement issue suggests that official savings estimates may be underestimates. This is because estimated savings were only calculated on the basis of savings in the year of cancellation of payment and on current savings from increased earnings. Any long-term effects in terms of time that would otherwise be spent on payments were completely ignored. Finally, while aggregate labour force data show no evidence of improved employment among lone parents, the programme was phased in during the worst recession in Australia for 60 years. This raises the question of what the counterfactual would have been if labour market conditions had remained more favourable, or if JET had not existed. While the employment of lone parents dropped in the early 1990s, their labour force participation did not, with the difference being made up by increased unemployment rates. In addition, while aggregate labour force data do not show increased employment, administrative data show that the proportion of benefit recipients with earnings stabilised at around 20% in the early 1990s (compared to 15% in 1989). When economic recovery started around 1993, the proportion with earnings again started to increase to 26% by 1999 (Whiteford, 2000).

Making work pay for lone parents

The most distinctive feature of the Australian income support system is its reliance on targeting. One of the most salient issues with targeting is that income testing produces higher 'effective marginal tax rates' (EMTRs) over the income range where benefits are withdrawn. Over the past 15 years there have been many initiatives to address concerns about the potential impact of EMTRs. As part of general tax reforms in 1987, the government removed the separate income test on rent assistance, and increased free areas, and the income disregards for children.

Another strand of policy development also contributed to concerns about high EMTRs. Benefits for low-income working families were introduced in 1983 and expanded in scope from 1987 onwards as part of an anti-child poverty package. Improvements in in-work benefits allowed increases in income support for families with children, since it was possible to do both without increasing replacement rates. However, these in-work benefits extended the income range over which high EMTRs applied. In combination with the policies to reduce poverty traps for assistance recipients, the provision of in-work benefits extended high EMTRs further and further into the family income distribution. One indicator of this is that by the middle of the 1990s more than 40% of Australian children were living in families receiving income-tested family assistance. In essence, successive reforms were successful at reducing the 'poverty trap', but at the cost of creating 'low income traps'. This was subsequently highlighted in Australian policy analysis and debate, most comprehensively by Ingles (1997).

This problem has become the focus of government policy initiatives, with major reforms to family assistance in July 2000. In this package accompanying the introduction of a Goods and Services Tax, and including income tax cuts, the withdrawal rate on pensions was reduced from 50 to 40%. The withdrawal rate on family assistance was also reduced from 50 to 30%. In addition, increases in family assistance provided the largest increases for lone parents, particularly for those with a youngest child under five years of age.

Following the most recent changes, lone parents can keep about A\$80 out of their first A\$100 per week of earnings. Above this level they keep between A\$30 and A\$40 per week out of each A\$100 increment, and for lone parents with two children, net gains fall as low as A\$21 per week – a marginal tax rate of 79%. Even after these reforms, lone parents with two children face an average effective tax rate of around 60% on incomes between A\$100 and A\$800 per week. The receipt of rent assistance extends the range of income over which high EMTRs operate, and the range is greater for those with more children. For those renting public housing, effective tax rates could be up to 25% higher. Childcare costs are additional, and where Childcare Assistance is being income-tested (above A\$28,200 per year), EMTRs rise by an extra 10 percentage points (or more with additional children). Those who have older children receiving Youth Allowance also experience further stacking of income tests.

There have also been incentives to make work more attractive in other ways. In 1988, lone parents with a Pensioner Health Benefit Card were allowed to retain this for three months after their income exceeded the cut-out limits (by less than 25%). In 1991, two new supplementary payments were introduced – the Employment Entry Payment for lone-parent pensioners (and Disability Pensioners), and the Education Entry Payment for lone parents alone. The Employment Entry Payment (currently A$100) is payable to people who get full-time employment after they advise of their return to work. It can be paid once in a 12-month period. The Education Entry Payment (currently A$200 in a calendar year) is payable to assist with the costs of taking up study, such as purchasing books, student fees and course fees. In addition, those studying in an approved course can be paid a Pensioner Education Supplement, with higher rates for heavier study loads. In 1996, a more general system was introduced of allowing pensioners (including lone parents) to receive an advance of up to A$500 of their future pension entitlements, for a range of purposes including those relating to work.

Childcare and long day care

The age at which children start school is variable across states, but is usually in the year that the child turns either five or six, so long as the birthday is within four or five months of the beginning of the academic year (in February). Some states have an earlier pre-school year provided publicly, but this may be part-day and part-week only.

Over the past 20 years, there has been a substantial increase in assistance with childcare costs. The Commonwealth Childcare Programme funds the majority of childcare services in Australia, although it does not directly provide services. Between 1991 and 1998, the number of funded places increased from 168,000 to 399,000. In 1998, around 130,000 of these were in for-profit long day care centres, with a further 65,000 in community or employer provided long day care. Another 65,000 were in family day care, with 134,000 places funded in after-school hours care. Between 1991 and 1997, real government expenditure on children's services increased from around A$290 million to nearly A$1,200 million (in 1997 prices). (In the following year real expenditure fell by about 10%, because of budget cuts, mainly in operational subsidies and reduced Childcare Assistance.)

Long day care centres may be approved for payment of Child Care Benefit, which is a subsidy towards the cost of fees for low- and middle-income families. This subsidy is paid direct to centres, which then charge reduced fees to eligible families. Family day care centres may receive an operational subsidy and may also be eligible for Child Care Benefit.

Outside school hours care and vacation care may be subsidised, and there is support for new outside school hours services for the first two years of operation. Occasional care centres may receive operational funding.

Child Care Benefit provides a maximum assistance for 50 hours of care of A$120 per week (A$2.40 per hour) per child (for approved care). Actual levels of assistance depend on the number of children in childcare, hours of care, types of care and family income. If family income is less than A$28,200, families are eligible for the maximum rate of benefit. Above this level, taper rates are 10% for one child in care, 15% and (above A$66,000) 25% for two children in care, and 15% and (above A$66,000) 35% for three or more children in care. The income test does not apply for incomes above A$81,000. Families with income above this level are only eligible for the minimum rate of Child Care Benefit of A$20.10 per week. In 1997, 77% of families using long day care were receiving some fee relief, with 60% of these receiving the maximum relief. At December 1998, a family eligible for maximum assistance and paying the average fee of A$162 in private long day care would have received a government subsidy of A$109.60, paying A$52.40 privately.

Children in lone-parent families are over-represented in funded services. Children of lone parents account for 16% of children under four years of age and 19% of children aged five to 11 years. However, they account for 20% of children in long day care, 27% of those in family day care, and 22% of those in before or after-school care.

Family-friendly employment

Family-friendly provisions and practices can include on-site childcare centres, family rooms, brochures containing referral service numbers and contact details for employee assistance programmes, as well as conditions such as paid parental leave, career breaks and purchased leave schemes. Provisions such as flexitime, control over start and finish times, influence over the pace of work, access to a phone at work to use for family reasons and access to regular part-time work can assist in promoting a flexible workplace that directly benefits employees with families.

There is no statutory paid maternity or parental leave in Australia, although there is a right to one year's unpaid maternity leave for all workers covered by industrial awards. Just over one third of all workplaces with 20 or more employees offer paid maternity leave, and just under one fifth of these workplaces offer paid paternity leave. The conditions of this leave vary across workplaces, dependent on industrial awards and workplace conditions (DEWRSB, 1999).

It is difficult to make definitive statements about other family-friendly work conditions, although there is increasing consciousness of its importance. DEWRSB (1999) argue that there is evidence of progressive cultural change in approaches to work and family matters over the last decade. For example, 72% of organisations reporting to the Affirmative Action Agency provide paid leave to care for dependants. Between 1994 and 1997, the proportion offering permanent part-time work increased from 70 to 81%. In nearly two thirds of these organisations job-sharing opportunities existed. Two thirds of certified agreements include one or more family-friendly measures, such as flexible working hours, banking/ accrual of rostered days off, and time-off in lieu of overtime at ordinary time rates. Large workplaces in the public sector are most likely to have a range of family-friendly provisions.

Available research does not appear to consider the position of lone parents, who may have different perceptions, because all the need for time flexibility falls on one person rather than two. In addition, while organisations may report that they have family-friendly provisions, perceptions by employees may differ. In particular, someone who is seeking work, or thinking about seeking work, may not be aware of these flexible time provisions, and may not feel confident about asking about family leave provisions when applying for a job. It can also be noted that the absence of paid maternity leave as a universal right may indicate a lack of family friendliness. On the other hand, it could be considered that paid maternity leave is not relevant to the bulk of lone parents (as most become lone parents because of separation rather than new births).

Conclusion

Why do Australian lone parents have a comparatively low level of labour force participation?

One answer to this question is that it is actually not as low as often thought. While point in time data indicate that less than half of all lone parents have a job, over the course of a year the figure is more than 60%. Similarly, over the course of a year the labour force participation rate of lone parents is 75%, not under 60%. Correspondingly, complete non-participation in the labour force is 25%, not more than 40%. These differences are important. For example, in Australia it is common to make statements along the lines that "x per cent of children are being brought up in households with no one in paid employment". It is common to then go on to conclude that this proportion of children has no positive role models from whom to learn commitment to jobs. Underlying this characterisation is the image that all the lone parents who do not have a job at a point in time will never and have never had a job. From a longitudinal perspective, it is clear that this x per cent will almost inevitably be an overestimate. Indeed, it would seem fair to conclude that what children in these circumstances learn from their parents' labour force experience is that it is hard to find and keep jobs, since roughly one third of lone parents experience unemployment in the course of a year. Many also learn that their parents value employment strongly, or they would not keep looking.

The time dimension emphasises that policy makers may need to think in terms of disaggregated groups, not of lone parents as a homogeneous mass, who all require the same form of assistance to learn employment skills. It is also necessary to think of lone parents as disaggregated in terms of time. What is appropriate for one lone parent at a particular point in time may not be appropriate for an otherwise similar lone parent who happens to be at a different stage in their relation to the labour market.

Another answer to the question, why do lone parents have a comparatively low level of labour force participation, is that the system is designed to allow this, through relatively generous eligibility criteria and income-testing arrangements. But a further important result of the design of the benefit system is that the proportion of the population exposed to high EMTRs may well be higher than under a more restrictive social assistance scheme. That is, the disincentive effects may be less strong, but they will affect more of the population. As discussed earlier, most of the employment gap for lone mothers compared to partnered mothers is in part-time work. It seems reasonable to argue that this is no more than what could be expected from the potential disincentive effects of the benefit system.

It is also notable that Australian lone parents are paid to be parents, in a programme that equates them to partnered mothers. This appears to reflect a long-standing community support for mothers not to be 'forced' into work. Many Australian debates about childcare, for example, are based on the premise that it is best for mothers to provide childcare, particularly for young children. It seems reasonable to conclude that the most common view in Australia is that women with young children, including lone mothers, should have the right to combine motherhood and employment, with more emphasis on their role as mothers than workers (McHugh and Millar, 1997). While there is support for increasing labour force participation, this emphasises part-time rather than full-time work.

Ultimately, there are internal contradictions at the core of current policies. On the one hand, recent reforms of taxation and family benefits significantly increased assistance for lone mothers and mothers in single-income families, particularly for those with children below school age. In the case of mothers in low-income, single-income families, if they start to work they will face very high effective tax rates, as they will lose this assistance in addition to income testing of family benefits.

On the other hand, the most recent report on welfare reform (Reference Group on Welfare Reform, 2000) signals a move away from this approach, at least in the case of mothers whose children are of school age. However, as discussed earlier, the employment gap for lone mothers is largest for those with young children, but this is the group that would not be affected by the proposed participation activities. It would seem reasonable to conclude that Australian policy makers have not yet fully accepted the argument that it is paid work that is the only solution to poverty for lone parents.

Notes

[1] I am grateful for comments received from David Stanton and Jane Millar. The views expressed are my own and not those of the Organisation of Economic Co-operation and Development (OECD).

[2] In population statistics, dependants include all family members under 15 years of age, children aged 15-19 and attending school, and those aged 15-24 years attending a tertiary institution full time, and living in the same household as their parent (and who are not themselves classified as a husband, wife or sole parent). Dependants for payment purposes include all family members under 16 years of age, plus some older children with disabilities. Until 1987, the policy definition included dependent students up to 24 years of age.

[3] This may understate the role of separation, as it is not clear from published statistics how many of the 30% of lone parents who were never married were in *de facto* relationships before becoming lone parents.

[4] Coverage rates are difficult to estimate, because the age of children qualifying their parents for income support payments differs from the age ranges in population statistics. In addition, the definitions of dependent children both for programme purposes and statistical purposes have changed over time. Arguably, the figures used here underestimate coverage rates. Calculating coverage rates using a more restrictive age definition would increase the coverage rates, but would be an overestimate, and would also make the series less consistent over time.

[5] The major exception are those who have migrated to Australia as lone parents, and who are in the first two years of residence. Those who migrate to Australia and subsequently become lone parents are covered.

[6] All amounts are given in Australian dollars. As of September 2001, one Australian dollar was equal to £0.34 British pounds.

[7] Jobseekers included unemployed people, those working under 10 hours per week and who wanted a job with longer hours, those not in the labour force but likely to enter in the near future, and those discouraged from looking for work.

[8] This has subsequently been replaced by a competitive network with private sector providers (see Webster and Harding, 2000).

FIVE

Lone parents and employment in Norway

Anne Skevik

Introduction

During the 1990s, a number of changes have taken place in the benefit system for lone parents in Norway. The aim of this chapter is to give an outline of these changes, and to discuss their background in terms of historical developments, demographic changes, and the prevailing discourse on mothers and employment. Since the most important changes were introduced in January 1998 and phased in over a three-year period, it is still too early to give a full review of the consequences of the reforms.

'Activation' was the central keyword in Norwegian social policies in the 1990s. All social benefits, including those for lone parents, were to be redesigned in the light of the activation principle (cf Hvinden, 1999; Drøpping et al, 1999). Paid employment was to be the "natural first option" for people of working age, and social insurance benefits should only be paid to those who were unable to work due to "circumstances related to health or social situation" (St meld no 35, 1994-95, p 17). For lone parents, this new principle came to imply a controversial redefinition of their responsibilities as earners and carers. The key question was, under what circumstances is being alone with a dependent child a 'social situation' that requires an exception from the general duty to work outside the home? As I will show below, Norwegian politicians dealt with this question by introducing a relatively strict division between 'lone parents as carers' and 'lone parents as workers', with the age of the youngest child as the crucial dividing line. Lone parents with children younger than three received more financial support by the end of the1990s than they did in the beginning, while those with older children received far less. A second important question was what are we to do about those lone parents who must be expected to work, but who are unable or unwilling to do so? In answering this question, little if any weight was placed on the creation of financial incentives, which would make employment more tempting in financial terms. Rather, this concern inspired an innovative move in the form of local 'help to self-help' groups, whose chief aim was to motivate and enable lone parents to take up education or employment.

In what follows, I will first chart the background for the 1990s' emphasis on activation in terms of demographic changes and lone parents' situations. Second, I will give a brief overview of the history of lone-parent benefits in the Norwegian welfare state, and place the 1990s' changes in this context. In doing so, I will emphasise the re-definition of the supported group, as well as the 'self-help' networks. Having outlined the changes, I will consider the political climate in which they took place, with an emphasis on the normative conceptions of motherhood among politicians, lone mothers and the population in general. In the final section, I will consider some possible effects of the 1990s' changes in terms of labour market participation and income distribution.

Lone parents in Norway: numbers and circumstances

As in most other Western industrialised countries, family practices have changed rapidly in Norway over the past few decades. Divorce rates have increased, the proportion of children born outside marriage has increased, and cohabitation seems to have replaced marriage as the most common way of living together for younger cohorts. Tables 5.1 and 5.2 illustrate these trends.

The divorce rate increased relatively quickly in the 1970s and 1980s, peaked – so far – in 1993 and stabilised at a relatively high level through the second half of the 1990s. The Norwegian divorce rate of about 11% is one of the highest in Western Europe (Millar and Warman, 1996, Table 2.1). The extra-marital[1] birth rate increased strongly in the 1980s, and continued to increase at a slightly slower pace in the 1990s. However, it is estimated that less than 5% of all children in Norway are born by 'genuinely single' mothers, and this proportion has remained relatively stable since the 1960s (Noack and Keilman, 1993, p 292; Jensen and Clausen, 1999, p 288). The increasing extra-marital birth rate is therefore almost fully explained by the increase in cohabitation rates. As Table 5.2 shows, cohabitation became more common than marriage among women

Table 5.1: Divorce rates and proportions of children born outside marriage, Norway (1960s-1990s)

	Divorce rate (per 1,000 existing marriages)	Extra-marital birth rate (%)
1961-65	2.9	4.0
1971-75	4.9	9.0
1981-85	7.9	20.0
1986-90	9.5	33.7
1991	11.2	40.9
1993	12.1	44.4
1995	11.7	47.6
1997	11.3	48.7

Source: Statistics Norway: Yearbook of Statistics (1999, Tables 49, 73). Proportions born outside marriage: computed by author

Table 5.2: Women aged 25-34 living in cohabiting or married relationships (1977-98) (%)

	Cohabiting				Married			
	1977	1988	1994	1998	1977	1988	1994	1998
25-29	5	24	35	37	81	53	35	30
30-34	2	12	22	27	87	71	60	53

Source: Statistics Norway: Yearbook of Statistics (1999, Table 67)

in their late 20s in the 1990s. Similarly for women in their early 30s, cohabitation rates increased while marriage rates fell.

The prevalence of lone parenthood in Norway, measured as lone parents as a proportion of all families with children under 16, is shown in Figure 5.1. Until 1994, this statistic included parents who cohabited with a partner who was not the child's other parent. From 1994 onwards, parents who have cohabited with a new partner for more than one year are excluded. This change caused the statistics to drop by about five percentage points. It can be seen that the curve rose more steeply in the 1980s, and has remained stable after 1994 at about 18%. Thus in the latter half of the 1990s, just under one in five Norwegian children under 16 lived in a lone-parent family.

Statistics on the characteristics and circumstances of lone parents are not published regularly in Norway, and the figures that are published are

Figure 5.1: Lone parents as a proportion of all parents with children under 16

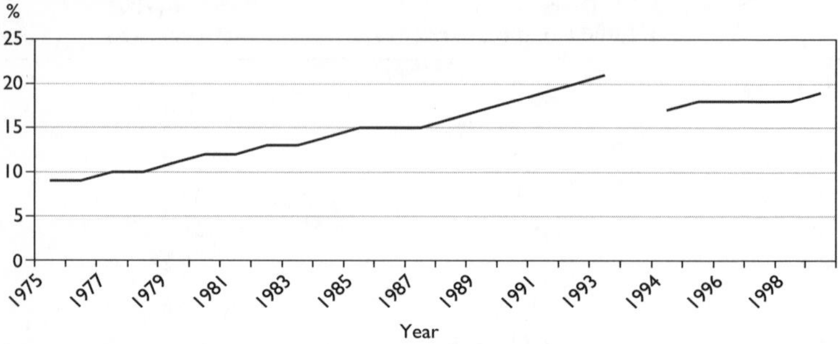

Note: These are the proportions who received extended child benefit. It includes families with children under 16.

Source: Yearbook of Social Security Statistics (various years). Proportions computed by the author

often misleading, given the insufficient registration of cohabitation. In the large-scale surveys, the sample of lone parents is normally much too small to analyse. Lone parenthood does not generally attract the kind of interest among Norwegian politicians or in the media which creates a demand for constantly updated information; generally, lone parenthood is not regarded as a social problem. However, when the government began to reconsider the benefit arrangements for lone parents in the late 1980s (see below), the lack of information was seen as problematic. A special sample of lone parents was therefore drawn in the 1991 Survey of Level of Living. This survey is the latest set of high-quality data available regarding the situation of lone parents[2]. Some key characteristics of lone parents in 1991 are presented in Table 5.3. Although this data is from the beginning of the 1990s, there is no reason to believe that the picture has changed notably in later years. As the table shows, the majority of Norwegian lone mothers are separated or divorced, while 43% have never been married. The vast majority of these will be ex-cohabitees. Almost half are 35 years or older, while only 13% are under 25. Two out of three have only one child, and only about one in four have children under five years of age.

The age of the mother, the age of the youngest child and the number of children in the family all tend to influence lone mothers' labour force participation (cf Bradshaw et al, 1996). Judging from the demographic data presented in Table 5.3, therefore, we would expect Norwegian lone mothers to have relatively high labour market participation rates. However,

Table 5.3: Characteristics of lone parents in Norway (1991) (%)

Lone fathers	Lone mothers						
	Single	Separated/ divorced	Widowed	Under 25	Over 35	Child under 5	With one child
9	43	52	6	13	47	27	65

in the early 1980s the employment rate of lone mothers fell below that of married and cohabiting mothers, and remained at a lower level throughout the decade (Kjeldstad and Rønsen, 2000, Figure 4). Only about two thirds of all lone mothers in Norway were in employment in the early 1990s, as shown in Table 5.4. Employment rates fell slightly in the early 1990s, but show a steady increase between 1993 and 1998. About half the lone mothers who were in employment worked full-time, that is more than 35 hours (Kjeldstad and Rønsen, 2000, Figure 7). Married and cohabiting mothers had higher employment rates than lone mothers throughout the 1990s, but only about 40% of those employed in this group worked more than 35 hours per week. These full-time/part-time proportions have been relatively stable over time in both groups.

An important finding in the 1991 Survey of Level of Living was that lone parents were among the most vulnerable groups in Norway in terms of poverty. Twenty-five per cent of the lone parents interviewed said that they often had difficulties in managing current expenditure, and 56% said they would have no possibility of paying an unforeseen bill of NK2,000 (approximately £160). The corresponding figures for couples with children under seven years of age were six and 14% respectively (NOS C43, 1993). It was also known from other studies that lone parents were the group of claimants within the National Insurance system who most often needed social assistance to supplement their rights-based benefit (Terum, 1993). The relatively low labour market participation rates of Norwegian lone parents, combined with their economic vulnerability, indicated that something needed to be done with the existing benefit system.

Table 5.4: Employment rates for lone mothers in Norway (1990-98) (%)

1990	1991	1992	1993	1994	1995	1996	1997	1998
65	64	63	65	66	67	70	70	69

Source: Bradshaw et al (2000, Table 8)

Mothers and employment in the 1990s: the end of ambiguity

Non-employed and low-paid lone parents in Norway have two forms of public support available to them: social insurance and social assistance. Norway is unusual in Europe in having a separate set of benefits for lone parents within the rights-based social insurance scheme. The reason for this can be found in the history of the Norwegian welfare state: the modernisation of welfare provision in Norway consisted of 'lifting' as many categories of claimants as possible out of the Poor Law-descendent social assistance. The social assistance scheme could thus be allowed to remain a system of last resort, characterised by means testing and local discretion (Lødemel 1997). There are no national scale rates for Norwegian social assistance, and the legal framework determining what kind of needs are covered is very loose. This creates a stark contrast to the National Insurance system, which is regulated in detail on a national level and where entitlement criteria are very clear. Residents whose National Insurance entitlements end are therefore not left to live on the streets, but are transferred to a branch of social security which is regarded as highly inferior to the main system.

Lone parents were one of the groups that were lifted out of the means-tested social assistance through the creation of a separate benefit. Initially, when the benefit was introduced in 1964, it included only widows and unmarried mothers. Unlike most other countries, Norway never created a separate widows pension and unmarried mothers were included from the start (Skevik, 1999, pp 226, 229-31). Widowers were included in 1967, when the 1964 Widow's and Mother's Pension Act was integrated in the unifying National Insurance Act. Divorced and separated parents got statutory benefit rights in 1971, albeit under a temporary Act (the 1971 Temporary Act on Separated and Divorced Parents) where benefits were to be administered by the social assistance offices (Skevik, 1999, p 228). The temporary Act was suspended in 1980, when all categories of lone parents (including unmarried fathers) were integrated in the National Insurance Act.

It can be argued that the initial 1964 benefits for widows and unmarried mothers were 'activation-oriented' from the start. The new scheme included a subsistence-level benefit (named Transitional Allowance for unmarried mothers and Widow's Pension for widows), and two benefits which were intended to ease the recipient's transition into employment: Childcare Allowance and Education Benefit. Childcare Allowance was paid as a fixed amount to all widowed and unmarried mothers who needed childcare, while the Education Benefit was intended to cover extra costs incurred by education. Moreover, both Transitional Allowance and Widow's Pension were designed to encourage the recipient to combine benefits and earnings. If the recipient took up employment, the benefit was withdrawn at a rate of 40% above an earnings disregard. This created a long taper, and implied that even recipients with close to average earnings could claim a small amount of benefit. The documents preceding the Act are all very clear: the new benefit was not to be a substitute for earnings. If a widow was working outside the home at the time of bereavement, she was expected to continue to do so. Young non-employed widows were to be encouraged to enter paid employment as soon as possible, as were unmarried mothers as soon as the child was old enough. At what age the child was 'old enough' was, however, not determined in the Act. Determining whether or not the benefit should be granted, as well as when it should be withdrawn, was up to the discretion of the local social security committees. However, during the debates in the Storting (Norway's national legislative assembly) it was strongly emphasised that this discretion should be exercised with 'generosity', and that the claimant's domestic responsibilities had to be given due recognition (Skevik, 1999, p 232).

At what point domestic responsibilities ceased to be a legitimate justification for not taking up paid employment was thus not clarified in the Act. The 1964 Act, which had been bold and original in its definition of the supported group, entirely avoided this vexed question. So did the 1967 National Insurance Act, which merely stated that "benefits included in this chapter should be stopped when the child reaches an age where childcare responsibilities no longer provide an obstacle to paid employment" (1967 National Insurance Act, §12-4). We do not know how this extremely vague rule was implemented in the 1960s and 1970s. A committee working on reforming lone-parent benefits in the early 1970s maintained that the common practice was to withdraw benefits when the youngest child turned three (NOU, 1975, p 18). The Ministry of Social Security, in a White Paper from the 1979-80 session, believed it was common to withdraw benefits "no later than" the child's tenth birthday unless the child had special needs (Ot prp no 4, 1979-80, p 15, cf Terum, 1993, p 39). When the law was changed in 1980 to include separated and divorced parents, it was delegated to the Ministry to determine an age limit by guidelines. The 1980 guideline stated that benefits should normally be withdrawn when the youngest child finished third grade schooling, when the child would normally be 10 years old – "provided the child is by then sufficiently self-contained in practical matters such as dressing, eating and so on" (quoted in Terum, 1993, p 41).

This story illustrates the fundamental ambiguity towards mothers' employment in the Norwegian welfare state. The Acts from the 1960s clearly saw paid employment as the primary option for all adults. But the politicians preparing these Acts also recognised the difficulties inherent in integrating paid and unpaid work, and thus created a loose legal framework, which allowed for wide-ranging local and individual adjustments. When an upper age limit for children was finally introduced, this happened with almost no debate in the Storting and without any systematic research into the prevailing practice. The 10 year cut-off point therefore appears to have been set rather arbitrarily. Norwegian politicians almost systematically refused to turn this issue into a political matter; the decisions were left to the administration. To a large extent it was therefore up to the lone parents themselves to determine at what point childcare responsibilities "no longer provided an obstacle" to paid employment.

All this changed in the 1990s. The low employment rates of lone parents compared to married and cohabiting mothers caused concern, as did the economic vulnerability among lone parents documented most convincingly in the Survey of Level of Living. The challenge was twofold: increase the employment rates, and increase the level of income among lone parents. For some, incomes could be increased through employment. For others, employment was not really an option and incomes would have to be raised through higher benefit rates. Drawing the line between these two categories was to become one of the big social policy debates of the 1990s.

The first attempt to encourage more lone mothers to take up employment came in 1990, and was relatively unrelated to the later changes. During the 1970s and 1980s, it had become increasingly disadvantageous to combine Transitional Allowance and earnings. The lack of synchronisation between benefit increases and deduction rules had led to a very high marginal tax rate for low earnings. In 1968, a lone parent would retain 60% of her income above the earnings disregard. In 1988, she only retained 37.2% (Hatland, 1992, p 184). This was not a deliberate policy – indeed there is little evidence politicians were aware of this effect. The benefit increases had happened solely in order to combat poverty. The rules were changed in 1990 so that the benefit reduction was reset at its initial level of 40%. This was intended to make the combination of earnings and Transitional Allowance a more tempting solution for lone parents.

However, the 1990 alteration of the benefit deduction rate was merely a patching up of the existing system. It did nothing to tackle what came to be seen as the main problem, that is, the discretionary approach to lone parents' employment inherent in the social insurance system. The upcoming changes were signalled in the 1993-94 Budget, but it was the 1995 Welfare White Paper (St meld no 35, 1994-95) that really galvanised the debate. The changes proposed by the Labour government were eventually passed in 1997 with the support of the Conservative party and the right-wing Progress Party, and were implemented from 1 January 1998. The 1998 changes represent the end of the Norwegian ambiguity with regards to lone parents and employment. After 1998, a straightforward solution to the mother/worker dilemma was applied. A new rhetoric was introduced, where a distinction was drawn between 'active' and 'passive' benefit recipients. 'Active recipients' were those who combined benefit receipt with full-time or part-time employment, or who were undertaking education to increase their qualifications. 'Passive recipients' were full-time carers.

The key philosophy of the 1998 reform was that paid employment could be promoted through restricting eligibility to out-of-work benefits, that is Transitional Allowance. A number of new conditions were introduced in the Transitional Allowance. First, the upper age limit of 10 was lowered to eight. Second, and more crucially, a maximum duration period was introduced. Nobody should, in principle, receive Transitional Allowance for more than a maximum of three years, or five years if undertaking education. Thirdly, for lone parents whose (youngest) child had turned three, there was to be an 'activity requirement'. It was to be a condition for further receipt that the parent was either undertaking education, in employment, or actively seeking work. This was a relatively severe restriction on the previously rather generous entitlement criteria. An exception was made for 'up to one year after the break-up', during which time the parent could receive Transitional Allowance, provided she had children under 10 years of age. To meet the problem of poverty among recipients of Transitional Allowance, the allowance was increased from approximately NK63,000 (£5,000) to NK70,000 (£5,600) per annum. Transitional Allowance, in short, was transformed from 'little to many' towards 'more to a few'.

Childcare benefit was still to be available until the child was 10 years old. However, the calculation of the level was changed. Under previous legislation, childcare benefit was payable as a flat-rate allowance to all parents who had a need for childcare, regardless of whether or not they paid for this service. Under the new system, childcare allowance would cover 70% of documented childcare expenses, provided the parents' incomes fell below a (high) ceiling. The targeting in the new system was clearly better, but some lone parents would nevertheless lose some money on this reform. Education benefit was maintained without any significant alterations.

The 1998 reform was initiated and passed under a Labour government. Labour, however, lost the election in 1997, and was replaced in office by a centre-right coalition dominated by the Christian People's Party. One of the causes closest to the heart of the Christian People's Party was the Cash for Child Care reform. The reform implied that parents who were not using state-sponsored childcare should receive an amount in cash which roughly corresponded to the estimated state subsidy per child in state-sponsored day care. Arguments for the reform were phrased both in terms of fairness in distribution and in terms of "giving parents back their time" (cf Ellingsæter, 1999, pp 46-7). Opponents argued that this reform would reverse the trend towards gender equality and equal parenting, and that it would create a number of practical and social problems to pay parents in cash for *not* using a public service (cf Leira, 1998a). Cash for Child Care was introduced from 1 August 1998. From this day onwards, parents with children between one and three years old would receive NK3,000 (approximately £240) per month per child if the child was not in state-sponsored childcare. This benefit is also payable to lone parents. Although the Labour government and the centre-coalition may be seen as pulling in different directions with regards to the mother/worker dilemma their efforts taken together have created a clear-cut distinction between lone parents as 'carers' and lone parents as 'earners': the dividing line is the child's third birthday.

The most important aspect of the 1998 reform was that the right to out-of-work benefit was seriously limited. Because research had indicated that lone parents on average only received Transitional Allowance for three years (Terum, 1993), the architects behind the new system rejected claims that the new rules would cause widespread problems. For the majority, it was argued, there would be no changes in practical terms. It was recognised, however, that a minority might find it difficult to make the transition into paid employment. The 1991 Survey of Level of Living had showed that many lone parents felt lonely, had limited contact with friends and family, and suffered from depression and other psychological problems. For lone parents in this situation, taking away their benefit entitlement might only create deeper misery. Some active measure was needed to help each and every lone parent overcome the obstacles. With this concern in mind, the government looked with great interest to a local project which had been in place in county Akershus since 1992: OFO.

Overcoming the obstacles: social networks and individual guidance

Oppfølgingsordningen for enslige forsørgere (OFO), which literally translates as 'follow-up arrangement for lone parents', is a new creature in the multifarious Norwegian landscape of social security/social assistance/social care arrangements. The overall goal of the arrangement is to help lone parents make the transition from 'passive' to 'active' benefit receipt. The basic philosophy is to focus attention on the benefit claimant, and to integrate the services of the local National Insurance offices, the local social assistance authorities, and the local employment service into a unified package tailored to the claimant's needs. Initiatives should build on the resources the lone parents already have:'help to self-help' has been a key phrase. The ideology is captured in the rhetoric surrounding the arrangement: benefit recipients are consistently referred to as 'users', and the local benefit office is to be their 'service centre'. All lone parents in receipt of Transitional Allowance are targeted by OFO, but participation is entirely voluntary. Also, bereaved parents with children under eight may be approached. The OFO process has been divided into three phases: the mapping phase, the awareness phase and the action phase.

A key figure in OFO is the 'mediator' (*brukerkontakten*), who fills a vital role in all three phases. Mediators are recruited by the local benefit office from among the lone parents in receipt of Transitional Allowance, and their job is to provide a link between the benefit recipients and the National Insurance office. Since it is difficult to combine the work as a mediator with formal employment, the mediator will almost always be found among the 'passive' benefit recipients. The position is unpaid, but the mediator receives Transitional Allowance and Education Benefit for the period that she is undertaking the work. She is expected to work for 30 hours per week, out of which she will be available to the lone parents four days a week, and undertake training on the fifth day. Training the mediator, as well as supporting them on a daily basis, is the task of the local benefit office. It is important to note that mediators are not employed by the

National Insurance office, therefore they are not paid, and they do not know the claimant's case files. Similarly, they are not expected, or even allowed, to pass on information about the user to the benefit office. The lone parents should feel free to discuss anything with the mediator without fearing consequences for their future benefit receipt.

The initial phase of OFO is named the 'mapping' phase. The purpose of this phase is to chart any practical problems the lone parent might face, allowing the mediator and the benefit office to provide relevant advice and guidance. A key aim of OFO is to coordinate the activities of the different public institutions to which lone parents relate. The mediator will sometimes contact the user in their home and go on a visit as part of this initial phase, but this depends entirely on the lone parent's consent.

In the 'awareness' phase, the overall aim is to strengthen the lone parent's self-confidence and social network. This, it is argued, increases lone parents' opportunities in the labour market and also enhances their overall quality of life. In this phase, 'motivation courses' play an important part. According to the National Insurance directives, these courses shall "give the user a positive and constructive self-image, instigate the initiative to change her situation and enable the user to make choices leading to concrete action. The course shall end in a concrete plan of action for the individual" (Forskrift, 1998-10-00 no 60, p 10). In addition to motivation courses, the lone parents should be invited to participate in social activities as part of this phase. These are often organised by the mediator. A popular form of social activities have been evening gatherings organised around a particular topic, such as money management, parenting after divorce, and step-parenting. Other activities have included organising flea markets, boat-trips, going to the theatre, first-aid courses, and trips with children to chocolate factories or farms with animals. The purpose is simply to get lone parents out of the house and into some social activity.

In the 'action' phase, the plans made during the motivation courses are put into action. Lone parents, with or without the aid of the benefit office or the mediator, will apply for organised childcare, education, and/ or employment. As a form of assistance in this phase, some counties have organised particular classes for lone parents at secondary-school level. These classes accommodate lone parents' particular needs, implying that they may, for instance, allow the hours of schooling to follow the opening hours of the nursery.

The first OFO started in county Akershus in 1992 as a local project initiated by lone parents themselves and supported by the local National Insurance authorities. Following the project, more lone parents did take up education and employment. This fitted perfectly with the new activation approach. Similar projects were started in five other counties[3] in 1994, and were reviewed by the National Insurance Administration in 1996. The evaluation focused on three aims: activation, financial circumstances and self-esteem. The review (RTV, 1996a) concluded that among the participants in the project, 47% had changed from 'passive' to 'active' benefit recipients. However, only about 20% of those targeted by OFO chose to participate, implying that the overall effect on employment rates was low (RTV, 1996a, p 7). A more surprising finding was that in municipalities where OFO existed, higher proportions of all lone parents – whether they participated in the arrangement or not – made the passive to active transition. The effects were, however, much stronger among lone parents who had actively participated in OFO. The review (RTV, 1996a, p 9) suggested that the increased overall activity could be explained by the better routines for cooperation between the different bodies which dealt with lone parents at the local level. The importance of childcare was emphasised, as lone parents with young children or many children were less likely to become 'active' than others (RTV, 1996b). The combination of motivation courses and social activities was important – participating in just one form of activity did not give the same results. In terms of financial circumstances, the evidence was equally positive. About half the participants had received social assistance as lone parents, while only one in 10 did after the project. Among those who came off social assistance, 60% had received financial advice as part of OFO. OFO also had a positive influence on lone parents' self-esteem: among the users who described their self-confidence as low at the beginning of the project, about one third reported that their self-confidence had increased notably in the project period. Lone parents who started out with low self-esteem made the passive to active transition as often as those with higher self-esteem, but they needed more time and more extensive participation in the project (RTV, 1996b). Against this background of highly positive reviews, OFO was introduced on a national scale as an integral part of the 1998 policy changes.

Paid employment and the meaning of life: attitudes among politicians, the public and lone parents

The 1990s marked the end of Norwegian ambiguity towards lone parents and employment. 1998 brought a severe restriction of benefit entitlements, as well as an emphasis on local 'help to self-help' groups geared towards activation. This marked a break with previous policies. A clear-cut 'model of motherhood' (cf Leira, 1992) guided the new policies: the mother was to be supported as a full-time carer until the youngest child turned three, thereafter she would be supported as a worker. Why did this shift come in the 1990s, and how was it received by the electorate – and by lone parents themselves? Was this new policy a response to changing family practices, or was it a top-down approach that lacked popular legitimacy?

Norway has often been described as a laggard among the Scandinavian countries when it comes to facilitating the employment of mothers (for example Leira, 1992, 1993; Sainsbury, 1999). Norway's "Great Leap" (Skrede, 1999, p 188) with regards to mother-friendly employment policies did not come until the late 1980s/early 1990s, which was 15-20 years later than the neighbouring countries. The shift can partly be explained by the change in government in 1986, when a Labour government with a high proportion of female ministers took office. Under the so-called 'women's government' an active policy for public childcare was developed, encompassing both pre-school and school-age children, and parental leave arrangements were rapidly expanded (Koren, 1997, pp 33-6). The 1993-94 Budget suggested:

> When society invests these considerable resources on easing the situation for families with children, something which also benefits lone parents, the question may be asked if lone parents to a greater extent *should* utilise this offer from society. (St prp no 1, 1993-94, p 85; emphasis in original)

Given the active family policy, there was no longer any reason why lone parents should be exempt from the general obligation adults had to provide for themselves. But there was another line of argument that came to dominate the mid-1990s debate, in which employment was seen not so much as a duty, but as a right. This is captured in the following quotes, from the Welfare White Paper and the leader of the Storting's Standing Committee on Social Security respectively:

> Economic independence and social belonging through work is important for the individual. It gives greater freedom and more security. Welfare arrangements, therefore, shall not only give rights, they should also give opportunities and incite to participation and responsibility. (St meld no 35, 1994-95, p 12)

The main division today runs between those who do, and those who do not, have a job to go to. Therefore employment for everybody who desires it is still our most important task. Besides, we cannot accept, for moral and political reasons, that people are pushed out of employment due to age, disability or otherwise reduced working capacity. Employment shall not be a privilege for the so-called successful and those who are 100% healthy and between 25 and 55 years old. (Sylvia Brustad, Labour, St forh no 229, 1995-96, p 3451)

Arguments in favour of the new policy towards lone parents were phrased in these terms in the Storting debates: being out of employment for too long would lead to social exclusion and a difficult re-entry. Moreover, the activation policy towards lone parents was in line with the approach generally taken towards mothers' employment. The debate in the Storting reflected the increasing invisibility of unpaid work: not only had unpaid work ceased to be a legitimate reason not to work outside the home, it had also ceased to be an activity which could give meaning and fulfilment. Outside the realm of paid employment there was nothing but poverty, loneliness and passivity (cf Syltevik, 1996, pp 402-7; Skevik, 1999).

The child's third birthday was to be the new watershed between lone parents as 'earners' and 'carers'. Survey data from 1996 indicates that this age limit was controversial among the electorate (Figure 5.2; for further discussion see Skevik, 1996, 1998). Asked when they thought lone parents should be expected to take up employment, about one in four supported an age limit of three years. A larger group, one third of the sample, thought lone parents should be supported in the home as long as they had children under school-starting age[4], while 20% supported the existing age limit of 10 years. It is interesting to note, however, that these results seemed to mirror attitudes towards mothers' employment more than particular attitudes towards lone parents: in response to a question of when *mothers* should take up paid employment, people gave very similar answers (bivariate correlation .65). As can be seen from Figure 5.2, the curves for 'mothers' and 'lone parents' are almost identical.

Did lone parents in general support the idea of employment as desirable, or did they reject the values handed to them by the government? Information is scarce on the attitudes towards paid employment among lone mothers themselves, but the Survey of Level of Living 1991 contained some information. Respondents were asked to respond to six statements concerning employment, such as "it is very important for me to have a job" and "I would soon get bored if I did not have a job to do". For each

Figure 5.2: Opinions on when 'lone parents' and 'mothers' should take up paid employment

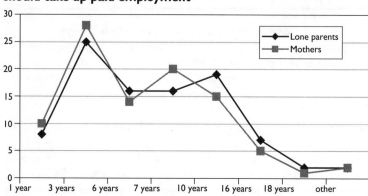

Source: Skevik (1996)

statement, the respondent answered according to a five-step scale, ranging from "agree strongly" to "disagree strongly" (see Skevik, 1998, pp 49-55 for a more detailed discussion). Analysis of this material indicates that lone mothers in Norway have overwhelmingly positive attitudes towards paid employment. Half – 49% – of the sample *agreed strongly* to five or more of these six statements (Kjeldstad, 1998, Table A19). The ideology of housewifery is clearly not very strong among Norwegian lone mothers, even though many of them may have found it difficult to take up paid employment at any given point in time.

The 1998 reform: incentives and distribution effects

When discussing activation policies directed at recipients of social benefits, it may be useful to separate three different strategies: politicians can focus on making employment *possible* by helping benefit recipients overcome the obstacles to employment, they can make employment more *tempting* by increasing in-work incomes relative to out-of-work incomes, and they can make employment *necessary* by restricting the availability of out-of-work benefits. The Norwegian strategy has been a combination of the first and the third strategy, where the OFO aims at creating possibilities while the benefit retrenchment makes work a necessity. Lone parents are subjected to strong pressure to take up employment at a much earlier stage than they have been before, but a lone parent who finds it hard to do so is not to be left on her own. A mediator from OFO will knock on her door and invite her to friendly gatherings and a motivation course, and as soon as she has figured out what she wants to do she will be assisted in applying for education and childcare. If she needs education, she can receive Transitional Allowance for an additional two years in order to finish schooling, and her child will often have priority in public childcare institutions.

What can be said of these changes in terms of the ratio between in-work and out-of-work disposable incomes? I have suggested that the 1990s reform package combined the stick with the helping hand, but can we also find some small carrots in this sack? It can be argued that the carrots were in fact already there. In particular, the rules for combining earnings and benefits introduced in 1964 were intended to motivate lone parents to get an income beside the benefit. However, over time the lack of coordination between benefit increases and deduction rules slowly ate the carrots, as described above. The 1990 reform reset this integration of earnings and benefits to its intended level. This happened even before the debate on activation for lone parents had really begun. The proportion of lone parents who combined earnings and benefits increased steadily after 1990, suggesting that this measure was appreciated by the recipients of Transitional Allowance (Yearbook of Social Security Statistics, 1999, Table 12.1). Due to some special taxation rules for recipients of National Insurance benefits, lone parents in receipt of reduced Transitional Allowance still face a higher effective marginal tax rate than other employees at some levels of income. This is not, however, being discussed as a problem. The tax system has not been utilised as part of the activation policy for lone parents in the 1990s.

The changes in the childcare benefit are difficult to interpret in terms of incentives effects. As long as childcare benefit was payable at a fixed rate to all lone parents who were undertaking education or employment, it was net gain for some. Lone parents who had free childcare with family members or friends could take the benefit and use it in full to cover other expenses. After 1998, this was no longer possible as the benefit is only paid if expenses are documented. In addition, under the old system lone parents with low incomes and high childcare costs could apply for an increase in the benefit to cover their childcare expenses in full. This is another possibility, which is lost under the new system, where the level of the benefit is fixed at 70% of documented expenses. The distribution effects inherent in the new system can thus be summed up: lone parents with medium and high incomes will gain, provided 70% of their childcare expenses represents a higher amount than the former fixed benefit level. Lone parents with low incomes and high childcare expenses will lose, since their benefit is reduced to cover 70% of their expenses instead of the full amount. Lone parents in all income brackets with very low or zero childcare expenses will lose the benefit entirely. This may negatively influence the willingness to work for lone parents who can only command low incomes but who depend on expensive childcare. However, it is unlikely to have an effect in other situations.

Employment rates for lone parents in Norway have increased over the 1990s, although not very strongly (see Table 5.4 above). Is this an indication that the activation strategy has worked? The answer is that it might be, or that the new policies may at least have played a part in this development. But it is worth noting that the increase in employment rates began before activation was really on the agenda for lone parents. There is evidence to suggest that economic booms and slumps influence lone parents' labour market participation rates more than changes in the benefit structure (Kjeldstad and Rønsen, 2000). This hypothesis is strengthened if we look at the developments in Sweden, where the early 1990s recession caused a steep fall in lone parents' (traditionally very high) employment rates (Bradshaw et al, 2000). Norway's economy was very strong in the latter half of the 1990s and the unemployment rates were very low. Given this background, the small increase in lone parents' employment rates may be no more than we might have expected.

As for the concrete 1998 changes, the new rules did not fully come into operation for all recipients until January 2001. At the time of writing, therefore, it is too early to say how they will work in practice. The OFO is the only part that has been evaluated so far. These initiatives have received a very favourable press, and they seem to help the target group not only to take up education and employment, but also to improve their financial situation and their self-esteem. The take-up rate is, however, low and the results are too limited in scope to really show on national statistics. As for the new eligibility criteria for Transitional Allowance, we are left to speculate about the effects. As noted above, a majority of lone parents never received Transitional Allowance for more than a few years anyway, and thus are unlikely to be severely affected by the new rules. The worries are, as usual, about the minority. Not all lone parents will have the capacity necessary to keep to the relatively strict deadlines inherent in the new system. The OFO may provide valuable help for some of them, but we cannot expect these arrangements to do miracles. We do not yet know how the 1998 rules will be implemented; some clauses are open to interpretation by the administration. But if the main rules are followed strictly, we may fear that the position of the most troubled lone parents becomes even more vulnerable.

Conclusion

When Transitional Allowance is being withdrawn, it is because a situation once identified as a 'situation of need' is no longer seen as such. When activity (as here defined) is now being required of lone parents with children older than three, it is because being a lone parent with children above this age is no longer seen as a situation requiring an exemption from the general duty to provide for oneself. This represents a change in the perception of what it entails to be a parent – the balancing of earning and caring responsibilities. Needs in respect of caring work are still recognised, but for a much shorter period than before. What is also new is the emphasis on paid employment as the one and only route to social integration. In the rhetoric of the debates in the 1960s, paid and unpaid work were portrayed as equally important and equally fulfilling. When benefits for lone parents were debated in the 1990s, the world outside the realm of paid employment was pictured as a black hole of social exclusion, populated by passive and miserable people. This linking of social and psychological factors to economic activity in the market provided a justification for the strong emphasis on 'activation', and is also the background on which the new state involvement in lone parents' self-esteem and social networks (through OFO) must be understood. Developing lone parents' personal resources is seen as a step towards a better life for them – and "the good life", ultimately, is that of the paid worker.

Notes

[1] 'Extra-marital' here refers to the proportion of children born to mothers who are not married at the time of birth, that is, cohabiting mothers and those who are genuinely on their own.

[2] The analysis presented here was undertaken in 1995 by Anne Skevik and Lars Inge Terum for the purposes of the project 'How and why do lone parents work outside the home', published as Bradshaw et al (1996).

[3] Østfold, Vest-Agder, Rogaland, Hordaland and Nord-Trøndelag.

[4] School-starting age in Norway was lowered from seven to six years from autumn 1997.

SIX

Does it work? Employment policies for lone parents in the Netherlands

Trudie Knijn and Frits van Wel

Introduction

For decades lone-parent families have accounted for only 10% of all families with children below the age of 18 years in the Netherlands and this was still the case at the end of the 1990s. From a social policy perspective, however, the Netherlands is a remarkable case. As in the US and the UK, Dutch welfare reforms are attempting to get lone parents into employment. Since the new General Assistance Act came into force in January 1996, mothers of school-age children have had an obligation to seek work. This had not been the case in the past. In this chapter we will conclude that these policies are less effective than was intended by the government at the time that they were introduced. Before we come to that conclusion, we will present demographic data and data on the employment rates of lone parents, and on opinions about welfare reform and orientations to work. We will also compare lone parents on welfare with lone parents not on welfare and analyse employment and care policies oriented to lone parents. This chapter is based on national data and two studies of lone parents in the Netherlands (Knijn and van Wel, 1999; van Wel and Knijn, 2000).

Characteristics of lone parents

The Netherlands has 258,000 lone-parent families, of which 228,000 (88%) were headed by a woman in 1997 (Ministerie van Sociale Zaken en

Werkgelegenheid, 1999). Although the percentage of lone-parent families, that is families headed by one adult who lives with at least one child below the age of 18, remained rather stable during the last 20 years, the composition of the group changed dramatically (see Table 6.1). The death of a partner was the main cause of lone-parent families in 1971, but today divorce is the main cause. The share of never-married lone parents seems to have been stable during the last decade. The number of lone-parent families is not expected to rise in the coming years, because divorce rates among parents are declining, while those of childless couples are increasing.

Demographic characteristics of lone mothers are rather similar to those of partnered mothers. They have the same age, educational level and number of children (Hooghiemstra and Knijn, 1997). For decades, the Netherlands has had very few unmarried teenage mothers (six per 1,000 teenage girls). Only among women from the Caribbean is unmarried teenage motherhood more prevalent, as is lone motherhood for adult Caribbean women (30%). Because many women from the Caribbean live in Amsterdam, this city has, after London and Dublin, the highest rates of teenage motherhood of all European cities (Bardsley, 1999). In contrast, women from other ethnic minority groups, in particular women from the Mediterranean, rarely live in lone-parent families (3%) (Hooghiemstra and Niphuis-Nell, 1995).

Unlike partnered mothers, almost half of lone-mother families depend on welfare (see Table 6.2). The 1965 General Assistance Act has offered them the opportunity to receive benefits without an obligation to work since the beginning of the 1970s. Since then the absolute numbers of lone mothers on welfare has almost doubled. In 1978 about 60,000 lone mothers received welfare benefits; this number increased to 105,000 in 1991, and to 115,000 in 1997 (Centraal Bureau voor Statistiek, 1998).

Table 6.1: Lone-parent families in the Netherlands*

	1981	1985	1989	1993	1997
As % of all families with dependent children	8	10	11	10	12
Proportion of whom:					
Widowed	27	16	9	8	3
Divorced/separated	62	67	67	68	74.5
Never-married	10	17	23	24	22.5

*Figures for 1981 to 1993 are based on WBO (SCP-Processing). Figures for 1997 are from the *Jaarboek Emancipatie*, Ministerie van Sociale Zaken en Werkelegenheid (1999) and based on CBS *Huishoudensstatistiek* (1997). The subcategories for 1997 come from the survey *Caring for work* (van Wel and Knijn, 2000)

Table 6.2: Sources of income per household (1997)

	Paid work (%)	Unemployment benefit/social assistance (%)	Health benefit (%)	Pension (%)	Total
Lone-parent families, children <18:					
Women	39.5	50	2.5	7	228,000
Men	66.5	20	6.5	–	30,000
Two-parent families, children <18	90	4.5	2.5	I	1,554,000

Source: CBS Inkomensstatistiek (1997) in Ministerie van Sociale Zaken en Werkgelegenheid (1999)

Long-term poverty is also more common among lone-parent families than among two-parent families (see Table 6.3). Lone parents on welfare receive a stable percentage (70%) of the level of benefit for two-parent families, which in turn is connected to the minimum wage. During the last 15 years the income gap between lone-parent and two-parent families increased; in 1985 the disposable income per person in lone-parent families was 25% less than in two-parent families, and in 1993 the gap was 35%. This is partly due to the fact that the uprating of benefits in line with inflation ended in the early 1980s. Also the labour participation rates of women in two-parent families increased, and more married women contributed to their family's income by getting a part-time job (Niphuis-Nell, 1997).

Table 6.3: Income and household composition (1997) (%)

	Low income	Long-term low income
Single women	31	18
Single men	23	8
Lone mothers	62	27
Lone fathers	26	9
Two-parent family	10	3
Couple without children	6	3
Others	8	2

Source: CBS Inkomenstatistiek (1997) in Ministerie van Sociale Zaken en Werkelegenheid (1999)

Lone-parent families, along with young and old single people, therefore belong to the poorest households in the Netherlands (Muffels et al, 1995; Engbersen et al, 1997). But not every lone-parent family lives in poverty; in particular widows, male-headed lone-parent families and higher-educated lone mothers are better off. Female-headed lone-parent families are the poorest; in particular when the mother is divorced or never married and when she has a lower level of education (Hooghiemstra and Knijn, 1997).

Moral stigmatisation

In contrast to the US and the UK, but similar to the Scandinavian countries, lone mothers in the Netherlands are nowadays not stigmatised for living without a male partner. This has not always been the case, as some historical studies show (van Stolk and Wouters, 1983; Wiemann, 1988; van Wel, 1992; Knijn, 1994). In the 1950s, lone motherhood was only perceived as an acceptable way of living when it was occasioned by the death of the husband. The taboo on sexuality before or outside marriage was very rigid and lone mothers were condemned as 'fallen promiscuous women' who did not respect marriage and the well-being of their children. Many philanthropic organisations supported lone mothers in 'lone-mothers' homes'. Their main remedy for helping these mothers was by 'developing a motherly and responsible attitude' that could help them find a decent man to marry. In the 1960s attention shifted toward teenage lone mothers. The new academic discipline of 'adolescent psychology' developed at just the time when the rate of teenage mothers was increasing slightly, as a result of the disconnection of sexuality and marriage at a time when the pill was not yet widely accepted for unmarried women. Adolescent psychologists and philanthropic organisations together developed a remedy that has disrupted many lives: adoption. Within a few years, hundreds of young women were morally forced to give away their children directly after birth. This remedy, which was perceived to be the best way for teenagers to reach adulthood without bearing the burden of motherhood, resulted in many traumatically hurt women and children.

At the end of the 1960s attitudes towards lone mothers changed again. The Netherlands went through a process of secularisation and anti-authoritarian protests that resulted in the opinion that everybody has the right to live according to one's own principles, at least when one does not harm another person. In this atmosphere the sociologist Millikowsky (1968) pleaded that lone-parent families should be seen as just an alternative kind of family. In his opinion their only problem is poverty. Therefore the government should take responsibility for guaranteeing the incomes of lone parents (that is, lone mothers) who should have the right to take care of their children while they lack a breadwinner. This statement contributed, among other factors, to the General Assistance Act including, from the 1970s on, a new category, namely the ABW-sec. The ABW-sec was mostly for lone-mother families who were exempted from the obligation to work until their youngest child reached the age of 18. Millikowsky's statement expresses the still prevailing attitude of the Dutch population towards lone-parent families; 79% of the population says that a female-headed lone-parent family is just another kind of family. Interestingly enough only 38% of the population says the same about a male-headed lone-parent family. The same poll shows that about 47% of the Dutch population has the opinion that it is more important for mothers to take care of children than to have a paid job (van der Avort et al, 1996). By implication the Dutch motherhood rationale still indicates that it is better to be a lone mother taking care of her children than a full-time working married mother.

Employment patterns and policies

The labour market participation rates of lone mothers are comparable to those of mothers in two-parent families. Since 1990 the employment rates of lone-parent families have increased significantly, although a few specific categories of lone parents are less likely to be employed than their partnered counterparts (see Table 6.4). These categories include lone mothers with young children and lone fathers with children of all ages.

Employed lone mothers work more hours per week than partnered mothers; they have to work more hours per week to avoid social assistance. But these different practices indicate that a part-time job for mothers is still the preferred practice for Dutch mothers. Our own research shows that, for instance, lower-educated lone parents either do not work or work more than 30 hours a week, while a third of middle- and higher-educated lone parents work between 21 and 30 hours a week (van Wel and Knijn, 2000; Table 6.5).

Since the beginning of the 1990s, there has been an increasing discrepancy between public opinion on lone-mother families and the political discourse. Politicians increasingly define lone-mother families as a social problem, both because of their poverty and because of their dependence on welfare benefits. The politically agreed remedy for both

Table 6.4: Employment by household type, men and women related to the age of children (%)

	Women			Men		
	1988	1990	1997	1988	1990	1997
Lone-parent families	26	28	42	63	65	72
Youngest child:						
0-5	16	18	29	–	–	–
6-11	23	27	45	–	–	72
12-17	34	37	50	63	65	74
Two-parent families	27	31	45	89	90	92
Youngest child:						
0-5	22	27	45	90	92	92
6-11	28	33	43	90	91	92
12-17	33	37	47	86	87	90
Total	36	39	47	70	71	74

Source: Jaarboek Emancipatie (1997)

Table 6.5: Working hours of lone parents not on welfare (%)

	Low educational level	Middle educational level	High educational level	Total
Not employed	32.7	11.2	7.6	12.2 (n=84)
1-19 hours paid work	6.1	9.1	7.6	7.8 (n=54)
20-21 hours paid work	18.4	34.0	41.5	36.0 (n=248)
32+ hours paid work	42.9	45.7	43.3	43.9 (n=302)
Total	98	197	393	688

Source: Knijn and van Wel (2000)

those problems is employment, as required under the new 1996 General Assistance Act. It is thought that getting lone mothers into paid jobs is a way to 'kill two birds with one stone': it will reduce welfare expenditure on the one hand, while on the other hand it will reduce lone mothers' poverty, as well as their social isolation.

The introduction of welfare reform in the Netherlands

The Dutch social assistance system offers income support to claimants who do not have other sources of income. A quarter of the claimants are lone-parent families (the majority of these being female headed). Others are artists, people with a drug addiction and people without past experience in the labour market, such as youngsters leaving school or long-term unemployed people. As a category, lone mothers occupied a specific position under the so-called ABW-sec, which meant that they had no obligation to seek work. Since January 1996 the Netherlands has implemented a new social assistance law, called the *nieuwe Algemene Bijstandswet* (nAbw/new General Assistance Act). The objectives of the law are twofold (Algemene Bijstandswet, 1995):

• to offer minimum income support to those people that really need it;
• to stimulate welfare recipients to earn their own living as soon as possible.

Decentralisation of responsibilities towards the local level and the activation principle were central elements in the new General Assistance Act. All claimants were given an obligation to seek work, including lone parents. Some parliamentary debates focused on the status of lone mothers, in particular on the question of at what age of the children could the mother be expected to earn her own living. At first it was suggested that mothers of children below the age of 12 should be exempt. The Parliamentary Under-Secretary of Social Affairs and Unemployment, Ter Veld, stated in 1992:

> The age of 12 years for the youngest child is included in the law. Albeit not as an absolute criterion but as an assignment to the mayor and aldermen to, in case a mother has to take care for one or more children below the age of 12 years, adjust the obligations to find work to the responsibilities concerning the care for and education of the children. (TK, 1992-93, p 83)

This age indication or guideline disappeared from the proposed law during the following years and was not included in the final text of the law that the government presented to Parliament. By an initiative of one of the very small orthodox Christian parties (the Calvinist Political Bond [GPV]), Parliament finally decided that such an open-ended criterion in the law was not acceptable. The government decided to introduce an obligation to work only for lone mothers with school-aged children, that is children over five years of age (Weuring, 1996). On 1 January 1996 the welfare reform acquired the force of law. Parliament might have accepted the age indication of the youngest child, but many other aspects of the law were still open for interpretation. The law says: "the new rules are in principle applicable to all welfare claimants", but it also states that:

> Municipalities will have to consider the presence of young children. This will give the municipalities the opportunity to attune the re-entrance to the labour market to the individual possibilities of those involved. In particular women, who are the main category of claimants of the ABW-sec, might benefit from this new law. The current welfare regime too often results in an automatic denial of their work potentials if they don't have the obligation to work. A needless dependence on welfare is in the end not in the interest of these claimants. (TK, 1993-94, p 23)

So while the government at a national level made policies about obligations to work, there was still considerable discretion available at a local level to grant exemptions.

At the time the law was implemented, no provisions were available to support lone mothers in their double responsibilities. The law does not include the right to childcare as a condition for accepting a job, and there is a shortage of childcare for pre-school children. After-school care is developing very slowly (only 4% of all children are covered), and if it is available it is of a poor quality. Municipalities were given discretion to implement the law and to interpret the phrase that mothers' caring responsibilities have to be taken into consideration. It is assumed that they use the law to help lone mothers out of poverty by finding a job, but it was expected that they would have problems in deciding how to weigh up care responsibilities with employment.

The situation is more complicated since the same Ministry of Social Affairs and Employment promotes a part-time work strategy for men and women who have children. This strategy was promoted by the Commissie Toekomstscenario's Herverdeling Onbetaalde Zorgarbeid (Governmental Advisory Committee for Scenario's for the Future) (1995) and has been accepted as the official emancipation strategy of the government. In several ministerial papers such as '*Kansen op Combineren*' (Chances to Combine, Ministerie van Sociale Zaken en Werkgelegenheid, 1997) and '*Naar een nieuw evenwicht tussen zorg en Arbeid*' (Toward a New Balance of Work and

Care, Ministerie van Sociale Zaken en Werkgelegenheid, 1999a) the so-called 'combination scenario' is promoted. This scenario implies a working week of a maximum 32 hours for both men and women in order to give each of them the chance to combine work and care, under the assumption that as a couple they will share work and care. With regard to lone mothers this policy evokes unforeseen effects; does what counts for partnered parents also count for lone parents, and if so, how should lone parents' part-time work be supported in cash and care? Municipalities are thus facing two problems. First, they have more local discretion, but they lack strict criteria for getting lone mothers off welfare. Second, they have to stimulate lone parents into employment but they hardly know anything about the work capacities of these welfare recipients, and they also lack the means for improving childcare and after-school care.

Shortly after the implementation of the welfare reform the Dutch government introduced some additional provisions to support lone mothers' re-entrance into the labour market. The new administration (a coalition of social democrats, social liberals and right-wing liberals) became aware of the cultural shock the reform occasioned. Already by the start of 1996 the government had increased the untaxed part of employed lone-parents' income from 6 to 12% (comparable to Earned Income Tax in the US). In addition, an earnings disregard for part-time work of 250 Dutch Guilders a month (£85 a month) was introduced and national budgets to support local childcare provisions were offered an amount of 85 million Dutch Guilders (£25 million) a year (*Staatscourant 43*, 29 February 1996). Lone parents by these means were for the first time treated as a specific category of welfare claimants in need of additional support. In other respects, for instance labour market programmes, they have the same rights and duties as other welfare beneficiaries.

It is worth stressing that this welfare reform implies a major shift in the Dutch motherhood rationale. Instead of perceiving mothers as the main carers of their children, they are now considered as providers. This changing image of lone mothers, however, is not shared by the population at large and certainly not by lone mothers themselves, and nor by the local 'street level' bureaucrats who have the discretion to implement the law. The majority of lone parents themselves, whether they depend on welfare or not, disagree with the full obligation to work (see Table 6.6).

The main resistance to the law can be attributed to the fact that lone mothers want to make the decision to get into paid work for themselves. They defend their autonomous right to decide as a mother whether they are capable of combining work and care or not, and to decide whether

Table 6.6: Opinion about lone mothers' obligation to work

	Lone mothers on welfare (n=452)	Lone parents not on welfare (n=688)
No obligation at all	52	34
20 hours or less per week	31	37
21-36 hours per week	4	9
Partly (not specified)	5	8
Full obligation	6	8
Unknown	2	3

Source: van Wel and Knijn (2000)

their children are capable of coping with a working mother and alternative carers. The majority believes that the government should not intervene in these decisions, the more so since most of them feel that they have the right to receive welfare benefits as long as their children need their care. This internalisation of the right to receive benefits on the basis of mothering is the main reason for lone mothers' rejection of the new welfare reform. Another reason is that married mothers still have the choice to stay at home because breadwinner families benefit from all kinds of advantages in taxation, social security and health insurance to date. In particular, those lone mothers that have been married housewives before divorce (these are mostly lower-educated mothers) can hardly accept that after divorce they suddenly have the obligation to work.

This is not to say that lone mothers do not want to have a paid job. The majority of employed mothers (84%) and many lone mothers on welfare (56%) agree that the combination of work and care brings variation in their life, contributes to self-esteem and self-development, social contacts and autonomy. However, lone mothers on welfare, unlike employed lone parents, do not expect that paid work will contribute much to their income. They also see more disadvantages in combining work and care than do employed lone parents. They stress that it could harm the children and that it is only the mother herself who can decide about the right moment and the right conditions to go out to work (van Wel and Knijn, 2000).

Labour market and activation programmes

Labour market programmes are one of the main instruments municipalities have to help welfare recipients move into paid work. Other incentives are the work requirements, sanctions, tax reductions and financial compensation for part-time work and for childcare. Evaluations of the nABW show that of all these instruments, the labour market programmes and the work requirements seem to be the most effective, although only small proportions of people on welfare participate (Engelen et al, 1999). An evaluation report from the Ministry shows that lone parents leave welfare to a much lesser degree than other categories since the implementation of the law (11% compared to 23% of two-parent families) (see Table 6.7). Since the new law the number of welfare recipients has declined by about 90,000 persons (20%). Only among older people (aged 57-64) has there been an increase (Ministerie van Sociale Zaken en Werkgelegenheid, 2000).

The new law seems to be rather successful in another respect; because fewer people have got onto welfare, fewer people leave – there is less circulation. In general this means that the proportion of people on welfare who are the most difficult to get into a paid job increases; older people, lone parents and other people who are a long way from the labour market are the ones that still have to rely on social assistance. The welfare pool is creamed off, as policy makers say.

After the welfare reform, lone parents gained access to labour market programmes, but they have not participated in these very successfully. Most lone parents on welfare never gain access to labour market programmes because it is decided that they are exempt from the obligation to seek work. Although a majority of the municipalities officially state that lone parents are included in the work requirements, in almost 80% of these same municipalities most lone parents are labelled as category 3 or 4 of the welfare law. These categories mean 'hard or impossible to

Table 6.7: People on welfare by household composition (1995-98) (%)

	1995	1996	1997	1998	Reduction per household type 1995-98
Two-parent families	19	18	18	18	-23
Singles	57	58	57	56	-21
Lone-parent families	24	24	25	26	-11
Lone-parent families children <5	–	–	8	8	–

Source: Ministerie van Sociale Zaken en Werkgelegenheid (2000)

intermediate for work' (see Table 6.8) (Ministerie van Sociale Zaken en Werkgelegenheid, 2000, p 37). Thus the first 'hurdle' is not the local labour office, but the caseworker in the welfare office who decides on the work requirements. In the interviews with the caseworker a majority of lone parents with children between the age of five to 18 years are exempted from the full obligation to work and are labelled as belonging to category 3 or 4.

Our own studies, based on a survey among 452 lone mothers on welfare in five cities, found that none of the lone mothers on welfare with a child under five years of age have an obligation to seek work. Of the mothers with children above five, only 40% have a full-time work requirement, while 25% have a part-time work requirement. In total, about 60% of all lone mothers targeted by the welfare reform are exempted from the full obligation to seek work (van Wel and Knijn, 2000). These results are similar to the findings of Engelen et al (1999), who analysed about 2,000 files of welfare recipients in 15 local welfare offices. They conclude that 37% of lone mothers on welfare with children over five have a formal exemption from the obligation to work, while another 18% have a *de facto* exemption. Municipalities legitimise these exemptions by stating that lone mothers' capacities and demands do not fit with the work requirements in the local labour market. They also stress that the national incentives (free childcare, rise of the untaxed part of income and part-time disregards) are insufficient and hard to apply, that they have low expectations of lone mothers' capacities to become economically independent, and that there is a lack of good childcare (Knijn and van Wel, 1999).

Being exempted from work requirements implies that neither the lone parent nor the caseworker invests in improving the lone-parents' skills and capacities. Re-assessments are, in practice, delayed for a period of about 18 months. Invitations to participate in work trajectories or courses are often omitted. The arguments for the exemption are diverse and mainly based on a combination of medical and social indications, the

Table 6.8: Social assistance classification

Category 1:	directly available for paid work
Category 2:	available for paid work after some additional training and guidance (three months)
Category 3:	not directly available for paid work, additional training and schooling will take about a year
Category 4:	not available for paid work in the near future

well-being of the children, a very low educational level of the mother, the lack of childcare, and a lack of motivation to find work. Although caseworkers should ignore these arguments, they are not very motivated to enforce lone mothers to seek work if they prioritise mothering above employment (Knijn and van Wel, 1999). Interestingly enough there is no relationship between lone mothers' work motivation and welfare status, or between welfare status and participation in labour market programmes. About half of the lone mothers with children over five, and also half of the lone mothers with children under five who are categorically exempted from the obligation to work, intend to have a job. However, most of them say that they do not want a job in the coming year. In particular, lone mothers of young children participate in labour market programmes although they are not obliged to do so. They seem to want to make use of the possibility to improve their work capacities before they have a work requirement (Engelen et al, 1999; van Wel and Knijn, 2000).

Lone parents who do have a (part-time) work requirement are expected to visit the labour office to report that they are looking for a job, or to get additional training and guidance. At that time a whole world of courses, trajectories, subsidised jobs and activation programmes is potentially available to them. Because of the very complex and differentiated character of this field, the caseworkers often lose sight of what happens with their 'client' who has a work requirement. Policy makers (and similarly researchers) can hardly keep a grip on the process. Labour market programmes are not provided by the local social assistance office itself but by the regional labour office. This office sometimes contracts out programmes to public or private providers working on a profit or non-profit basis. A growing market of so-called reintegration programmes is developing, albeit more in the field of unemployed people (social insurance) than in the field of welfare recipients (social assistance) (Aarts and Velema, 2000). Only a minority of these programmes are exclusively directed at lone parents; sometimes programmes are for women only, but half of the programmes do not differentiate between the subcategories of welfare recipients (Engelen et al, 1999).

Organisations providing programmes for lone parents are either sub-departments of the labour office or independent organisations. The latter includes temporary work offices, many national and local for-profit organisations, '*vrouwenvakscholen*' (female vocational schools founded by the trades unions and subsidised by the state) and welfare organisations that work on a non-profit basis. A complication is that not all trajectories attempt to get lone mothers directly into employment. Descriptions of courses and projects show that they have a very broad and varying scope, including rational emotive therapy, raising self-consciousness, improving language skills, learning to know what you want and who you are, and orientation on the labour market and on voluntary work. Such courses are not funded solely by labour departments, but can also be subsidised by the local welfare departments or by the European Union. In general one can conclude that improving lone parents' human capital dominates work-first objectives, but only in as far as resistance against, or fear of, being employed is assumed to be the main obstacle in getting a job. However, there is a snake in the grass; the labour market programmes are not meant to improve work skills and capacities to higher levels of schooling. The courses put the accent mainly on improving self-esteem and on eliminating psychological constraints. They only teach a very basic knowledge of the Dutch language and vocational skills such as computer typing, cleaning in corporations and home care, and lower administrative skills (Mandos and van der Werf, 1997). Lone parents that only lack good qualifications and therefore need courses to get a better position on the labour market hardly benefit from these programmes. In contrast, they often complain that the welfare reform does not allow them to get additional education, because they are supposed to be ready for leaving welfare.

Few evaluations of all these programmes are available. Some studies are rather local (Mandos and van der Werf, 1997), others give indications of the effects on labour market participation on the basis of welfare files (Engelen et al, 1999), or are based on large-scale surveys (van Wel and Knijn, 2000). None are very effective in indicating what kind of programmes are the most successful. In their study of welfare recipients' files, Engelen et al (1999) conclude that about 40% of welfare recipients take part in some labour market programme, mainly schooling and training. However, the effects of the labour market programmes are not very strong. Of all the participants of these programmes only 9% left welfare within 18 months, while of all those who left welfare, 60% participated in labour market programmes and the other 40% did not. Van Wel and Knijn (2000) find that mothers with younger children, mothers whose care ethic dominates over their work ethic, and mothers who have medical and social problems participated less in such programmes than other mothers. They also conclude that lone mothers on welfare have more chance to reach financial independence after following some courses and training programmes. More decisive, however, is their motivation to leave welfare, the intensity of looking for a job and the experience of having combined some kind of paid work with additional benefits. Several bottlenecks prevent the labour market programmes for lone parents being more successful. First, due to the booming labour market hardly any unproblematic welfare recipient is left. All people who are still on welfare need extra attention to find a job. Lone mothers are considered to be a problematic group, and a majority are exempted from the obligation to work, therefore they participate less than other groups in labour market programmes. Second, only a minority (15%) of the municipalities offer labour market programmes specifically focused on lone parents; about 20% have programmes for women only (Engelen et al, 1999). Because of their particular problems in combining care and work it is recognised that categorical programmes for lone parents would probably do better than the current programmes. A third problem is that caseworkers and local policy makers do not expect too much of all kinds of investments in welfare recipients. They state that "when the economy goes down we'll get all of them back", and argue that the current welfare recipients cannot earn a wage high enough to remain off welfare, in particularly through part-time jobs (Knijn and van Wel, 1999). Organisational problems also undermine caseworkers' enthusiasm for stimulating lone parents into paid jobs. Once they have directed their 'clients' to the regional labour office, they lose control of the route their clients are taking. Finally, a lack of caseworkers, miscommunication within offices and reorganisation of the social assistance offices do not contribute to well-developed projects.

This is not to say that labour market programmes do not work at all. They have some positive effects for a small group of lone mothers who are a long way from the labour market, in particular those mothers who have very low educational levels and/or great difficulties in perceiving themselves as workers (see Table 6.9). Almost all labour market programmes focus on this type of lone mother and do good work in improving the mother's self-esteem, contributing to reintegration into their neighbourhood (for instance as 'neighbourhood-mothers' helping other mothers), or by helping them to find a (subsidised) job (van Berkel and Brand, 1999; van der Zwaard, 1999).

Getting better off

In addition to getting lone parents into paid work, a second objective of the Dutch government has been to get lone parents out of poverty. In view of the high poverty rates among lone-mother families this is not a

Table 6.9: Integration and reactivation projects for women only

Into	Step in Arnhem 30 participants[a]		Homecare Heerlen 21 participants[b]		Orientation Middelburg 12 participants[c]		Prima Overijssel 139 participants[d]	
Regular job	–		–		2	(16%)	9	(6%)
Subsidised job	6	(20%)	9	(43%)	6	(50%)	7	(5%)
Other courses	20	(67%)	–		–		3	(2%)
Still in the programme	–		6	(29%)	1	(8%)	102	(73%)
Psychiatric care	–		4	(19%)	–		–	
Disappeared	1	(3%)	2	(10%)	3	(25%)	10	(8%)
Back to caseworker	3	(10%)	–		–		8	(6%)

[a] A five-week project (half a day per week) for lone mothers who lack the motivation to get into paid work. Seven courses for 10 participants per course were planned, the first courses started in 1996.

[b] A seven-week project (1.5 days a week), directed at the older (average age = 38) and rather motivated lone mothers, offers orientation, apprenticeships, mediation and follow-up care. Three groups of 10 participants each have started.

[c] A twelve-week course (taking one day a week), for not very motivated lone mothers, offering reorientation to the labour market.

[d] Local pilots at three locations, subsidised by the European Union, a cooperation of local social work organisations, social offices and labour offices. The attempt is to support women in the process of reorientation on the labour market.

minor objective. Lone-mother families are among the poorest Dutch families (alongside older single women), and in international comparisons, Dutch lone mothers tend to have low incomes (Hooghiemstra and Knijn, 1997; Plantenga, 1999). This is rather embarrassing when one takes into consideration the booming Dutch economy and the rising prosperity among other categories of the population. The efforts to get lone mothers into employment have to be evaluated at least partly from this perspective. As stated before, two financial incentives are offered together with the welfare reform: the increase of the untaxed part of the income of working lone parents (from 6 to 12%) and an earnings disregard for part-time work. One can keep 300 Dutch Guilders (about £85) a month of the earned income in addition to the benefit, although this disregard is not excluded from taxation. Both incentives are meant to bridge the poverty gap. This is still a major problem in reactivation policy. Alongside their main benefits, all welfare recipients can apply for housing benefits, and additional benefits (for public transport, children's swimming lessons, museums and also for new glasses, furniture or household equipment), and they do not have to pay municipal taxes. Lone mothers in particular can apply for paid childcare as long as they are on benefits. So, if they work part time and stay on benefit, they keep the possibility of getting childcare paid for by the municipality and, in addition, all other 'advantages' of being on welfare. If they are in full-time work they lose this. As a consequence, the gap between being on welfare and the potentially earned income by paid work widens further. The consequence is that a part-time job could increase their net income slightly, but only if the municipality grants a part-time work disregard.

Part-time work disregards are given by some municipalities to all people on welfare who work part-time. Some only give them to specific categories such as clients who have a medical or social reason to work part-time, older clients, clients who are on welfare for a long period, or lone mothers with children aged from five to 18 years (Engelen et al, 1999). In addition, municipalities can give premiums for leaving welfare and for schooling. About a third of the municipalities give one or two of these premiums, only a few give all three premiums and some give none at all. An argument for not giving a premium to people who leave welfare is that "it is 'normal' to accept a job if one can" (Engelen et al, 1999). One consequence of the increasing discretion of local authorities is the unequal treatment of welfare recipients according to where they live. A fifth of the municipalities do not spend their whole budget for premiums. Evaluations show that the disregards do not work very well as an employment policy because not many parents know about them, and if they do, they do not perceive them as being high enough to make a difference. Also caseworkers do not like to use the disregards because they take a lot of administrative work and in the end do not help lone parents enough, or even limit their motivation to find a full-time job. From the files of welfare recipients Engelen et al (1999) conclude that no more than 4% get some disregard, despite the fact that 10% of the welfare recipients work part time. Knijn and van Wel (1999) find that this percentage is significantly higher among lone mothers (12%), although 40% of the lone mothers who work part time do not get a disregard. Lone mothers' problems with getting out of poverty result from their preference for part-time work and are also due to their low educational level; they can only earn low wages in the highly segregated female jobs in the lowest segments of the labour market. Van Wel and Knijn (2000) show that lone parents (in the majority mothers) not on welfare are in general well educated in contrast to lone mothers on welfare, who on average have very low educational levels. They find that the less-educated lone mothers earn per hour exactly half of the wage of the highest educated lone parents – 13.35 versus 27.50 Dutch Guilders per hour (approximately £3.80 versus £7.90). Thus lone mothers who have at maximum a lower vocational education will have to work at least 32 hours per week to earn an income compatible to the welfare benefit, while lone mothers with a higher professional or academic level can do so with 21 hours a week. For less-educated lone mothers the decision to get a job is, from a financial perspective, not very rewarding. They have to work full time to have any financial advantage, and that is exactly what they do not want.

Childcare

In order to stimulate lone-parent employment the government offered, shortly after the introduction of the new General Assistance Act, a budget for childcare for which the municipalities could apply. The annual budget was 85 million Dutch Guilders (£25 million). The Childcare and After School Care for Lone Parents on Welfare Measure offers municipalities the possibility of buying childcare in already existing childcare centres or of developing new childcare centres for lone parents with children under 13 years of age (*Staatscourant 43*, 1996). Part-time working lone parents and those lone parents who participate in courses and activation projects can make use of such childcare for free. However, they do not have the right to child care; the decision is up to the municipality. In 1999, 490 of the total 538 municipalities made use of this childcare budget. The ones that did not make use of it legitimised this by ideological motives – they did not want parents to make use of strangers for childcare – or by stating that it was not necessary because lone parents work only during school time. An evaluation of this childcare measure shows that 70% of the parents who make use of it have increased their hours of work or have started courses (van den Akker et al, 1998; Ministerie van Sociale Zaken en Werkgelegenheid, 2000).

Nevertheless, local caseworkers are not very satisfied with this measure because applications take a lot of very complicated administrative work, especially because every change in a lone mother's need for childcare requires a new application to be made. Since lone mothers follow many different trajectories before they get into paid work, caseworkers are not very willing to start the procedure to apply for childcare budgets. Another complaint at the local level is that there are already long waiting lists for childcare, including for working parents not on welfare. Municipalities state that they do not have the budgets to develop new childcare centres and their opportunities to buy childcare places in existing childcare centres are very limited. That is why social assistance offices and their caseworkers often allow lone parents to pay informal childminders when they get into paid work, although this is in fact against the rules of the childcare measure. In studying the implementation of the childcare measure for lone mothers we found striking differences between cities. Some cities very generously pay all the childcare costs for every lone parent on welfare with school-age children who takes any initiative to get back into paid work, whether it be schooling, voluntary work or part-time paid work. Also when lone parents leave welfare for paid work these social assistance offices still pay the costs for childcare. Other cities are less generous and set all kinds of limitations; for instance, they only pay two months of childcare after the lone mother has left the social assistance scheme. Some social assistance offices do not pay childcare directly, instead the lone mothers have to apply for additional benefits to get the childcare costs paid. Such a rule denies the intention of the measure, because the lone mothers then experience childcare benefits as a favour and not all of them will apply for it (Knijn and van Wel, 1999).

About half of the lone mothers on welfare who make use of formal – acknowledged – childcare receive a subsidy from social assistance to reduce the costs. A majority, however, also contribute to the costs of childcare themselves (van Wel and Knijn, 2000). The parents who make use of the childcare measure are rather satisfied with it, but evaluation studies show that a majority of lone parents do not know about it. They are not well informed by their caseworker or think that their caseworker lacks information about how to access the childcare (Ministerie van Sociale Zaken en Werkgelegenheid, 2000). Interestingly, only a minority of lone parents make use of formal institutionalised childcare, in particular those with a lower educational level rarely use such care (see Table 6.10). This is partly due to the fact that after-school care is hardly developed in the Netherlands and lone parents of pre-school children do not have the requirement to be employed. On the other hand most (lone) parents prefer informal childcare above childcare centres or after-school care. This is less so for (lone) parents with a higher educational level. In addition, the costs of childcare temper the ambition of lone parents with a lower educational level to use formal childcare. They already have to find a balance between work and care and are rather reluctant to pay for childcare.

Table 6.10: Sources of care used by lone parents (%)

Sources of care	Lone mothers on welfare (n=452)	Lone parents not on welfare			
		Low educated (n=98)	Medium educated (n=197)	High educated (n=393)	Total (n=688)
Ex-husband/co-parent	10	14	20	44	33
Family, friends	27	31	48	48	45
Formal childcare	15	15	20	29	24
Paid childminder	6	4	12	32	22

Source: van Wel and Knijn (2000)

Conclusion

Five years after the introduction of the new 1996 General Assistance Act it is clear that, of all categories of welfare recipients, lone mothers are least likely to leave welfare. On the one hand, lone mothers on welfare are especially likely to have a lower educational level and they are rather anxious about receiving a requirement to find a paid job. On the other hand, the government insists that the requirement for lone mothers to get a paid job will be maintained. In practice, however, one is confronted with local social assistance offices exempting the majority of lone mothers from this requirement. In this chapter we explained the lack of success of the welfare reform for lone parents by evaluating three incentives that are intended to stimulate lone parents on welfare to get paid work. Each of these incentives only marginally contributes to welfare independence of lone parents. This is mainly because of bureaucratic and administrative complexities, but it is also because lone mothers, local caseworkers and local policy makers do not agree with the intentions of the welfare reform for lone parents. The dominant motherhood ideology in the Netherlands is still that mothers should give a priority to care and that they should work only when they decide that this fits with their caring responsibilities.

This is why a new parliamentary debate about welfare reforms has started. The new Minister of Social Affairs and Employment, Vermeend, intends to extend the working of the law to lone mothers with children below the age of five. According to his proposal these mothers will not have to seek for work actively, but will have to accept a labour market programme or a job if this is offered by their caseworker. This enforcement is mainly inspired by the enormous labour force shortages, in particular in the public care services such as home care, nursing and education.

Many working women are needed to fill the labour force gap. New plans include more serious efforts to support lone mothers on their way back to the labour market, such as higher tax reductions for working parents, additional budgets for childcare and extra premiums for people who leave welfare. It is recognised by the government that only lone parents who have a very low educational level and who have little work experience and who struggle with caring are the ones on welfare now. It is also agreed that lone parents who are willing to leave welfare are not supported enough by the current measures. Parliament has not accepted these proposals yet and is rather concerned about the plan to extend welfare reform to mothers of children under five. The majority in Parliament claims that the government (among others) should guarantee good quality childcare for lone mothers with young children, and make greater investment in education for lone mothers. They also demand that the government makes clear agreements with local government about guiding lone mothers into employment. Thus far, Parliament is not satisfied with the government's initiatives in this respect and therefore the decision to oblige lone mothers with children below school age to work is not accepted.

SEVEN

Lone parents, employment and social policy in France: lessons from a family-friendly policy

Christine Chambaz and Claude Martin

Introduction

As in many other European countries, the number of lone-parent families has considerably increased in France over the past three decades (Martin, 1997; Chambaz, 2000). As a group, they became more visible with the adoption of a new terminology to identify them. The expression 'single-parent' or 'lone-parent family' (*famille monoparentale*) was adopted by sociologists in France relatively late (the mid-1970s), compared to Anglo-Saxon countries, to describe the situation where one parent takes care of one or several children. Such families were previously divided into narrower and more confused categories[1] according to marital status and moral standards, or mixed together in the category of 'dissociated families' (except widows) (Lefaucheur and Martin, 1993, 1997).

During the same period, the mid-1970s, French family policies were reformed to support these more fragile households. A new allowance, the *Allocation de parent isolé* (API) (Lone parent allowance), was created in 1976 to guarantee a minimum income for all lone-parent families (mainly with young children) whose resources were under a pre-defined threshold. We may consider this new policy as a real turning point in French family policy, in the sense that the objective became more to support poorer families, and less to compensate for the cost of children, regardless of the household's level of resources. Other means-tested benefits were created at the same time, like the 'new school year allowance' (*allocation de rentrée scolaire*), to give additional support to the more disadvantaged.

The API was firmly criticised in the mid-1980s. Some argued that it has pernicious or perverse effects. The beneficiaries of the API were suspected of hiding the existence of a new partner or even that they would 'schedule' a new birth to continue to receive the benefit. Dependency on this lone-parent benefit, mostly by young lone mothers, was firmly condemned (Sullerot, 1984) and some plans to abolish the API were formulated, but never enacted. One of the main issues was the apparent failure of that policy to encourage access to work and thus the possibility that it would create a risk of reinforcing the economic dependency of these women on the state. This issue of disincentive to work still exists in the 1990s, but the percentage of employed lone parents (including lone mothers), which is still high, has weakened the argument. Employment rates have not declined and, as in 1990, almost seven in 10 lone mothers were working in 2000.

So, contrary to what is happening in many other European and non-European countries, where many lone mothers are dependent on the welfare state, because they are not in the labour market, lone parenthood is not considered at the moment as a major social problem in France. No significant reform has happened in the past 10 years towards these family situations. The political agenda is more concerned about the social exclusion of lone men (without family) and by the problem of the working poor than it is about lone-parent families. One of the main reasons for the lack of interest by the government in this category of family is their relatively good integration in the labour market in quantitative terms, compared with all mothers, even if they are, on average, integrated in precarious (fixed-term contract, unchosen part-time, temporary) and poorly paid employment and face many daily difficulties in terms of incompatibility between work and family life.

The main policy reform debate relevant to lone parents concerns the financing of the API and whether and how to bring together this specific lone parent benefit with the general minimum income benefit, *Revenu minimum d'insertion* (RMI) into a single system, in order to obtain a more coherent policy towards the most fragile households. This is discussed below.

In this chapter, we will first concentrate on the main trends in lone parenthood over the past decade. We will then present the latest data concerning the employment of lone parents and their specific conditions of work, before tackling the question of their financial resources. In the last section, we will expound the main policy reform issues about lone parenthood discussed in the two past decades.

Lone parenthood in France: facts and trends

In 2000, there were approximately 1,423 million lone parents in France, which represents 16% of families with children aged under 25. Lone parents are more and more lone mothers, who represent about 86% of all lone parents (Tables 7.1 and 7.2). The number of lone-parent families has increased significantly from 720,000 in 1968 to 1.1 million in 1990. The percentage of minor children (defined as aged under 18) living in a lone-parent family also increased significantly, from 8.4% in 1986 to 11.5% in 1994 and 14% in 1999.

However, the major changes concern the distribution of lone parents by marital status. The share of widows among lone parents dropped from 54% in 1968 to 12.7% in 2000, compared with the percentage of divorced parents, which rose from 17% in 1968 to 47.3% in 2000, and the percentage of single parents, which rose from 8% in 1968 to 31.5% in 2000. Thus, for the last decade, the most important increase concerns these single (that is, never-married) parents whose number has more than doubled, from 217,000 to 449,000[2]. As a matter of fact, the growing number of single parents relates mainly to the increase in cohabitation in the new generations and the fragility of these cohabiting couples.

The category of single (unmarried) parent also changed significantly in terms of age (Table 7.3). In 1990, just over one single parent in three was under 30 years old and only 8.1% were more than 45. In 2000, only one in five is under 30 and almost 18% are more than 45 years old (Figure 7.1). So, contrary to the situation in most Anglo-Saxon countries, lone parents in France are rarely young single mothers with babies. Most of them are divorced or separated mothers aged 35 plus and with pre-adolescent or teenage children.

Table 7.1: Number of lone-parent families in France in 1990 and 2000

	1990		2000	
	000s	%	000s	%
All families with dependent children	890	100.0	880	100.0
Lone-parent families	100	12.2	140	16.0
Lone-mother families	925	10.4	120	13.8
Lone-father families	162	1.8	201	2.3

Note: Dependent children are single, under 25.
Source: Labour Force Survey (1990-2000)

Table 7.2: Number and proportion of lone-parent families in France in 1990 and 2000, by marital status and age

	1990		2000	
	000s	%	000s	%
Marital status				
Single	217	20.0	449	31.5
Divorced	555	51.2	673	47.3
Separated	78	7.2	121	8.5
Widowed	234	21.6	181	12.7
Age				
Under 25 years	33	3.0	28	1.9
25-29 years	88	8.0	84	5.9
30-34 years	146	13.4	174	12.2
35-39 years	185	17.0	249	17.5
40-44 years	249	22.9	318	22.3
45-49 years	149	13.7	296	20.8
50-54 years	105	9.7	181	12.7
55 years +	134	12.3	94	6.5

Source: Labour Force Survey (1990-2000)

Table 7.3: Lone parents in 1990 and 2000, by marital status and age (%)

	Under 25	25-29	30-34	35-39	40-44	45-49	50-54	55+	All
1990									
Single	13.3	23.1	23.3	17.8	14.3	3.6	1.9	2.6	100.0
Separated	0.4	8.3	15.1	17.9	25.8	13.1	9.2	10.0	100.0
Divorced	0.5	5.1	13.8	20.5	29.4	16.0	8.4	6.2	100.0
Widowed	0.1	1.1	2.8	7.5	14.6	17.6	19.9	36.2	100.0
2000									
Single	6.0	14.3	23.3	21.7	16.7	10.9	5.3	1.5	100.0
Separated	0.5	5.1	14.3	15.4	21.2	20.0	15.4	7.9	100.0
Divorced	0.0	1.6	7.2	17.7	27.9	25.6	14.1	5.8	100.0
Widowed	0.0	1.4	2.0	7.2	16.1	27.8	24.2	21.2	100.0

Source: Labour Force Survey (1990-2000)

Figure 7.1: Lone parents' marital status according to age in 1990 and 2000

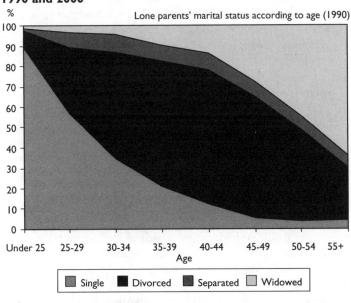

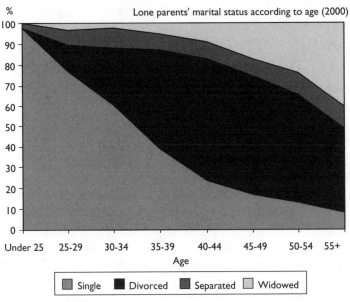

Source: Le Corre (2000)

Because of their age, lone parents much more often have children whose age is between six and 17, the school age, than children aged under three. Eight lone parents in 10 have no child under six years old (see Table 7.4), while one lone mother in four has no child under 18, which means that they are much more concerned with adolescents and young adults. Of the 3.3 million families with a child aged under three, 300,000 (10%) are lone-parent families. The age of the children may have a serious impact on the working conditions of these mothers, but also on the weight of domestic activities in their daily life. Compared with working mothers living in couples, lone mothers devote less time to domestic activities. They receive more help from their children, who are, as we just underlined, more often adolescents or young adults than they are young children. And many of them do not have their children, who stay with their fathers, during the weekends.

Nevertheless, in 2000, 160,000 children under three were living in a lone-parent family, which accounts for 7.6% of the under three age group. There were also 217,000 children between three and five years old living with a lone parent, equivalent to 10% of the children of that age category. The under six-year-olds living in a lone-parent family were 376,000, which is almost 9% of the under sixes in France (Avenel, 2001).

The level of qualification of lone parents, and particularly lone mothers, is quite low, but given the progression of the rate of staying on at school in each new generation, the percentage of lone parents without any qualification or with the minimum level of schooling, *Certificat d'études primaires* (CEP), is decreasing (Table 7.5). In 1990, 47% of lone parents had no qualification or only the CEP. In 2000, this was the case for 35%. Nevertheless, compared with partnered mothers, lone mothers still have a lower level of qualification, which has an impact on their level of employment. With this qualification profile, they are much more likely to be found in precarious jobs in the service sector, than in permanent and qualified jobs.

Lone parents and employment

A decrease in lone-mothers' employment rates?

We now focus on mothers, as they form a large majority of lone parents. The main noticeable change in their activity rates between 1990 and 2000 may represent a kind of convergence between lone mothers' and partnered mothers' behaviour.

Table 7.4: Number and age of children of the lone-parent families in 1990 and 2000

| | All lone-parent families | | | | All mothers | | | |
| | 1990 | | 2000 | | 1990 | | 2000 | |
	000s	%	000s	%	Lone mothers (%)	Partnered mothers (%)	Lone Mothers (%)	Partnered mothers (%)
Number and age of dependent children								
No child under 18	333	30.6	385	27.0	28.7	18.6	24.7	18.4
One child 6-17	360	33.1	511	35.9	32.9	21.9	35.7	21.5
One child 3-5	70	6.4	83	5.8	6.6	5.9	6.4	5.7
One child under 3	44	4.0	51	3.6	4.5	7.4	3.9	7.9
2 children, youngest child 6-17	144	13.2	203	14.3	13.5	17.4	14.5	17.5
2 children, youngest child 3-5	37	3.4	57	4.0	3.7	7.5	4.3	7.7
2 children, youngest child under 3	17	1.6	33	2.3	1.7	6.0	2.6	6.6
3 children or more, youngest child 6-17	44	4.0	52	3.6	4.1	6.1	3.9	6.2
3 children or more, youngest child 3-5	21	1.9	29	2.0	2.2	4.9	2.2	4.5
3 children or more, youngest child under 3	19	1.7	20	1.4	2.0	4.4	1.7	4.0
Number of children under 6								
0	880	80.9	1,151	80.8	79.2	64.1	78.9	63.6
1	178	16.3	240	16.8	17.7	27.9	18.5	28.4
2 +	30	2.8	33	2.3	3.0	8.1	2.6	7.9

Source: Labour Force Survey (1990-2000); DREES calculations (2000)

Table 7.5: Level of qualification of lone parents and lone mothers compared to partnered mothers in 1990 and 2000

| | All lone-parent families | | | | All mothers | | | |
| | 1990 | | 2000 | | 1990 | | 2000 | |
	000s	%	000s	%	Lone (%)	Partnered (%)	Lone (%)	Partnered (%)
Highest qualification								
No qualification or CEP	494	46.0	482	33.9	46.7	41.6	34.6	27.8
BEPC	96	9.0	123	8.6	9.4	9.7	9.1	8.6
CAP, BEP	226	21.1	379	26.6	20.0	23.6	25.3	27.2
Baccalauréat or BP	111	10.3	178	12.5	10.7	10.9	12.9	14.2
Baccalauréat +2	71	6.6	153	10.7	6.9	8.6	11.2	12.7
Higher degree	68	6.4	101	7.1	5.7	5.0	6.4	8.8
Still at school	6	0.6	9	0.6	0.7	0.6	0.7	0.7

Source: Labour Force Survey (1990 2000); DREES calculations (2000)

In 2000, about two thirds of all lone mothers were in employment and this had hardly changed at all over the past decade (Table 7.6). Lone mothers were still slightly more likely to be employed than partnered mothers (66.8% compared with 65.7%), even though the employment rates of partnered mothers had risen since 1990 (from 58.8%). However, lone mothers with at least one child aged under six years were less likely to be employed than partnered mothers with children of this age (48.9% of lone mothers compared with 57.8% of partnered mothers)[3].

In fact, the stability in overall employment rates for lone mothers is hiding a rising gap in employment rates between those with older and those with younger children. The employment rate of lone mothers whose children are all aged 18 and above (the mothers of young adults) has risen from 65.2% in 1990 to 71.7% in 2000. By contrast, the employment rate of lone mothers with at least one child aged under six has fallen from 52.1 to 48.9% over the same period. This fall in employment rates for lone mothers with young children does not depend on the number of children and is specific to lone mothers. As Table 7.6 also shows, the employment rates for partnered mothers with at least one child aged under six rose slightly from 54.7% in 1990 to 57.8% in 2000.

In fact, among these partnered mothers, the employment rate fell for

Table 7.6: Proportion of lone mothers and partnered mothers working according to International Labour Office (ILO) criteria (%)

	Lone mothers		Partnered mothers		Odds ratio	
	1990	2000	1990	2000	1990	2000
No child under 18	65.2	71.7	56.9	67.7	0.35	0.19
All children 6-17	74.2	71.5	62.9	71.3	0.53	0.01
One child or more under 6	52.1	48.9	54.7	57.8	-0.10	-0.36
All	67.0	66.8	58.8	65.7	0.35	0.05

Note: The odds ratio gives a difference between lone mothers and partnered mothers at each date. It is calculated as the difference of the logarithms of the ratio between the likelihood of working and the likelihood of not working for each group of mothers. It is like postulating a logistic model where the reference situation would be those of 'partnered mothers' at each date. The odds ratio would then give an indication of 'overpropensity' of lone mothers to work. So it takes direct account of the differences between 1990 and 2000.

Source: Labour Force Survey (1990-2000); DREES calculations (2000)

only one specific group: those with two children including at least one aged under six. This can be attributed to the extension in 1996 of the *Allocation parentale d'education* (APE) (parental education allowance) to families with a second (rather than a third) child. This provided an opportunity for some mothers in this family type (two children, one aged under six) to withdraw, or reduce, their employment participation. However, lone mothers are less likely to receive this benefit than partnered mothers. In June 1999, fewer than 20,000 lone parents benefited from APE at a full rate (which means that they did not work), that is about 7% of lone mothers with at least one child under six, as against 13% for mothers in couples.

Thus, as the 'odds ratios' (the gap between employment rates of lone and partnered mothers) show, lone mothers with older children are now only slightly more likely to be employed than partnered mothers, and lone mothers with younger children are increasingly less likely to be employed than partnered mothers.

Table 7.7 shows unemployment rates in 1990 and 2000, using both the ILO (seeking work) and self-declared measures. On the ILO measure, lone mothers are more often unemployed than partnered mothers (14.7% and 7.5% respectively in 2000)[4]. The unemployment rates of both lone and partnered mothers rose during the last decade and so the gap between them stayed about the same. But while the unemployment rates of all mothers of children aged over six increased, the unemployment rates of

Table 7.7: ILO and self-declared unemployment among lone and partnered mothers (%)

	ILO				Self-declaration			
	Lone mothers		Partnered mothers		Lone mothers		Partnered mothers	
	1990	2000	1990	2000	1990	2000	1990	2000
No child under 18	6.9	10.2	3.8	5.3	7.3	11.9	4.0	6.0
All children 6-17	13.0	15.7	6.7	7.7	13.0	17.7	5.8	8.2
One child or more under 6	23.3	17.7	8.5	8.3	26.5	23.9	9.4	9.6
All	13.4	14.7	6.8	7.5	14.2	17.6	6.7	8.3

Source: Labour Force Survey (1990-2000); DREES calculations (2000)

mothers of younger children could have fallen for lone mothers[5], whereas it increased for partnered mothers.

However, this relative stability could be hiding a change in lone parents' wishes. Among lone mothers with children aged six to 17, ILO unemployment increased by about two percentage points between 1990 and 2000 (from 13 to 15.7%), but self-declared unemployment increased by about four percentage points (from 13 to 17.7%). Inactivity decreased by the same proportion, and especially inactivity involving looking after home or family. Comparing 1990 with 2000, people in general have become more likely to declare themselves to be unemployed when they are not unemployed according to ILO criteria. This is more likely to be the case for lone mothers than for partnered mothers, and the gap between the two unemployment measures between 1990 and 2000 has also become greater for lone mothers than it has for partnered mothers. Non-employed lone mothers are, it seems, increasingly perceiving themselves as attached to the labour market, and as unemployed rather than as inactive. More than ever, the situation of lone mothers in the labour market is becoming difficult to measure and this suggests that the situation itself has become more complex and difficult.

The high employment rate of lone parents and particularly lone mothers in France is strongly related to the public services devoted to young children. As with many other employed mothers, lone mothers have access to pre-elementary school, even for two-year old children (Martin et al, 1998). They also often have priority in respect of local day care services because of the difficulties they have to manage their daily life between work and care.

In 1998, 100% of three- to five-year-old children were in a pre-elementary school, and even 35% of two-year-olds. The French situation is particularly good in this respect, compared to other European countries, even if many needs are not covered. Pre-elementary schools, day care centres (*crèches collectives*) and childminders' homes (*crèches familiales*) offered almost 500,000 places in 1999 for the 2.2 million children under three, which meets almost 20% of the number of places required. To these services, one may add the *crèches parentales*[6] (8,500 places) and the day nursery (*halte-garderies*) (70,000 places) (le Corre, 2000).

As the European Observatory on National Family Policies stated:

> The most important factor in explaining the very high rates of labour force participation amongst lone mothers in France seems to be the availability and quality of free pre-school childcare and the priority of access to it given to lone parents. (Bradshaw et al, 1996, p 78)

Conditions at work

About 5% of working lone mothers work under a special scheme linked with training or reducing exclusion. This proportion is twice as high as for partnered mothers. This does not mean that non-employed lone parents are required to participate in specific work incentive programmes. But those lone mothers receiving a minimum income such as API or RMI have priority for insertion jobs, as do all other beneficiaries.

Part-time work is less developed among lone mothers than among partnered mothers: in 2000, 73% of employed lone mothers worked full time, but this was true for only 63% of partnered mothers. This gap has been narrowing since 1990, linked to the broad expansion of part-time work. Moreover, there is an important difference between lone and partnered mothers working part time: while more than seven partnered mothers out of 10 chose to work part time, fewer than half of lone mothers are in this situation. Just under half of lone mothers who work part time would rather have a full-time job (Table 7.8).

Working lone mothers face difficult schedules, as do partnered mothers. Almost four out of 10 lone mothers follow rotating or changing shifts from day to day. Almost half of them may work on Saturday, and a quarter on Sunday. These proportions are very close to those observed

Table 7.8: Lone mothers' working conditions (%)

	1990		2000	
	Lone mothers	**Partnered mothers**	**Lone mothers**	**Partnered mothers**
000s	628	4,606	824	4,912
%	67.9	58.9	67.4	65.8
Duration of work				
Full-time work	84.5	72.8	73.4	63.4
Part-time work	15.5	27.2	26.6	36.6
less than 15 hours per week	2.0	4.1	2.9	3.8
15 to 29 hours per week	9.6	16.0	15.8	20.6
30 hours per week or more	3.9	7.1	7.9	12.2
When part time work				
would rather work full time	41.3	15.6	42.4	17.0
would rather work more but not full time	12.6	10.7	13.1	10.4
chose to work part time	46.1	73.7	44.5	72.5
Hours of work				
The same every day	66.9	66.0	64.7	65.2
Rotating schedule	6.1	5.5	7.1	6.9
Changing schedule	27.0	28.5	28.2	27.8
Work on Saturday				
As a habit	29.0	30.5	25.1	25.9
Sometimes	24.3	19.2	23.5	22.0
Never	46.7	50.3	51.4	52.2
Work on Sunday				
As a habit	6.8	9.6	8.1	8.9
Sometimes	15.8	12.3	17.0	16.9
Never	77.5	78.1	74.9	74.2

Note: Dependent children are single, under 25.
Source: Labour Force Survey (1990-2000); DREES calculations (2000)

for partnered mothers and so could remain unnoticed. But for the people concerned, such a disturbed agenda implies difficulties in the organisation of everyday life, especially when the children are quite young and the need for caring is great.

Even if these situations may be considered as extremes, some lone mothers are working on rotating shifts with irregular changes of working hours, sometimes beginning at 6 o'clock in the morning and sometimes finishing at 10 o'clock in the evening. This causes very difficult and unstable caring arrangements, mostly requiring the help of grandmothers. Employers do not get involved in these domestic problems. They transfer these social costs to the family network and/or onto the local authorities, which are sometimes experimenting with childcare alternatives, such as irregular and atypical timetables.

As a consequence, lone mothers are far less satisfied with their working conditions than partnered mothers. According to the European Community Household Panel (ECHP) for 1996, a quarter of lone mothers declared themselves dissatisfied (level one or two on a six-point scale) with their earnings, 7% more than partnered mothers. In the same way, lone mothers were unhappy with their job security (17%) and working time (9%), compared with respectively 12 and 7% of other mothers (Table 7.9).

The small size of the sample does not allow us to derive robust statistics on part-time workers, but it seems that the mean score of each of the items could be particularly low for lone mothers both in absolute and compared to partnered mothers.

Resources and poverty rate

The benefits granted to lone parents

Table 7.10 summarises the main benefits available to lone parents (and other families with children). Even if they usually participate in the labour market and, as a consequence, very often have income from work,

Table 7.9: Satisfaction with working conditions of mothers in paid employment (1996)

Item of satisfaction	Proportion of less satisfied workers (%)		Mean score	
	Lone mothers	Partnered mothers	Lone mothers	Partnered mothers
Earnings in present job	24	17	3.28	3.61
Job security	17	12	4.07	4.29
Working time	9	7	4.32	4.35

Source: Eurostat, ECHP wave 3 (1996); DREES calculations (2000)

lone-parent families are also very likely to benefit from social transfers. In 1997, 84% of lone parents received some form of social transfer, a very much higher figure than that for the whole population (49%), and than that for couples with children (75%). Lone-parent families represent an important target group for means-tested benefits: they draw housing benefits twice as often as other families (62% compared to 30%), and are (relatively speaking) the main beneficiaries of the *Aide à la scolarité* (school allowance) and of the *Allocation de rentrée scolaire* (new school year allowance). However, only a third receive *Allocations familiales* (family allowances), which are distributed to families with two children or more but not to one child families, (and so are received by about half of all families), but nearly 8% benefit from *Complément familial* (means-tested family allowance), a higher proportion than for other families (less than 1%).

In addition, a third of lone parents benefit from *Allocation de soutien familial* (ASF), an allowance aimed to support families who do not get any alimony/child support or who only get a small amount, and 154,000 lone parents (8% of all lone-parent families) were receiving API in 2000. This is a minimum income explicitly dedicated to lone parents with young children aged under three. Almost all – 98% – of the beneficiaries of API are women, most are very young (60% are less than 30 years old, and 36% are under 25), and they are mainly single (63%) (Avenel and Algava, 2001). When their children grow up, some of these lone parents move onto RMI (the minimum income for adults). In total, about 200,000 (10% of all lone parents) are beneficiaries of RMI.

So, even though most lone parents do have a job, about one in five remain under the legal thresholds for benefiting from income support schemes. It is estimated that 10% of working lone parents are poor, even though the threshold for benefiting from minimum income usually exceeds the poverty threshold (defined here as 50% of the median equivalised income). Lone-parent families are also over-represented among the working poor (Lagarenne and Legendre, 2000). However, it is important to recognise that the proportion of working poor is lower in lone-parent families than in couples where only one of the partners has a job (16% of whom are poor according to this measure).

On average, lone-parent families have a standard of living about 25% below that of the population as a whole (Table 7.11), but also below that of couples with children, who lie very close to the average. So it is not surprising that only a third of lone parents have to pay income taxes, which is quite low compared to the whole population (58%). Not only do lone parents have low incomes, but also the French system of *Quotient*

Table 7.10: The French system of social benefits for families and especially for lone-parent families

1. Benefits for families

Allocations familiales: for all families with at least two children aged under 16 (or 20 according to the child's activity and resources). Some premiums for children aged 10 to 14 or 14 and above.

Complément familial: an income-related family allowance complementing the *Allocations familiales*. The household means are compared to a ceiling taking account of the household composition, lone-parent families being dealt with in the same way as dual earner couples and so granted a heavier weight.

Allocation pour jeune enfant (APJE): an income-related family allowance given to families with at least one child under the age of three. Women can also benefit from it from the fourth month of pregnancy. The income ceiling is the same as for *Complément familial*.

Allocation de rentrée scolaire: a new school year allowance to compensate families with children from 6 to 18 years old for the expenses at the start of the new school year. Means-tested and paid annually.

Aide à la scolarité: an income-related school allowance for families with children 12 to 16 years of age.

Allocation d'éducation spéciale: a special needs allowance for disabled persons under 20.

Allocation parentale d'éducation (APE): a parental education allowance to compensate parents for the income loss due to the reduction or interruption of paid activity at the birth of a child. First provided for the third and subsequent child, it was extended to the second child in 1996.

Revenu minimum d'insertion (RMI): this benefit provides a minimum income to adults, the level of which depends on the structure of the household. Lone-parent families may benefit from it until their children are more than three years old (otherwise they can claim for API which is more generous). In 1999, almost a million people were receiving the RMI.

Allocations logement: there are two housing benefits, the aim of which is to pay part of a tenant's rent. Their benefit depends on the family structure, the nature of the housing, the level of income and the rent.

2. Allowances for child care

Allocation de garde d'enfant à domicile (AGED): this allowance is paid to working parents who employ a mother's help or nannies in the home for children under the age of three or six. It compensates for a part of social security contributions, the level (50% or 75%) depending on the family income level and the age of the child.

Allocation familiale pour l'emploi d'une assistance maternelle agréée (AFEAMA): this allowance is paid to families whose children are cared for outside the home by approved nannies. It makes families concerned free of social security contributions for this job, and gives them an additional benefit, whose amount was income-related from January 2000.

Tax credits also reduce the cost of child caring.

Table 7.10: Contd.../

3. Lone-parent benefits

Allocation de soutien familial (ASF): a means-tested family support paid to the surviving spouse, lone parent or family taking on the responsibility for raising an orphaned child. It is also paid for children to lone-parent families when the missing parent does not pay alimony, or less than the amount of ASF.

Allocation de parent isolé (API): this means-tested lone parent allowance is paid to lone parents with a child under the age of three. It is part of the minimum incomes system. The income ceiling is higher than for RMI. The API is a differential and transitory benefit which rounds up the income of the lone parent or pregnant lone mother to a certain subsistence level (about 60% of the minimum salary for a lone parent or a lone pregnant woman), for one to three-and-a-half years, depending on the child's age. It is available during pregnancy, for the first year after the separation of a couple, and/or until the youngest child reaches the age of three. More than 9 in 10 beneficiaries of the API are women. In 1999, 150,000 lone parents were receiving the allowance.

4. Tax quotient familial

The French income tax is calculated once a year for the whole family or *foyer fiscal*. The choice of the tax rate depends on the *Quotient familial*, which is more or less the ratio between the taxable income and the structure of the family. This latter is estimated as follows: each of the spouses counts for one, and each child for a half, except for the third child who counts for one. For lone-parent families, the calculation is slightly different, as each child counts for one. The tax paid by lone-parent families is consequently lower than that paid by couples with the same level of income and same number of dependent children.

---

familial (family coefficient) used in the calculation of taxes on income, awards a higher weight to children when living in a lone-parent family. So it is recognised that the cost of children represents a heavier burden for lone parents than for partnered ones. And among those who do pay tax, lone parents pay on average less than other households. It should be noted that this *Quotient familial* is also used for granting means-tested benefits, so that a lone-parent family is more likely to draw such benefits than a couple with the same income and the same number of children.

Income from social transfers makes up about a quarter of lone-parent families' gross income, about twice as much as for other families. For beneficiary lone-parent families, social transfers represent 32% of their total gross income (also twice more than for other beneficiary families), but for each family, the lower the total gross income, the higher the share of social transfers. Likewise, the share of minimum incomes in lone-parent families' total income is hardly significant (4%) for lone parents as a whole. But for the 20% of lone parents drawing minimum incomes, the minimum incomes account on average for 33% of their total. The remainder consists of other social transfers (48%, about half of this being accounted for by housing benefit) and 11% comes from wages, three times less than for other families. If the standard of living of most lone-parent families relies on incomes from work, the dependency on benefits of the few drawing minimum incomes is quite strong.

In spite of social transfers, lone-parent families remain more exposed to poverty than do other households. With a low-income threshold defined as 50% of the median equivalised income, and measuring poverty by reference to low income, 14% of all lone-parent families are poor. That means that their monthly standard of living is less than 3,430 French Francs (€523). With a higher low-income threshold, defined as 60% of the median (4,110 Francs, or €627), 27% of lone-parent families are poor. These proportions are higher than those of the whole population and those of other families. However, this is more to do with the number of employed people in the household than it is with lone-parent status as such. As previously noted, using the 50% threshold, about 10% of employed lone parents are poor. This is similar to the rate for couples with one or two children where only one of the spouses is employed, and even lower than the poverty rate for one-earner couples with large families. When considering non-employed lone-parent families, the poverty risk is much higher: 28% of these families are poor, more or less the same as for non-employed couples with children. This does not change with the 60% threshold.

Thus lone parents are confronted with the very serious problem of poverty. Lone parents represent 11% of the poor households and account for 24% of poor households living in low rent social housing (*Habitation à loyer modéré* [HLM]) in 1997 (social housing) (Observatoire national de la pauvreté et de l'exclusion sociale, 2000).

Main policy reform issues

Contrary to what happened in the mid-1980s, lone parents are not now generally considered as a major social problem and no specific reform has been scheduled in the past decade. They do, however, represent one of the most fragile groups in the population and form an important percentage of the poor households at the end of the 20th century.

In 1986, a project was formulated by the right-wing government to abolish API, which is one of the main elements of family policy towards lone parents. Even at that time, the project was not enacted. API is no longer a main policy reform issue, except in the prospect of harmonisation of the French minimum incomes[8]. Three recent official reports have

Table 7.11: Lone-parent families' structure of income

	Proportion of beneficiaries (%)			Share in the gross income (%)		
	Lone-parent families	Couples with children	All households	Lone-parent families	Couples with children	All households
Housing benefit (ALF,ALS,APL)	61.8	30.2	25.8	7.5	1.8	1.8
Allocations familiales (family allowances)	33.8	52.5	18.7	4.0	3.5	1.6
Complément familial (means-tested family allowances)	7.7	9.5	3.5	0.6	0.4	0.2
Allocation pour jeune enfant (allowances for young children)	9.4	15.3	5.7	0.9	0.8	0.4
Allocation de rentrée scolaire (new school year allowance)	51.1	27.2	11.8	0.9	0.4	0.2
Aide à la scolarité (school allowance)	17.8	5.3	2.8	0.1	0.0	0.0
Allocation d'éducation spéciale (disabled children benefit)	0.8	0.7	0.3	0.1	0.0	0.0
Allocation parentale d'éducation (parental education allowance)	2.3	6.2	2.1	0.6	0.8	0.4
Allocation de soutien familial (family support)	32.6	0.9	2.2	1.9	0.0	0.1
Allocation parent isolé (lone parent allowance)	7.6	0.3	0.5	1.4	0.0	0.1
Minimum vieillesse (minimum income for older people)	0.7	0.6	3.3	0.1	0.1	0.3
Revenu minimum d'insertion (minimum income for adults)	10.4	2.7	3.5	2.0	0.3	0.5
Allocation adulte handicapé (minimum income for disabled adults)	2.5	1.7	1.9	0.7	0.3	0.4

Table 7.11: contd.../

	Proportion of beneficiaries (%)			Share in the gross income (%)		
	Lone-parent families	Couples with children	All households	Lone-parent families	Couples with children	All households
CAAH (minimum income for disabled adults bonus)	0.8	0.5	0.5	0.0	0.0	0.0
Unemployment benefits	23.8	23.1	16.3	4.2	2.8	2.9
All benefits	*83.8*	*74.9*	*49.0*	*24.9*	*11.2*	*8.8*
Pensions	45.8	11.6	41.6	10.5	2.5	22.7
Income from work	79.0	96.5	67.5	62.5	83.6	64.0
Capital income				2.1	3.0	4.7
Total gross income				*100.0*	*100.0*	*100.0*
Income Tax (IR)	33.3	60.3	58.4	3.6	5.5	6.4
Average standard of living (net)				*75.9*	*98.6*	*100.0*
Poverty rate						
(threshold = 50% median equivalised income)				13.6	7.0	8.1
(threshold = 60% median equivalised income)				27.3	12.8	14.1

Source: Taxes and Incomes Survey (1997); DREES calculations (2000)

suggested harmonising API and RMI (Fragonard, 1993; Join-Lambert, 1998; Belorgey, 2000). However, there are some quite important differences between these two minimum incomes. First, API gives access to almost 60% of the guaranteed minimum wage (*Salaire minimum interprofessionnel de croissance* – SMIC), compared to 46% of SMIC for the RMI and for a lone person. The proposition is therefore to increase RMI up to the level of API. However, the difference is not just monetary, it is also symbolic. API is conceived as a replacement income or as a 'maternal salary', without any obligation to enter or come back immediately to the labour market. It is mainly received by younger lone mothers (61% of recipients are less than 30 years old) and the main objective of the benefit is to give recipients the opportunity to take care of their child. By contrast, RMI is a general minimum income benefit, available to all those aged over 25 without other adequate means. So, to move from API to RMI is perceived very negatively, like a failure. Nevertheless, about 45% of the ex-beneficiaries of API are receiving RMI. This type of trajectory is very common, mostly for those who received API up to the end of the legal period of entitlement[9] (about six in 10 of all terminations). Where API ended before the maximum legal period of receipt, it was due to re-partnering in almost 25% of the cases. These trajectories of re-partnering mainly involve young people with few children. The exit from API was due to an increase of income in only 11% of the cases of termination before the end of the legal period of receipt (Chaupin and Guillot, 1998). Similarly, when we consider the beneficiaries of RMI, the end of the benefit is due in only half of the cases to a resumption of work. The other cases are mainly due to a modification in the family situation. Those who return to the labour market mainly find a part-time job, whose duration is less than 30 hours a week.

To avoid the negative work incentives of minimum incomes, since 1988 it has been possible to receive API or RMI with an earned income (known as the *mécanisme d'intéressement*). This provides an incentive to return to the labour market because there is no immediate cancellation of the benefit. The whole of the earned income can be drawn concurrently with the benefit during the first three months. Then, for the following nine months, 50% of the earned income is taken into consideration in the assessment of the benefit. This mechanism works only when the earned income is lower than 4,400 Francs (€670) (which is less than the full-time SMIC), so it only concerns poorly paid or part-time jobs. In 1999, 132,000 people receiving RMI (12% of the beneficiaries) were using the mechanism of *intéressement*. This was the case for 13% of the lone-parent families receiving RMI. In August 1998, almost 30% of the

220,000 lone-parent families on RMI were also receiving an earned income. This amounts to around 60,000 households, which again indicates the importance of the working poor lone parents.

However, there remain other disincentives to work for RMI recipients. Up to 2000, when a lone parent received RMI, they could claim for the *Allocation logement* at the maximum rate. If they got a job, they would lose part of this means-tested benefit. The *Allocation logement* has just been revised to lessen this disincentive. Until 2003, all incomes below RMI will be identically regarded. But another disadvantage will be the reactivation of debts, which are suspended during RMI. In summary, the incentive for lone parents receiving RMI to get a job is weak, even if many beneficiaries prefer to have one.

The current reform proposals concern all French minimum incomes: particularly API and RMI. The objective is to maintain a minimum income and to sustain all the initiatives for the beneficiaries to go back to the labour market. Like the two previous reports, the recent Belorgey (2000) report suggests merging the API and RMI, with an increased rate for people taking care of a child. It also suggests revising the scale of the RMI benefit to give a better bonus for children in the household and to extend the period of the *intéressement*, without taking into account the *Allocation logement*. It is proposed that it would be possible to receive RMI and an earned income over six months, without loss of benefit (instead of three months as now).

These projects are still on the agenda. In addition, France is on the way to adopting a new fiscal mechanism called *Prime pour l'emploi* (bonus to work). It is actually a tax credit for working people whose earnings are less than 1.4 times the (SMIC) guaranteed minimum wage but who have had a minimum period of employment activity during the year. The tax credit is given to individuals but takes account of the family's resources. Beneficiaries with children get a bonus, the first child of lone-parent families counting twice, which is quite consistent with the fiscal law that counts children of lone-parent families as a higher financial burden than other children.

However, as we discussed above, lone parenthood is not a significant policy issue in France at the moment. For example, the recent report of the Observatoire national de la pauvreté et de l'exclusion sociale (2000) does not give much attention to lone-parent families. And it is also noticeable that very little research has been devoted in the past decade to lone parenthood. The problem of single homeless men is giving more cause for concern. Nevertheless, one could notice the comeback of the 'old evil spirit', with growing interest in the issue of parental responsibility or, as it is more often expressed, parental irresponsibility. Lone-parent families are in the middle of this recurrent rhetoric underlining their incompetence, their lack of authority and the problem of the behaviour of children of divorce, and so on. It could be suggested that France is in a transition period on these issues and that lone-parent families may again become the focus of policy.

Notes

[1] Like 'mères sans conjoint' (mother without a partner), 'femmes chefs de famille' (women heads of families), 'femmes seules' (lone women), and so on.

[2] The increase is also significant for separated lone parents, whose numbers rose from 78,000 to 121,000. Couples seem to separate more often before divorce has been pronounced.

[3] The economic situation of children under six years old living in a lone-parent family is lower than in other families: 73% of them are living with a lone parent who is an employee or belongs to the working class, compared to 54% of children living in a two-parent family (Avenel, 2001).

[4] Other mothers, when they are not employed, are more likely to be defined as 'inactive', rather than unemployed.

[5] The conditional tense is for the small size of the sample for this category of lone mothers.

[6] Created after 1968, and officially recognised during the 1980s, the 'crèches parentales' are run by parents' associations. The requirements are less stringent than for 'crèches collectives' and they are smaller (between 10 and 15 children). Parents are co-producers of the service and contribute between 6 and 8 hours per week.

[7] The 'quotient familial' is a natural figure used to calculate tax allowances. It is the outcome of dividing the incomes of a household by a given number of 'shares' which correspond to its size and financial position.

[8] The global cost of API at a national level is relatively stable from 1988: between 4.6 and 4.9 billion Francs (Thélot and Villac, 1998).

[9] After 12 months or at the third birthday of the youngest child.

Part 2: Cross-cutting approaches

EIGHT

Orientations to work and the issue of care

Jane Lewis

The paid work/unpaid work equation

Modern welfare states have been constructed around the paid work/ welfare relationship. Just as governments have always been most concerned about the structure of incentives and disincentives that impinge on the able-bodied worker, so the core social policies of modern income maintenance systems have hinged on the relationship of the individual to the labour market. Carol Pateman (1988) has argued that the very definition of citizenship in the modern state rests on the idea of independence, which is defined in terms of the ability to earn a wage. But this raises in rather an acute form both the welfare and citizenship status of those who have been and are marginal to the labour market, especially if they are able-bodied adults with no obvious reason not to be in employment.

Historically, many countries did not expect mothers to go out to work. Central to the post-war welfare settlement was the idea of a male breadwinner model family, in which it was assumed that women would in the main be dependent on their husbands, an assumption that was inscribed in the whole social security system. Under such an assumption, lone mothers as a group posed particular problems. As women with children and without men, were they to be treated as mothers or workers? In strong male breadwinner countries, they tended in the post-war period to be treated as mothers (Lewis, 1998). Thus in the UK and in the Netherlands lone mothers in receipt of benefits were not required to register for work so long as they had a child under 16 years of age. In countries where the male breadwinner assumptions were rapidly modified, as in Sweden, or were less pervasive, as in France, lone mothers have been less likely to be treated categorically. There is evidence that in those countries that adhered to the male breadwinner-based assumptions longest and that chose to treat lone mothers as mothers there has recently been a pendulum swing in attitudes towards treating them as workers. This has been most striking in the UK and the Netherlands[1], where both governments moved in 1996 towards treating lone mothers in receipt of benefit as workers rather than as mothers (see Chapter Ten of this book).

This is part of a larger shift towards what might be termed a more individualised adult-worker model. In the UK case, the emphasis in the government's policy documents has been placed firmly on the notion that everyone who can is going to be in the labour market. How the care work that so many must do is going to be carried out is not explicitly addressed. Tony Blair's introduction to the document on welfare reform has been widely quoted – "[w]ork for those who can; security for those who cannot" (DSS, 1998, p iii) – and contrasted with the Beveridgean promise of security for all. Further on the document states that "[t]he welfare state based around the male breadwinner is increasingly out of date" (p 13). The notion is not only that all who can work will do so (an adult-worker model), but there is a growing idea that wages will allow for more self-provision (considerable optimism on this score continues to characterise the proposals for pensions in particular). This is an especially unreal assumption for women, given first, the unequal division of unpaid care work; and second, the fact that a disproportionate number of them are employed in low-paid, often care-related, jobs. It is additionally problematic for lone mothers, given the relative lack of attention paid to the demands of care work. The drive from 'welfare-to-work', begun by the Conservatives and developed so strongly by Labour, has by no means completely neglected the issue of caring work. The National Childcare Strategy and Childcare Tax Credit embodied in the Working Families' Tax Credit (WFTC) scheme are important initiatives, especially in a country where the issue of reconciling work and family responsibilities has been historically ignored. There is also the new strategy for carers and proposals for second pension credits for those caring for young children or adults, albeit on a more restricted basis than for the basic pension. These efforts are nevertheless limited, especially in the wider European context. Indeed, put alongside the fact that the long-term care issue has not been adequately addressed, Labour's political will to tackle the issues raised by care looks considerably weaker than its passion to promote paid work.

It is vitally important to promote and defend the right to work. However, the context in which this is done is crucial. The UK Labour government has put effort into the employment policy context for its welfare-to-work drive, with the enactment of a minimum wage and, as Glennerster (1999) pointed out, some active labour market policies that smack of Scandinavia and Australia more than the US. Furthermore, its policies in this arena are detailed. Care as an issue lies at the interstices of paid and unpaid work, public and private (in the sense of state and market), formal and informal (in the sense of public sphere and family), and of provision in the form of cash or services (Daly and Lewis, 2000). But policies for care are, thus far, much more limited and vague than policies in respect of 'work'. The Consultative Paper *Supporting families* (Home Office, 1998) put better services and support for parents first, but referred mainly to education and advice to be delivered via a national Family and Parenting Institute, a helpline and health visitors. The potentially extremely valuable Sure Start programme, providing childcare, family support, primary health care, early learning and play for young children is conceptualised as part of the attack on social exclusion. There is no coherent policy on the care of dependants, young and old, to match the policy on paid work. The care work side of the equation is thus largely missing. Yet this is also a crucial part of the context of a welfare-to-work programme. There is now a substantial body of evidence from this and other countries (see Chapter Six of this book) that many women want to prioritise care and that a majority will prioritise it in the absence of 'suitable' alternative arrangements, suitable in terms of accessibility, affordability and quality.

The point is that care work takes time and ways have to be found to take account of it. Some have advocated the idea of making social policy care-centred (for example, Knijn and Kremer, 1997). As a thought-experiment this has much value. Anna Coote's question "How shall we care for and support our children?" asked in 1981, has continuing value in pointing out the lacunae in our social provision. However, there is no reason why we should not try and transcend the paid work/unpaid work dichotomy by paying proper attention to *both sides* of what is a rapidly changing work and care equation. Tony Blair is certainly right in saying that the male breadwinner model is out of date, but the emphasis of New Labour has been skewed towards paid work and monetary incentives. In the case of lone mothers, there are of course three possible main sources of income: earnings, men and the state. After the 1991 child support legislation fiasco in the UK, it is not surprising that government has put more stress on wages as an alternative source of income to state benefits, but close consideration of the paid/unpaid work equation demands further interrogation of the role of men that stretches beyond their traditional role of breadwinner.

In what follows I first draw attention to the extent to which and the way in which the male breadwinner model has been eroded. How real is the idea of a fully individualised, autonomous adult-worker model? Second, I turn to the issue of the obligation to care, which exists alongside the obligation to work. There are ethical issues raised by care, which reinforce the case for policies to address it. The drive to an adult-worker model draws attention to the position of all those who have less leverage on the labour market, whether by reason of race, disability, low educational achievement (often related to poverty), or gender. It is lone mothers' sole responsibility for care and work that makes them particularly vulnerable.

An adult-worker model?

The male breadwinner model has substantially eroded in two key respects: the changing pattern of women's, and to a lesser extent men's, contribution to the family in respect of cash and care; and the changing structure of the family itself. In both respects there has been increasing individualisation, but nowhere is there a fully-fledged adult-worker model. Table 8.1 shows the spectrum of gendered patterns of paid work. In Western Europe there is evidence of substantial movement away from the male breadwinner model towards an adult-worker model (Crompton, 1999). However, it is more common to find some form of transitional dual breadwinner model than a full dual career model. There may therefore also be convergence between Western and Eastern European countries, as the latter move in the opposite direction, away to some extent from a full dual career model.

As Table 8.1 shows, the comparative data on women's post-war labour market participation for Western countries all show an upward trend and men's a downward trend. It is no longer only the Scandinavian countries that have virtually equal proportions of men and women in the labour market.

The British General Household Survey showed that in 1975 81% of men aged 16-64 were economically active and only 62% of women. But by 1996 this figure was 70% for both men and women (ONS, 1998, Tables 5.8 and 5.9). In other words, the rise in the proportion of female employees has been matched by a simultaneous fall in the number of male employees (Walby, 1997, Table 2.1). Married women are as likely to be employed as non-married women and the contribution by men to family income has fallen from nearly 73% in 1979-81 to 61% in 1989-91

Table 8.1: Selected Labour Force Statistics for 18 OECD countries ranked by female share of labour force (1994) (%)

Labour force participation as a % of population from the ages of 15-64

| | 1960 | | 1994 | |
	Male	Female	Male	Female
Sweden	98.5	50.1	78.1	74.4
Finland	91.4	65.6	77.1	69.9
Denmark	99.5	43.5	84.2	73.8
US	90.5	42.6	85.3	70.5
France	94.6	46.6	75.9	59.1
UK	99.1	46.1	83.3	65.6
Austria	92.0	52.1	81.0	62.1
Germany	94.4	49.2	80.8	61.8
Australia	97.2	34.1	85.5	63.8
Belgium	85.5	36.4	72.5	51.6
Netherlands	97.8	26.2	79.1	57.4
Italy	95.3	39.6	76.9	43.4
Ireland	99.0	34.8	81.8	43.9

Source: OECD (1996)

(Harkness et al, 1996). By 1996/97, women's contribution to a couple's joint lifetime earnings ranged from 41% for a low-skilled woman without children to 49% for a high-skilled woman, but dropped to 24% and 47% respectively with the addition of two children, reflecting the large earnings gap between equally skilled men and women due to motherhood that hits low-skilled women particularly hard (Women's Unit, 1999).

This figure varies widely across the European Union, for example, in the Netherlands, men's average contribution to the household income amounted to 76% in 1994. In West Germany in 1993 men contributed 73% of income in households with children under 18, whereas men in East Germany contributed 56% (Knijn et al, 2001: forthcoming). In the US, the much more dramatic deterioration in the economic position of manual male workers, particularly black men, has been linked to the growth of lone-mother families (Wilson, 1987).

The nature of women's participation in the labour market also varies considerably between countries. Table 8.2 shows the extent of women's part-time work. Men are still predominantly full-time workers, while in many countries women work part time. This is less true of France, where the female labour market participation rate is lower than for the UK or Scandinavia, but where women are more likely to work full time. But here too, recent increases in women's employment have tended to be part time (See Chapter Seven of this book).

But the meaning of part-time work differs considerably across countries. In the UK, short part-time working is very common. Almost a quarter of women with children under the age of 10 worked 15 or fewer hours per week in the late 1990s (Thair and Risdon, 1999), and 24% of all female employees worked under 20 hours a week (Rubery et al, 1998). In the Netherlands also, 80% of women work part time and 33% work less than 20 hours a week. And in Germany women's participation is mainly part time and a quarter work fewer than 20 hours a week (the social insurance threshold). In the Scandinavian countries, female part-time work is also common, but women usually work relatively long hours, often exercising their right to work part time while they have young children. This part-

Table 8.2: Part-time employment in 18 OECD countries ranked by part-time employment as a proportion of female employment (1995) (%)*

	Part-time employment as a proportion of total employment			
	Total		Female	
	1979	1995	1979	1995
Netherlands	16.6	37.4	44.0	67.2
Australia	15.9	24.8	35.2	42.7
Sweden	23.6	24.3	46.0	40.3
UK	16.4	24.1	39.0	44.3
Denmark	22.7	21.6	46.3	35.5
US	16.4	18.6	26.7	27.4
Germany	11.4	16.3	27.6	33.8
France	8.2	15.6	16.9	28.9
Austria	7.6	13.9	18.0	26.9
Belgium	6.0	13.6	16.5	29.8
Ireland	5.1	11.3	13.1	21.7
Finland	6.7	8.4	10.6	11.3
Italy	5.3	6.4	10.6	12.7

* Based on country definitions of part-time work. Data for the UK, Belgium, Denmark, Germany, Ireland and Italy are from the annual European Labour Force Survey. Data for all other countries are from national Labour Force Surveys (1994).

Source: OECD (1996)

time work attracts pro rata benefits and is not the 'precarious' employment that is so common in the UK.

Thus the *precise nature* of the erosion of the male breadwinner model is complicated. There has been no simple move from a male breadwinner to a dual career model. For the UK, Ward et al (1996) found that 78% of 33-year-old women contributed less than 45% of the joint household income and 46% did not earn enough to be self-sufficient. In addition, almost half of the married full-time women workers in their sample of 33-year-olds were financially dependent. In most Western countries some kind of dual breadwinner model has become the norm. Often, given women's lower earnings, this amounts to a more-or-less one-and-a-half earner model, in other words the dual-earner models (ii) and (iii) in Table 8.3. Model (iv) is a more gender equal model and has not been achieved in any country, but it is the official policy of the Dutch government, with its 'combination scenario' and the Netherlands has somewhat more part-time work for men (17% of Dutch men work part time, but a majority of these are either young or over 55 years old).

Thus the social reality is that while a high proportion of adult women are in the workforce in most OECD countries, they are not fully individualised in the sense of being self-sufficient and they still take responsibility for a large proportion of the unpaid care work that is done, supported to very varying degrees by collective provision. When, therefore, the UK and Dutch governments swung from treating lone mothers as mothers to treating them as workers in the late 1990s, they did so regardless of the fact that a majority of married mothers actually work part time. By contrast, French women have historically been both workers and mothers, and the French social welfare system has recognised this both by providing generous benefits for women as mothers (especially where there are three or more children) and by taking active steps to reconcile work and family responsibilities via the provision of care services. But in

Table 8.3: Patterns of male and female paid work

(i) Male breadwinner model	Male FT earner
(ii) Dual breadwinner model	Male FT earner, Female short PT earner
(iii) Dual breadwinner model	Male FT earner, Female long PT earner
(iv) Dual breadwinner model	Male PT earner, Female PT earner
(v) Dual career	Male FT earner, Female FT earner
(vi) Single earner	Lone parent FT or PT earner

Note: FT: full time; PT: part time

the UK context, as Alan Marsh asks in Chapter Two, should we expect more of lone mothers than of married mothers in respect of their engagement with the labour market?

Different patterns of paid employment in families and households are parallelled by different patterns of provision for care. We lack research on the precise nature of these patterns for different countries and on how and why particular configurations have developed. In the male breadwinner model it was assumed, for the most part correctly, that women would carry out the work of care on an unpaid basis. At the other end of the spectrum, we might anticipate that in the dual-career model, care and household services would be bought in. A small scale qualitative study by Gregson and Lowe (1994) showed this to be the case, but also found that couples who had previously had a fairly traditional division of labour used paid help to replace the woman's household labour. Those who had previously shared both childcare and housework used paid help to modify their division of unpaid work and tended to hire help with childcare rather than housework. It is hard to avoid the conclusion that this is because gender is in fact the key independent variable: the meaning of paid and unpaid work is different for men and for women.

The vast majority of dual-earner couples rely mainly on relatives and childminders to provide childcare; among British mothers with children aged 5-11, 37% only work while the children are at school. However, Labour Force Survey data reports that 90% of women with children who work part time did not want full-time work (Thair and Risdon, 1999). Indeed, it may be as the recent literature has stressed, that alternative moral rationalities underpin women's greater commitment to family work. Duncan and Edwards (1999) and Trudie Knijn and Frits van Wel (Chapter Six of this book) have suggested forcefully that this is the case for large numbers of British and Dutch lone mothers (see also van Drenth et al, 1999; Ford, 1996). If an alternative moral rationality of care does exist, it would run counter to the purely economic incentive of 'making work pay', which has been greatly stressed in UK and US welfare reform.

There is of course considerable evidence that women want to care. Hakim (1996) has argued strongly that the British female labour force divides into a group of committed career women and another group that is content to choose part-time work (and undertake care). Hakim's model is controversial because it highlights choice and underplays constraints. Nevertheless, if good quality, affordable day care were to be provided overnight, it is not clear that all women would want to work full time in countries such as the UK and the Netherlands. The proportion wishing to do so would be, it seems from Chapter Five of this book, much higher in Norway, while in the US an adult-worker model has long been accepted. As matters stand, the proposition is unlikely to be put to the test in the UK. The quality of childcare in the UK is often low and much of it is likely to be unaffordable. The fastest growing provider of childcare since the late-1980s has been the private sector (Land and Lewis, 1998).

The norm is now that women will engage in paid work, and attitudinal surveys in the post-war period have shown consistent increases in the acceptance by men and women of female employment at all stages of the 'lifecourse' (Dex, 1988). But to what *extent* – full-time or some form of part-time – varies considerably according to social class, ethnicity and sometimes region. Nor are the accompanying assumptions in respect of unpaid work predictable. Both in terms of behaviour and normative assumptions, we are very far from a fully individualised, adult-worker model and this has major implications for what can be expected of lone mothers and for the basis of social provision more generally.

The obligation to work and the obligation to care

The new view of work and welfare stresses the obligation of all citizens who are able to undertake paid work. In the mid-1980s, Lawrence Mead made the case in the US for the state to assert its moral authority in order to insist that welfare recipients fulfil their obligations as citizens to engage in paid labour. He presented this solution in terms of a model of equal citizenship and something that would bring about greater social integration. Welfare-to-work, implemented first in the US, embodied these ideas and was applied to all able-bodied adults, lone mothers included. Yet there is a huge amount of concern on both sides of the Atlantic about 'the family's' capacity and willingness to care and about the quality of care that is given to young and old dependants within it. In the debate over the family, care is lauded and there continues to be mixed feelings about the employment of mothers, especially if they have young children. Care is recognised as important, but the implications of the welfare-to-work agenda for the anxiety about the family have not been confronted. In the US, prior to the passing of the 1996 Personal Responsibility and Work Opportunity Reconciliation Act, it was openly argued that not only was there a fundamental obligation on the part of able-bodied people to enter the labour market (Mead, 1986), but it would be better in the case of lone-mother families for the children in those families to experience one breadwinner as opposed to none (Novak and Cogan, 1987). In respect of lone-mother families, the American Enterprise Institute arrived at a position roughly similar to that taken by many late Victorians: lone mothers should work but should also be brought into social settings where they might be taught 'mothercraft' (Novak and Cogan, 1987).

Social democrats have, like Mead but unlike more radical critics of welfare (such as Charles Murray), also stressed the overriding importance of employment as a means to social integration or inclusion. In the UK, the effort to get more lone mothers into the labour market has been justified as much by reference to the welfare of the mothers themselves as by condemnation of welfare dependency. But there has been little acknowledgement of the complicated relationship between independence and dependence. After all, the middle-aged woman who gives up her job in order to care for an older person and becomes dependent on benefits does so in order to allow the older person to retain a greater degree of independence. For Labour, welfare-to-work is an idea that is central to 'third way' politics and as Deacon (1998) has suggested, represents a combination of welfare conceptualised as self-interest, as authority, and as moral regeneration.

However, there is an equally strong literature stressing the importance of the obligation of 'the family' to care. Commentators from a wide range of political perspectives have drawn attention to the idea that people have become more individualistic, seeking the means to self-expression and self-fulfilment, the main evidence being patterns of family change with high rates of unmarried motherhood and relationship breakdown. While there is no agreement as to whether individualism is inherently selfish (Giddens [1992] for example, has argued strongly against such a position), the balance of opinion has tended to be pessimistic. In the US, David Popenoe (1993, p 528) stated bluntly: "People have become less willing to invest time, money and energy in family life, turning instead to investment in themselves". Men's failure to maintain their children after relationship breakdown and women's increasing participation in the labour market are cited time and again as further confirmation of concern for self rather than others within the family.

In this interpretation, any encouragement given to women to enter the labour market is part of the problem, not the solution. The arguments at the end of the 20th century were a little different from the older and more familiar ones about the impact of women's work on children. While these are far from dead, the concerns expressed in the 1990s revolved around the extent to which women's employment promotes relationship breakdown and the effects it has on men's behaviour. As Valerie

Oppenheimer (1994) has pointed out, people with very different politics can buy into the idea that women's employment is a key variable explaining family change. In addition, commentators in both the US and UK have expressed fears about the effect of women's employment on male work incentives and willingness to support their families. Geoff Dench (1994, pp 16-17) has argued that "[I]f women go too far in pressing for symmetry, and in trying to change the rules of the game, men will simply decide not to play.... The family may be a myth, but it is a myth that works to make men tolerably useful". Thus women's employment is blamed for undermining the traditional male role of breadwinner and for creating 'yobbish men' in the next generation (Dennis and Erdos, 1992; Phillips, 1997).

Most recently, Fukuyama (1999) has argued that the change in women's employment behaviour has allowed men to behave irresponsibly (resulting in the formation of lone-mother families). Most of these writers do not go so far as to advocate curbs on women's work. Fukuyama's solution relies on a 'spontaneous re-norming' of society, which he hopes will involve women recognising the importance of staying at home with young children. Galston (1991, p 281) has gone further and argued that the liberal state has to take action to protect and promote its distinctive conception of the human good: "[r]easonable public arguments for traditionalism" in respect of the family have been overlooked. These arguments in favour of women doing more care work tend to be tied to a strong desire to resuscitate the male breadwinner model family. As Iris Marion Young (1995) has observed, this is effectively to argue that women be prepared to make themselves dependent on men for the sake of their children and others who may be in need of care.

Thus, in respect of current government policy there are actually two questions, whether women have the right to choose to stay at home to care and if so must they inevitably depend on a male wage in order to do so?

Care: ethics and policies

Feminist work on care has argued that the ethic of care is based on responsibility and relationship and there is therefore a limit to the extent to which this work can be 'commodified' (Gilligan, 1982; Svenhuijsen, 1998). Some feminists have gone further and see care as part of an intrinsically female culture and value system that is represented as being of a higher moral order than that of the public sphere (for example,

Elshtain, 1981; Noddings, 1984). This is close to the position of those philosophers of welfare who seek to argue that the market and the family are structured by norms that express different ways of valuing people and things, and must therefore be kept separate (Wolfe, 1989; Anderson, 1993). Other feminist writers have concluded that the caring ethic should become the property of men as well as women and that caregivers need rights (Lister, 1997; Tronto, 1993). However, the shift towards a set of assumptions based on an adult-worker model implies a substantially greater commodification of care work, although this is not explicitly stated.

This issue becomes more difficult still when it is highly likely that a substantial proportion of women in employment will have low-paid caring jobs. In the course of the creation of a 'social care market' in Britain since 1993 (Lewis and Glennerster, 1996; Wistow et al, 1996), the conditions of work of many paid carers have deteriorated. J. Ford et al (1998) found that two distinct labour markets were developing, one employing women on very low wages, with poor working conditions to do 'routinised' tasks, usually in the private sector, and the other employing better qualified women to deliver more specialist services, usually in the public and voluntary sectors (see also Ungerson, 1999). Early work by Scandinavian feminists suggested that the process by which women in those countries had been drawn into the labour market from the 1970s to carry out care work in the public sector amounted to a form of public as opposed to private patriarchy (Siim, 1987). Later, Scandinavian feminists became more optimistic about the possibilities of a 'women-friendly' state (Hernes, 1987). However, for the most part British care jobs are characterised by poor wages and working conditions, especially for part-time workers. In the minds of many policy makers advocating the New Deal for Lone Parents in the UK, was the idea that lone mothers would find employment in the formal care sector.

Thus, taking gender into the picture, there are four main problems in moving towards a full adult-worker model. First, unpaid care work is unequally shared between men and women, which has substantial implications for women's position in the labour market. Second, given the lack of good quality affordable care in the formal sector, many women have little option but to continue to provide it informally (what Land and Rose [1985] referred to as 'compulsory altruism'). Third, a significant number of female carers want to/feel that it is 'right' to prioritise care. Fourth, women's low pay, especially in care-related jobs, means that full individualisation is hard to achieve, on the basis of long part-time or even full-time work. In such a context, women may resist the injunction to full individualisation so far as they are able, or substantial diswelfares may be visited on dependants, young and old.

However, an adult-worker model is not necessarily 'bad for women' and, given the extent to which social provision is becoming ever more related to individual effort, it may be necessary. Everything depends on the conditions under which such a model is implemented. There remain the questions as to 'who cares and on what terms?'. Just as policy assumptions based on a male breadwinner model disadvantaged women in particular, so assumptions based on a full adult-worker model are also likely to do so. Any idea that wages will enable more self-provision in the social arena, especially in respect of pensions, is fraught with danger for women. The new welfare contract is moving from social contributions to individually defined contributions, premised on the idea that adults are in the workforce, but this is an unrealistic assumption in respect of women. Assumptions regarding an adult-worker model pose threats to women unless issues to do with the unequal gendered division of work and hence of lifetime earnings, which are particularly grave for lone mothers, are addressed.

Furthermore, whether care is paid or unpaid it cannot be understood simply in terms of activity, tasks or tending. The love and duty that are involved are powerful elements in the gendering of care work. The injunction to care is felt more powerfully by most women than by most men and explains why women have tended to add their increasing hours of paid work onto unpaid care work. However, it is the understanding of care as process, human activity and moral orientation that makes it possible to challenge the policy making discourse and to seek 'equal billing' for care in the policy debate. The literature that develops an ethic of care proposes an alternative model of relationship and connection and makes a strong case for enabling all human beings to care. While the arguments for and against full individualisation, together with the policy trend towards assuming an adult-worker model, signal the importance of treating care as work in order properly to value it, the arguments that take a care-centred perspective highlight the importance of time to care.

It is therefore necessary to think more closely about how a balance between paid and unpaid work is to be achieved. It is useful to look at the Scandinavian and US models in this regard. Both have a fully individualised, adult-worker model that encompasses married and lone mothers. However, in the US case, the obligation to enter the labour market is embedded in a residual welfare system that sometimes borders on the punitive, whereas in Sweden and Denmark it is supported by an extensive range of care entitlements in respect of children and older people. The position of lone mothers is particularly instructive in this respect because of the problem of combining unpaid care work and employment. The US has gone much more wholeheartedly than the UK down the road of treating these women as paid workers, imposing time-limited benefits. Employment rates of lone mothers are high in the US; the push factor is strong. But employment rates are higher still in Sweden and Denmark and lone mothers' poverty rates are much lower than in the UK or the US. Indeed, Sweden comes closest to having achieved Mead's ideal in that all adult citizens are obliged to engage in paid work in order to qualify for a wide range of benefits, which then permit them to leave the labour market. However, Swedish lone mothers still get one third of their income from the state (Lewis, 1998). The system is based on a commitment to universal citizenship entitlements, rather than, as in the US, grafting equal citizenship obligations on to a residual welfare model.

Put simply, the Scandinavian adult-worker model recognises care and hence practices what White (2000) has called 'fair reciprocity'. All able-bodied adults are treated as citizen-workers, but after that permission to exit the labour market in order to care with wage replacement is granted, and formal care services are provided. As Anne Skevik's chapter (Five) states, needs in respect of care work are recognised in the Scandinavian countries. In effect, Sweden and Denmark operate a similar sex equality model to the US, but their systems have the capacity to graft on respect for difference that manifests itself in the form of an unequal division of care work (Lewis and Astrom, 1992). The family penalty experienced by female carers is less than most other countries, although there is still a penalty to be paid for moving between the models outlined in Table 8.3.

Different kinds of care policies are likely to have different incentive effects in respect of labour market behaviour. Conservative and communitarian commentators tend to favour cash allowances as a means of recognising care (Morgan, 1995). Thus Coleman (1993, 1995) has advocated 'bounties' that would both compensate 'parents'[2] for the costs of childcare and reward good childrearing outcomes. Cash benefits and allowances are often promoted as a means of permitting women greater 'choice' as to whether to care at home, or to hire a carer and work outside the home (as per Chapter Three of this book). In practice, the choice is usually a figment, because the costs of choosing one option over another are not equal.

The provision of care services in the formal sector tends to work in the reverse direction, providing paid employment for women and allowing female carers to enter the labour market. Bradshaw et al's (1996) cross-national study of lone mothers' employment showed affordable childcare to be the key variable explaining the differences in employment rates between the countries. But accessibility and quality are also key. In fact, genuine choice between caring work and employment requires the provision of both cash and services. In respect of children under school age, a carer requires good childcare services to carry on working, which even in European Union countries are available only in the Scandinavian countries, France, Belgium and some parts of Italy. To have a genuine option of taking parental leave, the carer must be able to return to her job and to receive cash compensation at a high replacement level. A policy like parental leave can be implemented such that it promotes female labour market exit (as in Germany) or as a way of promoting greater gender equality in respect of paid and unpaid work (Bruning and Plantenga, 1999).

Anything to do with care tends to be poorly valued. Wages in the formal sector are low and benefits and allowances for carers in the informal sector are also low. This means both that in a world in which individualisation and the capacity for self-provisioning is increasingly being assumed by policy makers, carers are profoundly disadvantaged. In a world where dignity as well as welfare in the broadest sense derives mainly from wages, it is crucial that care is valued. Some fear that commodification will undermine the motivation that inspires care (Himmelweit, 1995). But if care is not valued it is degraded and exploitative. The argument that gender justice requires care to be properly valued is strong (Bubeck, 1995; Nelson, 1999).

Thus far, the new approach to welfare by policy makers and academics (for example, Esping Andersen, 2000) has focused on the need for reforms to secure changes to the social security system that will promote labour market entry, but given the problem of reconciling paid and unpaid work and the unequal gendered responsibility for care, it is also important that reform and restructuring take account of people's lifetime relationships to the labour market, for example in respect of pension guarantees. Carers are particularly prone to low paid work and periods with no pay.

Given the existence of what is in most countries a one-and-a-half earner rather than a fully-fledged adult-worker model, more attention has to be paid to policies that:

- compensate for and encourage the more equal sharing of the care work that all societies need;

• promote transitions between different types of work, paid and unpaid, over the lifecourse.

There is, in addition, the need to provide life chance guarantees, for those (men as well as women) entering low paid flexible jobs (often in human services), so that they have the chance to leave them and so that those staying in them are compensated (Esping-Andersen, 2000). Assumptions regarding the existence of the male breadwinner model historically underpinned social insurance welfare systems. As these are called into question by family change and by the increasing flexibilisation of men's as well as women's work, so there is the major challenge of fundamentally re-thinking the building blocks of social provision. The danger is that new assumptions regarding an adult-worker model will underpin a move towards an individual contractualism that over-estimates women's economic independence and capacity for self-provision, and insists on an unfair reciprocity that ignores care work. This would be particularly disastrous for lone mothers.

Notes

[1] In Germany, another strong male breadwinner country, lone mothers have been more likely than married mothers to be employed, but this is, in a large measure, because the social security system operates differently. Lone mothers tend to have to resort to social assistance, which is much less generous than social insurance; they are therefore pushed into the labour market in a way that they are not by the more generous Dutch system of social assistance or by the much less generous, but more gender equal, British system (see Daly, 2000).

[2] Strangely, Coleman (1995) denied that his scheme carries any gender implications.

NINE

The social, economic and demographic profile of lone parents

Karen Rowlingson

Introduction

British lone parents are much less likely to be in paid work than their counterparts in other countries. One of the reasons for this is their social and demographic profile: British lone parents are more likely than those in other countries to be young, be never-married, have young children, and have three or more children. All of these factors tend to reduce employment rates for lone parents. But these are not the only reasons for low employment rates of lone parents in Britain. This chapter provides cross-national demographic data on lone parenthood in order to throw light on variations in employment rates. It begins by taking an overview of demographic change and its relationship to economic and cultural factors. It then presents cross-national statistics on a range of demographic aspects of lone parenthood such as marital status, gender, age, ethnicity and social class. It ends by reviewing the employment rates of lone parents across different countries and assesses the role of demographics in explaining variations.

Demographics, economics and culture

There are strong links between demographics and the economy, particularly as far as the labour market is concerned. In relation to lone parents, we know that people within this group are more likely to have paid jobs if they have certain demographic characteristics such as being older and having fewer and older children. This makes it seem as though demographic factors are responsible for the employment of lone parents and while this may be the case to some extent, the relationship between demography and employment is likely to be more complex. For example, perhaps lone parents who have chosen to have fewer children and have them at older ages are women who have better educational qualifications and have always had better employment opportunities than lone parents who have children at younger ages. Thus employment opportunities might be responsible for certain demographic characteristics as well as being a result of them.

The link between demography and economics is similarly complex at a macro level. With the decline of industrial society demographers now talk of a 'second demographic transition' characterised by high rates of divorce, cohabitation, births outside marriage and lone parenthood. It is argued by some that the changing nature of the labour market after the Second World War (including more women in paid work, fewer men in paid work, more service sector and part-time jobs) may in part be the cause of demographic changes during this period. The move to a post-industrial society may therefore have been a cause of the 'second demographic transition' that we are currently witnessing (Coleman and Chandola, 1999).

This 'second demographic transition' is occurring at the same time as major structural change in the economy and the labour market. It is also occurring at a time when there has been, according to Ingelhart (1977, 1990) a shift from conservative values emphasising duty, responsibility and order to values emphasising self-realisation and autonomy. This shift from a value system emphasising obligations to others, religious duty and respect for traditional authority towards a value system promoting individualised rights and personal self-fulfilment has, it is argued, affected both women's and men's attitudes and feelings of obligations towards partners and children. Thus culture and identity are also likely to be important factors driving the second demographic transition. This begs the question of the nature of the relationship between culture and economic structure – a question beyond the scope of this chapter.

Having outlined some of the broad demographic themes, this chapter now takes particular demographic variables to compare different countries in relation to lone parenthood.

Rates of lone parenthood

The growth of lone parenthood is only one aspect of the second demographic transition (which also includes increasing cohabitation, increasing divorce and increasing numbers of births outside marriage) but it is the aspect that causes most concern (in Britain at least) to politicians, policy makers, media and public. In 1990, Britain had one of the highest rates of lone parenthood in Europe along with Sweden, Norway and Denmark (Bradshaw et al, 1996). The European countries with some of the lowest levels include Greece, Ireland, Italy, Portugal and Spain (see Figure 9.1). This division suggests some combination of North/ South, rich/poor, Protestant/Catholic factors at work. Countries which are generally rich, Protestant and Northern European have much higher rates of lone parenthood than those that are mainly poor, Southern Catholic countries, though the UK cuts across this division as it is a relatively poor country but is Northern and Protestant.

The special demographic characteristics of Southern Europe (including low levels of divorce, cohabitation and births outside marriage) have been explained by some as the outcome of limited family welfare and unfavourable labour and housing markets (Tapinos, 1996). But the low levels of lone parenthood may not (only) be a result of limited family welfare but a cause of it, as there is perceived to be less need for such welfare. Alongside these economic factors, these countries are also characterised by religious and cultural opposition to illegitimacy as well as strong support for the extended family. Thus culture appears to be an important factor in explaining rates of lone parenthood. Countries with strong religious and cultural taboos on illegitimacy, divorce and cohabitation are much less likely to have high rates of lone parenthood.

If we look outside of Europe but remain within the developed world, Japan has a very low rate of lone parenthood, Australia has a slightly lower rate than Britain and the US has by far the highest rate in the Western world.

The figures presented in Figure 9.1 must be read alongside a statistical health warning (alongside all the comparative figures presented in this chapter). Reliable comparative data on lone parenthood is very difficult to find as definitions of lone parenthood vary quite dramatically in data sets from different countries. The most common sources of inconsistency are in the definition of 'a child', the treatment of cohabiting mothers, and the treatment of lone parents living in complex households. For example, in Figure 9.1, data for France defined lone parents as those with 'children'

Figure 9.1: Lone parents as a percentage of families with children

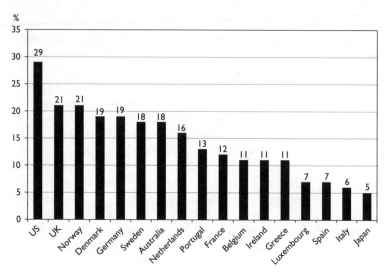

Source: Bradshaw et al (1996, p 12)

aged under 25 whereas data for Greece and Ireland only defined lone parents as those with 'children' aged under 15. Furthermore, data on lone parents from the Netherlands and Norway included cohabiting couples where the man was not the father of any child/ren in the family. The comparisons made in this chapter are based on the best available data but it must be borne in mind that these are not entirely reliable.

Nor is this data very up to date and it would be helpful to have more up to date comparable information for a wide range of countries but this does not appear to be readily available. Evidence presented elsewhere in this book suggests that the figure for Norway has remained relatively constant over the 1990s. It also suggests that the percentage of lone parents in the Netherlands has remained rather stable in the last 20 years and the Central Bureau for Statistics even expects a decline in the overall numbers of lone parents due to a decline in divorce among married couples with children. According to data for Australia presented in this book, the rate of lone parenthood has increased at a much faster rate during the 1990s than it did during the 1980s (from 15.4% of families in 1990 to 21.4% of families in 1999, compared with 12.6 to 14.6% during the 1980s). And in the US, the rate of increase was greatest in the 1970s and there has continued to be an increasing proportion of lone-parent families, but the rate of increase has slowed down somewhat.

As well as looking at different rates of lone parenthood it is also important to note that countries also differ dramatically in terms of the percentage of births outside marriage. This figure cannot be taken as a direct indicator of single motherhood as these births could be to cohabiting parents, and clearly usually are, but there does appear to be some correlation as the highest rates of births outside marriage are in Denmark, Norway and Sweden (Whiteford and Bradshaw, 1994). The lowest rates are in Greece and Italy. The UK and the US fall somewhere in between these two extremes. Divorce rates are also associated with lone parenthood. The highest rates are in Denmark, the UK and Sweden with the lowest rates in Greece, Ireland, Italy, Portugal and Spain. The US has by far the highest rate.

Routes into lone parenthood

Another interesting point of comparison between countries is the family marital status of lone parents or, in other words, their route into lone parenthood. These will be related to rates of non-marital births, cohabitation and divorce. Interpreting differences between countries is likely to be problematic because in some countries cohabitation may be very similar to marriage and yet mothers who separate from a cohabiting partner are usually placed in the 'single/never-married' lone-parent group rather than the 'separated/divorced' lone-parent group. But in other countries, where cohabitation takes on a different form and meaning, it may be more appropriate to combine ex-cohabiting mothers with single never-cohabited mothers. British data on lone parents now divides single lone parents into those who have never lived with a partner and those who have separated from a cohabiting one (see Chapter Two of this book).

The proportion of lone parents who are never married varies dramatically from about half in Sweden to about a third in the US and UK. Never-married lone parents are much less common in Portugal, Italy and Japan. Widowhood is a much more common route of entry into lone parenthood in these countries (see Figure 9.2). Routes into lone motherhood are strongly linked to employment participation as (young) never-married lone parents are less likely than average to be in paid work. This is because they are more likely to have pre-school age children and few educational qualifications. Thus they have a greater need for childcare, which they may have to pay for and yet they are

Figure 9.2: Routes into lone motherhood

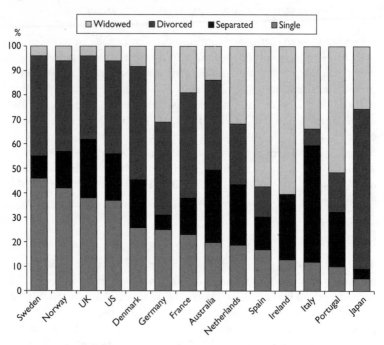

Note: Data for the Netherlands and Spain combine separated/divorced categories. For the purposes of this graph, the figures have been split evenly between the two categories.

Source: Bradshaw et al (1996, p 18)

unlikely to be able to find well-paid jobs due to the fact that they are more likely to come from poorer backgrounds (see below).

This is the current situation (as 'current' as the data allows) in terms of routes into lone parenthood but over the past 30 years there appear to have been two trends in operation. During the 1970s and 1980s, divorce and separation from a husband were the main causes of lone parenthood, increasing sharply during this time, with a decline in the proportions of lone-parent families caused by widowhood. But the late-1980s and 1990s have witnessed a growing number of single women having babies or cohabiting couples separating, according to data presented elsewhere in this book from Britain, Norway, France and the US. This change should be placed in the context of a more general increase in cohabitation and births within cohabiting relationships. Chambaz and Martin argue that the growing number of lone parents in France refers mainly to increases in cohabitation and the fragility of these unions (see Chapter Seven of this book).

Similar trends can be seen in the Netherlands though with some variation (see Chapter Six of this book). There has been a dramatic decline over the 1980s in the proportion of lone parents who were widowed in favour of more divorced/separated lone parents and single never-married lone mothers. Interestingly though, the proportion of single never-married lone mothers has remained fairly stable during the 1990s.

Marital status/routes into lone parenthood are commonly used as a variable for analysis but, as Alan Marsh argues in Chapter Two, this analysis should be carried out with some caution. Lone parents' lives are (increasingly) complex with movements in and out of lone parenthood making simple classifications likely to distort the realities of people's lives. Having signalled a need for caution, it must nevertheless be said that routes into lone parenthood are very important and are strongly linked to other demographic differences, such as the age of the lone parent, the age of her/his children and so on. And, as mentioned above, there are also strong correlations between routes into lone parenthood and employment.

Gender

Lone parenthood is a universally gendered phenomenon. In Britain and Norway at least nine lone parents in 10 are women. Countries with the highest proportions of lone fathers include Greece, Italy and Germany. Not surprisingly, lone fathers are more common in countries where the most typical routes into lone parenthood are through widowhood or divorce. Lone fathers tend to have higher rates of employment than lone mothers and this is probably due to gender. However, it also reflects the fact that lone fathers are more likely, on average, to be older and have older children than lone mothers. These factors also help to explain their higher employment rates.

Age of lone parent and age/number of children

Older lone parents are more likely to be in paid work. This is because the age of a lone parent is determined partly by their route into lone parenthood, which is itself linked to educational qualifications. The age of a lone parent is also linked to the age of their child, which means that it is easier for older lone parents to return to work if their children are at school or are able to look after themselves. According to Bradshaw et al (1996), in all countries, lone fathers tend to be older than lone mothers. And in countries where widowhood accounts for a high proportion of lone parents, the average age of lone parents will be relatively high. Compared with other countries, the UK has much younger divorced and younger single lone mothers.

The age of the youngest child is often thought to be crucial in determining the employment rates of lone parents in Britain. However, research among mothers in general does not always find this variable to be important once other factors (such as attitudes and socioeconomic background) have been taken into account (Thomson, 1994). In most countries, lone mothers are less likely than cohabiting/married mothers to have children aged under five, but in the UK and Ireland, the opposite situation occurs (Bradshaw et al, 1996). And the UK (in the early 1990s) had the highest proportion (46%) of lone parents with children under five or six (Figure 9.3). Countries with the lowest proportions included Spain (13%), Japan (13%) and Portugal (7%). Once again, these figures will be strongly related to routes into lone parenthood, as countries with

Figure 9.3: Percentage of lone-mother families with children under 5 or 6 years old

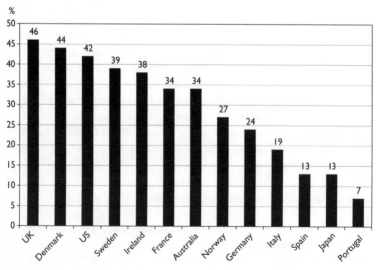

Source: Bradshaw et al (1996, p 19)

high rates of single lone mothers are more likely to have younger children in these families.

More recent data from Alan Marsh, reported in Chapter Two of this book, suggests that the percentage of lone parents in Britain with children under five has declined quite dramatically during the 1990s from 47% in 1991 to 37% in 1999. Evidence from France, presented in Chapter Seven of this book, also suggests a reduction in the percentage of lone parents with pre-school age children (though a much smaller one than in Britain). This trend is likely to be due to the ageing nature of the cross-section of lone parents, but it is occurring at the same time as an increase in the proportion of lone parents who are never-married mothers. This suggests (and other evidence confirms) that much of this increase is from cohabitation breakdown rather than women without partners having babies.

In all countries, lone-parent families are much more likely to have only one child than married/cohabiting couple families. Related to this, in most countries a smaller proportion of lone-parent families have three or more children compared with couple families. But Britain is the odd one out here – about the same proportion of lone-parent families have three or more children compared with couple families (Bradshaw et al, 1996). A possible explanation here is the important role of social class in the creation of lone-parent families in Britain – working-class families are generally more inclined to larger families and they are also more likely to result in lone-parent families.

Teenage lone mothers

Britain has one of the highest rates of teenage motherhood in Europe – about four times the West European average (Coleman and Chandola, 1999). In this aspect of demography, as with many others, Britain has much more in common with the non-European English-speaking countries such as the US and Australia. The rate of teenage pregnancy in the US is a considerable outlier – far higher than in other countries (Social Exclusion Unit, 1999). Fertility rates of women in their 20s have declined in the last 20 years throughout Europe and the fertility rates of teenagers have also declined – except in Britain. This has caused some divergence in fertility patterns between Britain and the rest of Europe.

The British government is particularly concerned about teenage lone motherhood or, more precisely, teenage *pregnancy*. A report by the Social Exclusion Unit (1999) reveals that there were almost 90,000 conceptions to teenagers in England in 1997. Roughly three fifths resulted in births (56,000), and 90% of teenage births were outside marriage (about 50,000).

According to analysis of the Family and Working Lives Survey (FWLS) data (Rowlingson and McKay, 2001: forthcoming), only 4% of lone mothers in 1994/95 were aged between 16 and 19 years. While this suggests that government attention on teenage lone parents is out of proportion to the scale of any 'problem', other statistics suggest the opposite. For example, no fewer than 31% of all lone parents had their first child when a teenager, compared with 9% of all mothers. Some of these births would have been within marriage and therefore they would not, at that time, have been teenage lone parents. But people who marry young have a much greater risk of separation and divorce. Analysis of FWLS data also shows that just over half (56%) of those who had been teenage mothers went on to become lone mothers, compared with 23% of mothers who had children later than their teenage years. There is, therefore, good reason for any analysis of lone parenthood to look in detail at the circumstances surrounding early parenthood, in the British case at least.

It is well known that teenage mothers tend to come from disadvantaged backgrounds. Analysis of the FWLS data confirms this (Rowlingson and McKay, 2001: forthcoming). Just 2% of women with fathers in social class A (top professionals), and 5% in social class B (senior managers and other professionals), became teenage mothers. This compares with 11% overall, and as many as 23% of women with unskilled fathers (class E) (see Figure 9.4).

This data therefore suggests that very few current lone parents in Britain are teenagers, but a high proportion of teenage pregnancies lead to lone parenthood and a fairly high proportion of lone-parent families were once teenage mothers. The Social Exclusion Unit (1999) justifies the attention paid to teenage pregnancy in terms of a number of factors including:

- higher infant mortality rates of babies and children born to teenage mothers;
- higher rates of accidents among children of teenage mothers;
- teenage mothers much less likely than other mothers to have no qualifications;
- teenage mothers much more likely than other mothers to be on benefit or to have low incomes at the age of 33;

Figure 9.4: Rates of teenage motherhood by social class of woman's father at age 14

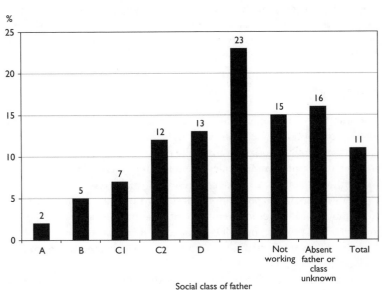

Source: Rowlingson and McKay (2001: forthcoming)

• daughters of teenage mothers more likely than other girls to become teenage mothers themselves (though as a reason for interest in teenage parenthood this is rather circular).

The report gives three reasons why Britain has such a high rate of teenage pregnancy and lone motherhood. These are:

• *Low expectations:* too many young people in Britain see no prospect of a job and fear that they will end up on benefit anyway – "put simply, they see no reason not to get pregnant" (SEU, 1999, p 7);
• *Ignorance:* young people in Britain lack accurate knowledge about contraception, what to expect in relationships and what it means to get pregnant;
• *Mixed messages:* British culture as far as teenagers are concerned is contradictory – it may seem to them that "sex is compulsory but contraception is illegal" (SEU, 1999, p 7).

The report goes on to suggest various approaches to reduce teenage pregnancy. Most of these approaches set out to tackle the problem of ignorance, and to some extent the problem of mixed messages. For example, the Social Exclusion Unit proposes various schemes giving out information and advice. But little is said about tackling the more fundamental issue of low expectations.

Ethnicity

The link between ethnicity and lone parenthood is an interesting and highly controversial one (Song and Edwards, 1997). The majority of lone-parent families in Britain are White but some ethnic minority groups are over-represented among lone-parent families (such as Afro/Caribbean women), while others are under-represented (such as Asian women). In 1996, 6% of the British population belonged to an ethnic minority group. According to Marsh et al (2000), 9% of lone parents were from ethnic minority backgrounds in 1999 – 3% were Afro/Caribbean, 2% Black African, 1% were Indian and 3% were from other ethnic minority backgrounds.

The Labour Force Survey also shows that just about two thirds of Afro/Caribbean mothers in Britain were lone parents in 1995-97, compared with 21% of White mothers (Holtermann et al, 1999). The largest subgroup among Afro/Caribbean lone mothers is single mothers (60%) compared with only 6% of Pakistani and Bangladeshi lone mothers. Lone motherhood is very widespread among Afro/Caribbean mothers but they only constitute about 4% of all lone mothers and only 6% of all single lone mothers (Holtermann et al, 1999).

There is little comparable information on lone parenthood and ethnicity across different countries. Bradshaw et al (1996) provide an excellent and comprehensive guide to cross-national data on lone parents and mention on page 23 in an endnote that they can say nothing about ethnicity as there is no comparable data on it. Trudie Knijn and Frits van Wel (Chapter Six of this book) comment that one of the few characteristics that distinguish lone mothers from partnered mothers in the Netherlands is ethnicity. Almost 30% of Caribbean women (from Surinam and the Antilles) are living in a lone-parent family. Teenage mothers (of whom there are relatively few in the Netherlands) are also much more common within the Caribbean community. This means that Amsterdam has one of the highest rates of teenage motherhood of all European cities (after London and Dublin).

In Australia, McHugh and Millar (1997) note that a survey in the early 1990s found that 29% of aboriginal and Torres Strait Islander families were headed by a lone parent – a much higher rate than for the rest of the population. But they caution about using these figures to make direct comparisons with Western family patterns as, for example, the concept of the 'nuclear' family may not be readily applicable to indigenous populations and so the idea of a 'lone-parent' family will also have greatly different meanings compared with the non-indigenous populations. Other research has suggested that the rate of lone parenthood among non-English-speaking Australians, born overseas, is lower than that for the English-speaking Australian-born women (McHugh and Millar, 1997).

While the issue of ethnicity has received relatively little attention in British research on lone parenthood, the issue is central in the US. In 1998, the share of children living with a lone mother was 18% for White mothers, 51% for African-American mothers and 27% for Hispanic mothers (Chapter Three of this book). There are also major differences in the routes into lone parenthood among different ethnic groups. In 1998, 28% of children living with White lone mothers were living with never-married mothers. The percentage for African-American women was 63% and 44% for Hispanics.

There is clearly a much higher rate of lone parenthood (and particularly single lone motherhood) among Afro/Caribbean women compared with White women and this seems to be true across countries (at least there is evidence of this in the US, UK and the Netherlands). Within this community, however, there is some variation in rates of lone parenthood by educational qualifications. Berthoud (2000) has found that only one in 10 Afro/Caribbean women with degree-level qualifications had become single lone mothers compared with almost half who had no qualifications. The same analysis applied to White women found only 2% of those with degrees had become single lone mothers compared with 12% of those with no qualifications. Economic and educational differences might therefore explain some of the differences between Caribbean and White women, but they can by no means explain it all. If these were the only important variables then we might expect a high rate of lone parenthood among Pakistani and Bangladeshi women in Britain, who have a very high rate of poverty and a relatively low level of educational qualification. But lone parenthood is very rare among this group. This points to the likely importance of culture in the creation and maintenance of lone-parent families.

Culture, tradition and religion vary considerable between the White,

Afro/Caribbean and South Asian communities. In West Indian life, 'visiting relationships' between fathers and their families has been a traditional feature and one which, it has been argued, might stem from the experience of slavery (Beishon et al, 1998). Matriarchal family structures have also been strong in this community and there is some evidence that more emphasis has traditionally been placed on individual choice and idealised marriage compared with the White community (Beishon et al, 1998). These characteristics of Afro/Caribbean culture, according to some, have much in common with the 'modern individualist' nature of life in Britain today. By contrast, South Asian culture generally has a more patriarchal family structure and heavily stigmatises divorce and illegitimacy, giving strong support to both the nuclear and extended families (Berthoud, 2000). This resembles, to some extent, the Victorian values from which Western society appears to be departing.

Whatever the reasons for the link between ethnicity and the rate of lone parenthood, there is clearly an important link between the ethnic background of lone parents and their employment rates. Afro/Caribbean lone mothers have much higher employment rates than White lone mothers (Holtermann et al, 1999). This is the case even though Afro/Caribbean lone mothers are more likely than White lone mothers to be single lone mothers. This, once again, hints at the importance of culture and identity in relation to labour market decisions.

Geographical distribution

This book is comparing nation states but there is also considerable variation *within* states in terms of the distribution of lone parenthood. This has important consequences for employment, as discussed below (see also Duncan and Edwards, 1999). There is, again, relatively little readily available comparative data on this and so this section concentrates on data from Britain. Analysis of the 1997 Labour Force Survey finds that almost half (45%) of all lone mothers live either in the South East or the North West (Holtermann et al, 1999). The North West has the highest rate of lone parenthood followed by Wales, the North and Yorkshire/Humberside. The lowest rates are found in East Anglia and the South West. If we look within regions, we find that the highest rates of lone motherhood can be found in the metropolitan areas – particularly inner London, sub-regions of Merseyside and Tyne and Wear. More than a third of inner London families (36%) are headed by a lone mother, compared with 21% in outer London.

One problem related to the spatial concentration of lone parents is that the areas in which lone parents tend to live (such as the inner cities of London and Liverpool) have far fewer employment opportunities than others. The late 1990s were generally an economic success in Britain. There was an increase in the number of jobs in the country leading some commentators to talk about supply-side problems such as skills shortages. However, some parts of the country, such as the inner cities of Liverpool and London are still suffering from a lack of labour demand. Turok and Edge (1999) argue that government policy has so far failed to address this issue sufficiently. Rather than focusing on supply-side issues (such as improving people's motivation to work, job-seeking skills and employable skills), the government should, in their view, be considering demand-side issues such as attracting employers to areas where joblessness is high.

The link between high rates of lone parenthood and lack of labour demand causes problems for lone parents in seeking paid work. There may also be another issue here – perhaps rates of lone parenthood are high in these areas because there are fewer opportunities for men to find decently paid jobs and therefore become potential husband-father-breadwinners. Improving employment opportunities in deprived areas for both men and women could therefore increase the labour market participation of lone parents, while at the same time reduce the number of lone-parent families.

Education and social class

Social class has received relatively little attention in relation to lone parenthood for a number of reasons (see Rowlingson and McKay, 2001: forthcoming, for a discussion), not least because social class has traditionally been based on the male head of the household (which is, by definition, absent in a lone-mother family). The rise of lone parenthood therefore appears to challenge the very basis of social class. In terms of cross-national analysis, it is very difficult to find comparable information about social class and lone parenthood from different countries. Despite these difficulties, this section will demonstrate that an analysis of lone parenthood by social class can be highly informative in stressing the backgrounds from which lone parents come, and the relationship this has to their future employment opportunities.

One indicator of social class is educational achievement and Bradshaw et al (1996) have compared lone parents in different countries according to whether or not they have post-school qualifications. Even this apparently straightforward indicator is problematic in terms of its comparability, but the data suggests that lone mothers are most likely to have post-school qualifications in the US and Denmark (38% and 31% respectively). About one lone parent in five has post-school qualifications in the UK, Sweden and Australia. Levels of education are lowest in Italy, Spain, Portugal, France and the Netherlands. Compared with married/ cohabiting mothers, lone mothers are generally less likely to be educated to this level and the gap between these two groups is greatest in the UK, with 21% of lone mothers having a post-school qualification compared with 32% of married/cohabiting mothers. This has important implications for their future employment opportunities, as those with fewer qualifications will only be able to command low wages. The educational background of lone parents may also be a reason why women become lone parents in the first place and so improving the education of all young women might reduce the number of lone-parent families and, where lone-parent families are still created, improve their job prospects.

Analysis of the Family and Working Lives Survey (FWLS) in Britain has looked at the chances that a woman will have a baby before marrying or cohabiting with a partner (Rowlingson and McKay, 2001: forthcoming). This is not the same as the definition of a 'single lone parent' in most official statistics (the official definition will include people who have separated from a cohabitation and then had a baby while living alone). The 'single lone mothers' in this analysis are therefore not only single at the point that they have their babies but have never lived with anyone.

Using this approach, 7% of women in the survey had, at some point in their lives, become a single lone mother. That is, they had given birth to a child prior to *any* marriage or cohabitation. But how does this vary by social class? Figure 9.5 illustrates the fact that the chances of becoming a single lone mother were very low among women of top professional fathers (group A) and increased down the social class scale towards unskilled manual workers (group E). A 14-year-old girl with an unskilled manual working father had six times the chance of becoming a single lone mother as a 14-year-old girl with a father in a professional occupation.

Social class has traditionally been measured by classifying the occupation of the (male) head of the household. With the growth of lone parenthood, however, not all households have a man in them. Analysis of the father's social class found that about one 14-year-old in 10 either did not have a father in the household or had a father whose social grade could not be classified. Girls in this situation had a much higher than average chance

Figure 9.5: Risk of having a pre-partnership birth by father's social class

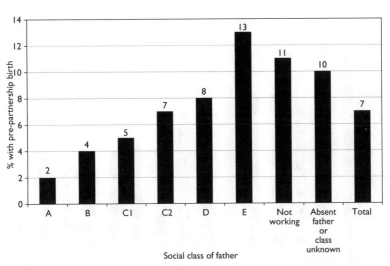

Source: Family and Working Lives Survey 1994/95 in Rowlingson and McKay (2001: forthcoming)

of becoming a single lone mother – but no higher than girls with unemployed or unskilled fathers.

The traditional focus on the male head of the household is also open to criticism due to the rise in women working and the apparent increase in equality between men and women generally. Thus the analysis was repeated, but this time the focus was on the social grade of mothers of 14-year-old girls. This shows a similar picture as the analysis of fathers – the chances of becoming a single lone mother are much greater for girls of working-class mothers as middle-class mothers.

The other main route into lone parenthood is through the breakdown of a marriage or cohabitation where there are children. Analysis of the FWLS showed that one in five couples with children separated to form a lone-mother unit. The rate of relationship breakdown to form a lone-parent family was much higher, at 31%, for those from an unskilled working-class background, and slightly lower (at 17%) for those from social classes B and C1 (junior professionals/managers and other non-manual workers).

This analysis illustrates the link between social class and lone parenthood. It is useful as a reminder that the relationship between lone parenthood

Figure 9.6: Employment rate of lone mothers in different countries

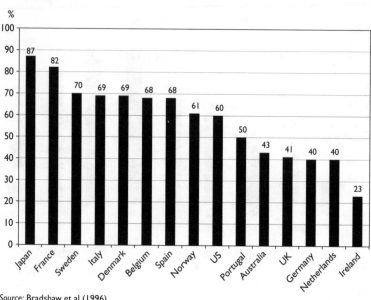

Source: Bradshaw et al (1996)

and poverty is not simply that lone parenthood causes poverty but that women from poor backgrounds are much more likely to become lone parents. Their poor backgrounds and poor educational achievement will also affect their labour market participation.

Employment

Given all that has been said so far in this chapter, it will come as no surprise that British lone parents have a very low rate of employment compared to lone parents in other countries (see Figure 9.6). These data (from Bradshaw et al, 1996) come from the early 1990s and there have been some increases in employment rates since then. For example, Alan Marsh (in Chapter Two of this book) presents data showing that 44% of lone parents were in employment in Britain in 1999, a rise of a few percentage points on the early 1990s. Peter Whiteford (Chapter Four) informs us that 49% of lone parents in Australia were in employment in 1999, a similar level of increase as in Britain. Trudie Knijn and Frits van Wel (Chapter Six) show a substantial increase in the employment of lone parents in the Netherlands over the 1990s, culminating in employment rates of 42% for lone mothers and 72% for lone fathers. Jane Waldfogel and her colleagues, also present evidence in Chapter Three of a substantial increase in employment of lone parents in the US, particularly never-married lone mothers, during the late 1990s.

It is well established that those lone parents who do have jobs in Britain are much less likely to work full-time than their counterparts overseas. Furthermore, the proportion of lone parents in paid work with children under five years of age in the UK is lower than that for married mothers with children under five, unlike most countries for which there is data (Bradshaw et al, 1996).

Demographic factors are clearly related to the low employment rates of British lone parents, as British lone parents are, compared with lone parents in other countries, more likely to:

- be younger;
- be single never-married lone mothers;
- have young children;
- have three or more children;
- have low educational qualifications compared with mothers in couples.

We have also seen that British lone parents are highly likely to come from working class backgrounds and be concentrated in areas with a lack of labour demand. All of these factors might be used to explain low employment rates. And in some other countries, such as Italy, demographic patterns might seem to explain *high* rates of employment among lone parents, as Italian lone parents are more likely to be separated/divorced rather than single, and they are more likely to be older mothers with older children and only one or two children. But the link between demographics and employment is not so apparent in other countries. For example, Sweden has a high rate of lone-parent employment despite having a high proportion of single lone mothers, a middling proportion of older lone mothers and a low proportion of older children in these families. Evidence also suggests that in most countries, lone parents with a similar demographic and educational profile to those in Britain are nevertheless more likely to have paid jobs.

The role of non-demographic factors must therefore be considered and this chapter has highlighted the role of culture. Culture and identity seem to be important across countries but also within them, as is evident from the fact that Afro/Caribbean lone parents in Britain have a demographic (and socioeconomic) profile that would suggest a low rate of employment and yet they are more likely to have paid jobs than White lone parents.

Bradshaw et al (1996) assessed the role of culture in explaining variations in employment patterns of lone parents and found that the correlation was not particularly strong. For example, Italy has a high rate of employment among lone parents but there was only weak support for mothers to go out to work in this country. So alongside demographics and culture, other factors are likely to be important in determining the employment rate of lone parents. These include the tax and benefit systems, the availability, affordability and suitability of childcare provision, the extent of family-friendly employment practices and the nature of the labour market. These issues are covered by other chapters in this book.

Conclusion

This chapter has presented cross-national data on the demographic characteristics of lone parenthood. There are two points to be made about the data itself. First, countries define lone parenthood differently in their data sets and so comparisons must be made with some caution. Nevertheless, these are the most reliably comparative data available. Second, the data are becoming rather old now and there is a need for a repeat of the study by Bradshaw et al (1996) to update our information on lone parents across countries.

Turning to the more substantive issues, it has been argued in the chapter that demographic characteristics go some way to explaining the low rate of employment among lone parents in Britain. But other factors are also very important, including culture/orientations to work, tax/benefit regimes, childcare provision, family-friendly employment practices and the nature of the labour market. There is also a complex relationship between social, demographic and employment factors. For example, the poor employment prospects of young working-class men and women in Britain is likely to be a key factor explaining why some women become single never-married lone mothers. Demographic factors affect employment rates, but the reverse is also true.

TEN

Work-related activity requirements and labour market programmes for lone parents

Jane Millar

Decisions about who should and should not be expected to support themselves through paid employment are central to all systems of social protection. This is an issue in which there has been a significant gender divide in most countries. For men, paid work is generally expected, unless for reasons of sickness, unemployment, or retirement. Of course, these are themselves all conditional and subject to change – retirement ages can be moved, unemployment and sickness can be defined more or less stringently – and there are examples of this sort of change in recent policy in many countries. But the changes affecting men tend to be at the margins, a shifting of boundaries between the economically active and inactive, rather than a fundamental change in the expectations driving policy. For women, in contrast, there seems to be a much more radical transformation taking place in a number of countries. Women with children are increasingly being defined as part of the labour force, as among those who are expected to support themselves through employment, rather than as primarily at-home caregivers.

This policy shift has particularly affected lone mothers and is reflected in two main sorts of changes: changes in the conditions under which lone parents can claim benefits without some form of work–related activity test; and the inclusion of lone parents in labour market programmes. This chapter examines both of these, drawing first on the material from the six national chapters to highlight key points for each country and then to make comparisons across the countries[1].

Activity requirements for lone parents

The division of lone parents into either 'mothers' (supported by benefits to stay at home and care for children) or 'workers' (required to be eligible for work in the same way as other benefit claimants) has often been used as an analytical frame for comparing different national systems of support (Millar, 1996; Lewis, 1997; Duncan and Edwards, 1997b). The six countries included here present a range of different approaches and in all, except France, the rules have either changed recently and/or are in the process of change[2].

Australia: Lone and married parents in Australia may be eligible for support under the same system (Parenting Payment), which is available to anyone caring for dependent children aged under 16. The benefit is partially means-tested on a partner's income, where applicable. There is no requirement for recipients to work or to seek work. However, in the 2001 Budget it was announced that Parenting Payment recipients with children aged 13 and above will be required to undertake around six hours a week of activities aimed at helping them return to work, and those with children aged six to 12 will be required to attend annual interviews to discuss preparation for work. Thus in future only those with pre-school children will have no labour market requirement at all.

France: Employment rates for lone parents in France are high and there have been no major policy changes in recent years. The *Allocation de parent isolé* is available to pregnant women, in the first year after a couple separate, and/or until a youngest child is three years old. Recipients are not required to seek paid work, although they can receive this benefit alongside wages. Once entitlement to this benefit is ended, lone parents may be eligible for the *Revenu minimum d'insertion*, the means-tested minimum income guarantee that is available to all those aged 25 plus. Individual 'insertion' contracts are part of the claim for this benefit, but as Enjolras et al (2001, p 51) note the "law is extremely ambiguous about the degree of obligation that goes with the right to insertion".

The Netherlands: Prior to 1996, there was no requirement for lone parents in the Netherlands to work or seek work. Since 1996, lone parents claiming social assistance are required to seek work or participate in labour market programmes once their youngest child reaches five years of age. Local social assistance officers, who can require lone parents to seek full-time work, or part-time work, or exempt them from a work requirement, administer these. Recent government proposals would make it obligatory for lone parents with children below the age of five to accept a place on a labour market programme or a job offer.

Norway: Prior to 1998 Norwegian lone parents were entitled to receive 'transitional allowance' with no work test as long as their youngest child was aged under 10. Since 1998, entitlement has been restricted to those with children aged under eight, with a maximum period of three or five years (if in education), and those with a youngest child aged over three are required to be undertaking education, in employment or actively seeking work as a condition of receiving the transitional allowance. Lone parents are exempt from activity obligations in the first year of lone parenthood, if they have a child aged under 10.

UK: There is no requirement for lone parents claiming Income Support to work or to seek work as long as the youngest child is aged under 16. However, since April 2001 new and existing lone-parent benefit claimants with school-age children are required to attend a 'work-focused' interview as part of the process of claiming benefits. They will then be required to attend annual reviews. From April 2002, compulsory work-focused interviews will be extended to all lone parents in receipt of Income Support, regardless of the age of the youngest child, and the reviews will take place at six-month intervals.

US: Since the implementation of the 1996 welfare reforms, lone parents in the US are required to be in 'work or work-related activities' as a condition of access to benefit support. There is significant variation across states in the way in which this is applied, but many states start to apply these work requirements once children reach three months of age. Federal law sets a five-year time limit for the receipt of cash assistance, although again states may set shorter limits than this.

Table 10.1 summarises the situation in these six countries across the two dimensions of age of youngest child and nature of the activity requirements. In general, lone parents with children who have reached school-leaving age are treated in the same way as other working-age benefit claimants and are required to fulfil the same sorts of work requirements. The table therefore focuses just on lone parents with children below school-leaving age. The activity requirements include: requirements to attend work-related interviews, to participate in education or training, requirements to seek full-time or part-time work, and requirements to participate in work or work-related activities.

France, however, is difficult to categorise in these terms, first because (as noted above) the *Allocation de parent isolé* is related to pregnancy and duration of lone parenthood, as well as the age of the youngest child. Second, the French insertion policies are based more on the concept of providing individuals with a right to work than on the concept of mandatory work participation. Thus, lone parents receiving the minimum income may have priority for work placements but not necessarily an obligation to take these. Insertion also covers a wider field than employment and training, and may, for example, include assistance with housing and health matters. We have therefore shown France as a separate category.

Looking at the other countries, the US stands out in respect of both of these dimensions. First, all lone parents – except those with very young infants – are included in the activity requirements. Second, the activity requirement makes it mandatory to *participate* in work or work-related activities, not just to be available for or seeking work. These other sorts of activities may also be required – job search, training, and so on – but they are not sufficient by themselves, except for limited periods. This is a 'workfare' model[3] and is not replicated in any of the other countries (a difference which should be borne in mind for the comparisons of the labour market programmes below). The introduction of these very strong work requirements in the US followed a long period in which 'welfare' was increasingly unpopular and perceived as a failure, as a system which had increased dependency, created disincentives to work, and which had failed to prevent poverty. The 1996 reform introduced radical changes, but there had been an increasing emphasis on work requirements at both federal and state level over the previous decade or more.

All the other countries currently start to apply some work-related activity requirements around about the time that children start nursery or primary school[4], although (as noted above) the UK is introducing some requirements for all lone parents and this has also been proposed in the Netherlands. School age is also the dividing line used in many other countries including, for example, Austria, Finland, Germany, Luxembourg, New Zealand and many provinces in Canada (Millar, 2000a). In many countries, therefore, there is a division in expectations between *pre-school children/care at home* on the one hand, and *school-age children/participation in employment* on the other.

Although the UK is planning to extend requirements to all lone parents, these are the least intensive of the various different forms of activity requirement. The requirement will be to attend a work-focused interview at the start of the claim for Income Support and then every six months. The UK government has set a target to increase employment rates among lone parents to 70% within 10 years and are pursuing this by policies intended to 'make work pay' financially and to make it easier for lone parents to combine part-time work and benefit receipt. These policies are part of a wider commitment to tackle worklessness (DfEE, 2001a). In Australia, the measures announced in 2001 are also fairly modest, introducing annual interviews for those with children aged six to 12 and six hours of work-related activities for those with children aged 13 plus. The types of activities that might be required are "education and training, confidence building courses or community work" (Vanstone and Abbott, 2001, p 16). These measures are also part of a wider welfare reform agenda in which it is argued that the system needs to be restructured around the concept of 'participation' and 'mutual obligations'.

In the Netherlands, the policy shift was also part of wider reform to social assistance in 1996, which had two main aims: to provide a minimum income guarantee and to activate employment. The reforms extended work obligations to a wider group of claimants, including lone parents. At the same time the government has been promoting a part-time work strategy for men and women with children – the 'combination scenario'. Thus the work requirement might be for full-time or part-time work. However, there is a lack of services, particularly childcare, to support parental employment in the Netherlands and the financial support for part-time work remains limited. There is also some ambivalence about whether or not lone mothers should be required to participate in work (discussed further below).

In Norway, the changes to the activity obligations for lone parents were not part of a wider reform of social security. The arguments made for the changes were twofold. First, that married mothers were increasingly employed outside the home and that state support for parental employment was high enough to enable lone parents to participate in the labour market. Second, it was argued that lone parents suffered social exclusion and social isolation as a consequence of non-employment. A contrast was made between 'passive' and 'active' benefit recipients, with the latter combining benefit receipt with employment or education. The aim of policy was to encourage more such activity. Anne Skevik, in Chapter Five of this book, suggests that there was an "increasing invisibility of paid work" in these debates and "not only had it ceased to be a legitimate reason not to work outside the home, it had ceased to be an activity which could give meaning and fulfilment".

Thus, these shifts towards the introduction of activity obligations for lone parents have entered the policy arena in various ways. For the US, an important factor was the perceived failure and unpopularity of the previous system. In other countries the measures have often been promoted as part of a modernisation of the welfare state, to meet changing needs and circumstances. Issues of gender equality and the position of women in the labour market have sometimes been part of the debates. In many countries, there is an increasing emphasis on the value on paid employment for all, both as the route out of poverty and the route into social inclusion. We return to some of these issues at the end of the chapter, but first we

Table 10.1:Activity requirements for lone parents as a condition of receiving financial support

Activity requirements	Youngest child is:		
	Pre-nursery/ pre-school	At primary school	At secondary school
None	Australia France[1] Netherlands Norway[1] UK		
Insertion		France	France
Prepare for work:			
• attend work- related interviews	UK (from 2002)	Australia UK	UK
• take part in education/training		Netherlands Norway	Netherlands Norway
Seek work	Netherlands[2]	Netherlands Norway	Netherlands Norway
Take part in work or work-related activities	US	US	US Australia[3]

[1] Also no activity requirements in first year of lone parenthood (for those with children aged under 10 in Norway).

[2] Proposed, currently under discussion.

[3] Six hours per week work-related activities.

look at one aspect of the implementation of these new activity obligations: the nature and operation of labour market programmes for lone parents.

Labour market programmes

As for the previous section, we start by summarising the key features of the labour market programmes for lone parents in each country and then compare these, especially in respect of outcomes. France, however, is not included here, as there are no specific programmes for lone parents there that can be compared in this way.

Australia: The Jobs, Education and Training programme (JET) started in 1989 and so has now been running for over a decade. It is available on a voluntary basis to lone parents and to various other groups with similar barriers to workforce participation (Department of Family and Community Services, 1999), including partnered mothers in receipt of Parenting Payment. An inter-departmental agency (Centrelink) is responsible for implementation of all labour market programmes on behalf of the relevant departments[5]. There are over 100 JET advisers located in local Centrelink offices and they pursue outreach activities as well as inviting lone parents to attend an interview. Any lone parent may come forward but there are three particular target groups – teenage mothers; those with a youngest child aged six and over who have been on benefits for at least 12 months; and those with a youngest child aged 12 and above. JET provides "structured assistance which includes a return to work plan; information, advice and referrals to government and community services including assistance with finding childcare; referrals to education and vocational training; and referrals to Job Network members for job search and assistance" (Peter Whiteford, Chapter Four of this book).

The Netherlands: Social assistance and labour market programmes in the Netherlands are both run by local municipalities, usually with separate administration. The first point of contact for lone parents is the social assistance office, where the caseworker decides on work requirements. There are four main categories or phases: immediately available for work; available after some additional training or guidance of up to three months; not available until additional training or guidance of up to one year; not available in the near future. If lone parents are assessed as not available for work they are not required to be reassessed for 18 months. Lone parents with a work requirement are referred to the labour office, where there are various training courses, subsidised jobs and activation programmes potentially available to them. These may be provided directly by the regional or local labour office or contracted out to private and non-profit contractors. Some offer special programmes just for lone parents, others more general programmes.

Norway: Although lone parents in Norway are required to be available for work, as described above, they are not necessarily obliged to participate in labour market programmes (that is, they can discharge their work obligations in other ways). In fact the main programme – OFO (translated as 'follow-up arrangements for lone parents') – is based on voluntary participation. This started in one county in 1992 and has since been extended throughout the country. It is the responsibility of the National Insurance Administration, with regional coordination and day-to-day operation at local office level. The goal of OFO is to help lone parents make the transition from 'passive' (receiving Transitional Allowance only) to 'active' (Transitional Allowance plus work/education) and this is pursued through the role of a 'mediator'. Mediators are themselves lone parents, recruited from those receiving the transitional allowance, and they are unpaid volunteers, working up to 30 hours per week. Their task is bringing together information and advice from across the various relevant departments (local national insurance offices, social assistance, employment services, childcare and education) and their activities include home visits and arranging social activities. The scheme targets all lone parents receiving Transitional Allowances and the OFO process includes three main phases: 'mapping' (assessing needs and providing information); 'awareness' (improving self-confidence and social networks, making plans for future activities); and 'action' (putting plans made in the second stage into effect).

UK: The main programme in the UK is the NDLP (New Deal for Lone Parents), one of the first of the New Deal programmes, which started as a prototype in 1997 and nationally from 1998. It originally targeted lone parents with a youngest child aged five years and three months, but the target group was later extended to those with children aged three and above. Participation is voluntary, with lone parents invited to attend an initial interview and then, if they wish, to take part in the programme. It is the responsibility of the Employment Service and run through local employment offices (soon to be merged with the benefits paying service). The main point of contact is the personal adviser, who offers information and advice about employment and training opportunities, childcare services, and about the financial impact of working. Participants draw up an action plan and regular contact is maintained with the personal adviser, which can include in-work mentoring and support.

US: Each state runs its own programme or programmes in the US, so there can be considerable variation. The Michigan programme, described by Jane Waldfogel and her colleagues in Chapter Three, is called the Family Independence Program (FIP) and is operated through local offices in which applicants complete a combined application form for benefits, pursue child support claims, and fulfil work requirements. The latter involves attending a Work First orientation session within two weeks, where information and advice about work requirements, childcare, training and employment possibilities are discussed. The key person here is the Family Independence Specialist, with whom the lone parent works to draw up a personal plan of action and this is put into effect within two months of the receipt of assistance. There are over 80 Work First programmes in Michigan, usually run by contracted organisations, and these fall into four main types: those which offer both job search/ motivation workshops, and job search support, making direct contacts with employers and setting up interviews; those which offer one but not both of these; those which make clients themselves responsible for job search; and those which offer little structured support. Those who fail to find work within four weeks may be placed in a work experience position or a vocational training course. Contact with those who find work and leave the programmes is maintained for up to 90 days.

Other states share some of these features but can vary in several ways, including the extent to which programmes are primarily work first or human capital oriented, in the number of hours of the activity that are required, and in the ways in which they apply exemptions and sanctions. The Manpower Demonstration Research Corporation (Freedman et al, 2000) has been following 11 programmes in seven locations over the past two years. They suggest that four main categories of welfare-to-work programme approaches can be identified: employment focused, with high enforcement and first assignments to job search; employment focused, with high enforcement and first assignments to job search or basic education/vocational skills training; education focused, with high enforcement and first assignment to basic education or skills training; and education focused, with low enforcement and first assignments to basic education or skills training. All states use case management methods, but some (like Michigan described above) offer an integrated welfare/labour market programmes service while others keep these as separate functions.

Comparing programmes

Table 10.2 offers a comparison of the labour market programmes in these five countries. It is necessarily impressionistic rather than systematic, but it does highlight a number of similarities and differences. Norway's programme – voluntary, operated by lone-parent clients, with social as well as labour market elements – is perhaps the most 'different' from the others, but each programme has its own characteristics and context. For example, there are no comparable labour market programmes for other groups, such as long-term unemployed people or unemployed youth, in the US and this gives a different context to the US programmes. In Australia and the Netherlands, lone parents do not have separate programmes. In the UK and Norway they do, although the UK has other very similar parallel schemes for disabled people and partners of unemployed claimants and may be moving towards programmes with combined client groups (Millar, 2000b).

The use of 'one-stop' services (that is, combining benefit and employment) plus an individual 'caseworker' model is found in Australia, the UK and the US, and the Netherlands is moving towards this approach. However, caseworkers may have very different caseload sizes across these countries, and this would affect how far they are able to carry out individual assessments in practice. Peter Whiteford (in Chapter Four of this book) suggests that caseloads are probably too high for such assessments in Australia. Norway is rather difficult to categorise along these same dimensions, since the 'mediator' role is not entirely analogous to a caseworker role. In all countries there is some contracting out to private and not-for-profit contractors (including lone-parent self-help organisations) and this is particularly strong in the Netherlands, the US and Australia.

In most comparisons of labour market programmes a distinction is made between 'work first' and 'human capital' approaches. But it seems useful to add another dimension, 'information and advice'. All the schemes offer this, but in the UK (and, to a lesser extent, Australia) it is probably fair to say that this is the primary focus of the programmes – brokering information for the lone parent, rather than specifically referring them on to particular schemes or finding jobs for them. Since 1996 the Australian government has been increasingly promoting a work first model in all their labour market programmes and this has also been applied to JET clients. About half of JET participants are referred to the Employment Service for job search activities. The Michigan scheme is work first (although, as described above, other US schemes are more human capital oriented). The Netherlands and Norway are the most human capital oriented of these programmes, and in Norway this could be extended to describe the scheme as promoting human and social capital[6].

All the programmes include elements of both 'job preparation' (for example, attending work-focused interviews; taking part in work preparation programmes; taking part in education/training and/or literacy/ numeracy courses; attending addiction/other treatments; arranging childcare) and 'job seeking' (for example, assessment of job-readiness by caseworkers; constructing a job plan/contract; fulfilling job search requirements; attending Job Clubs). In some countries (the Netherlands,

Table 10.2: Labour market programmes for lone parents: summary

	Australia	Netherlands	Norway	UK	US – Michigan
Programme name	JET	No separate title	OFO	NDLP	FIP
Designated lone-parent programme	No	No	Yes	Yes	Yes
Compulsory to attend programme	No	Yes	No	No	Yes
One-stop shop	Yes	Being developed	No	Yes	Yes
Caseworker model	In part	Yes	No	Yes	Yes
Private sector contracted out provision	Yes	Yes	No	No	Yes
Self-help/lone-parent organisation provision	No	No	Yes	No	No
Work/training focus*	IA/WF	HC	HC	IA/WF	WF
Staged approach	No	Yes	Yes	No	Yes
In-work mentoring	No	No	No	Yes	Yes

Notes: * IA = information and advice; HC= human capital; WF = Work First

Norway and the US – Michigan) this is formalised into various 'stages'. Lone parents are first assessed by a caseworker and then activities – job preparation or job search – are required according to their 'employability' status. In the US, the Wisconsin 'self-sufficiency ladder' is another example of this sort of approach, with four steps of the ladder running from supported activity, to community service, to trial jobs to regular employment (Meyer, 2001). The UK and the US schemes can follow people into work and offer in-work mentoring and support.

Labour market programmes: 'outcomes'

With such different schemes and also different types of evaluations, it is not possible to quantify and rank the differences in outcomes and make statements such as 'country x achieves better results than country y'. Here, as in previous sections, we therefore start by summarising the national picture on outcomes and then attempting some overall (again impressionistic) assessment.

Australia: There are regular statistics published on the numbers going through JET but there has been no formal evaluation since 1995-97 (DSS et al, 1997). The statistical monitoring shows that almost 400,000 people took part in JET interviews between 1989 and 1998, the vast majority of these being lone parents. Over the whole period of operation of the programme, about 100,000 (25%) have taken up employment; 95,000 (24%) have undertaken educational courses; and 129,000 (32%) have participated in training programmes (Department of Family and Community Services, 1999). The evaluation of JET in the mid- to late-1990s found that take-up rates varied from about 20% for teenage mothers to 41% for lone mothers with school-age children. After joining the programme, JET clients were more likely to have income from earnings than non-JET clients were, although part-time employment was more common than full-time employment. Income support benefits can be paid to people both in and out of work and so lone parents are very likely to *combine* work and benefits. Many people took part in education/ training but these were often at fairly basic levels, and in 'women's jobs' (McHugh and Millar, 1997).

It was estimated that JET was breaking even in terms of cost, and in general the government has considered the programme a success, "instrumental in assisting workforce entry for a substantial proportion of

JET customers" (Department of Family and Community Services, 1999, section 4.5.2). This point was reiterated by the Minister for Family and Community Services in July 2000: "JET is a demand driven programme which ... has an important role in helping people to overcome the barriers of entering the paid workforce by helping with access to education, training and employment, and where required, child care" (Newman, 2000). Peter Whiteford (Chapter Four of this book) notes that the 1996 evaluation showed JET to be more successful than many of the US schemes in operation at that time, and argues that this success has been in spite of the rather low levels of resources invested and the unfavourable labour market conditions at that time.

Also of interest in respect to Australia is a recent study of a pilot programme for Parenting Payment recipients (Pearse, 2000). This pilot programme – the Parenting Payment Intervention Pilot – was intended to trial 'more active' interventions to help the target group (mainly, but not exclusively, lone parents) to 'reduce their reliance on income support'. These more active interventions included a compulsory interview for some people (on a random allocation basis) and a 'more structured and holistic' approach, including information about the advantages of returning to work. The study allowed for a comparison between voluntary participants, people who were invited but declined to take part, and a control group. There was a large difference in take-up between the voluntary (14%) and the compulsory interview groups (88%), although once in there was little difference in how they responded to the interview, which was generally positive. About 30% said that the interview had helped them to change their plans and that they now planned to try and increase their employment. The 11 JET advisers who were responsible for implementing the programme seem to have been won over to the compulsory approach, with five agreeing with this at the start and 10 by the end. Among respondents, 59% thought an interview should be compulsory for all Parenting Payment recipients and 26% supported an interview for some, but not all, recipients.

The Netherlands: The evaluation of the new policy in the Netherlands found a very limited impact on employment rates. There has been some reduction in benefit receipt because of people finding it more difficult to get onto benefits in the first place (as in the US, discussed below). However, lone parents have the lowest exit rates from benefits than any other category of claimant. There seem to be a number of reasons for this. First, there has been a relatively high rate of exemptions from work requirements. In one study in five cites it was found that about 35% of lone parents were exempt from work requirements, 25% had a part-time requirement and 40% a full-time work requirement (quoted by Trudie Knijn and Frits van Wel in Chapter Six of this book). Second, there was little by way of practical measures to support the work obligations – a lack of suitable work programmes for lone parents, difficulties in cross-agency working, a lack of knowledge about the in-work benefits that might be available, and lack of available and affordable childcare. Many lone parents had little previous work experience and faced significant barriers to work. Third, there were the attitudes of both the caseworkers and the lone parents themselves, who did not necessarily accept that compulsory work requirements were acceptable and appropriate. All these factors reduced participation and made it difficult to achieve immediate employment outcomes. However, those who did participate reported some gains in confidence, self-esteem and social reintegration, and these programmes seem to have been more effective in enhancing aspects of employability than in achieving higher rates of employment (at least in the short term).

Norway: The OFO programmes in five counties were reviewed in 1996 and this showed generally positive results. Among participants half changed their status from 'passive' (that is, receiving Transitional Allowance only) to 'active' (also participating in training or working part time). About half of the participants had received social assistance, but only one in 10 were in receipt after taking part in the project. Many of these had received financial advice as part of their OFO package. Many reported increases in self-confidence. Certain characteristics slowed down the transition from passive to active, such as having very young children, large families, and low self-esteem. There were two particularly interesting findings. First, in areas where the schemes operated, more lone parents made the transition from passive to active, whether they were participants or not – an apparent synergy effect. Second, it was the combination of social and individual activities that achieved the good results – lone parents who took part in both gained the most benefit.

UK: Information about the operation of the NDLP includes the regular statistical monitoring, the evaluation of the prototype programme, and the ongoing evaluations of the national scheme. By October 2000 about 195,000 lone parents had attended an initial New Deal interview, of whom nine out of 10 went on to take part in the programme. About 68,500 people had found employment. Of the lone parents who found work, about four in 10 were continuing to receive support from their New Deal personal adviser while in work (DfEE, 2001b).

The evaluation of the prototype found that take-up rates were low with only about one fifth of those invited participating. However, this does not necessarily mean that all the non-participants were actively opting out. Lone parents are relatively new target groups for labour market programmes and this seems to have been reflected in the way that they responded to the schemes. Many had not heard of the programmes before and so were unsure what was being offered, whether it was required of them or not, and what impact it might have on their benefits. Some of those who did not participate were not actively opting out – they did not remember receiving a letter, or the letter came at a time that was difficult for them, or they somehow just did not take up the interview offer. There were also substantial numbers of volunteers from outside the target group.

Participants were generally very positive about their experiences, valuing the contact with the personal adviser and the information and support they were offered. A quarter of those who found jobs said that the personal adviser had given them significant help and there was a 'small but positive' effect on numbers in receipt of Income Support – about a 3% improvement in the rate of leaving Income Support (Hales et al, 2000). Dead weight (that is, those who would have found jobs anyway, without the benefit of the programme) was estimated to be about 80%. But this may be an over-estimate, since there is some evidence that participation did provide an extra 'push', which can benefit even the most work-ready and actively seeking. As in Australia, these outcomes have to be seen in the context of the fact that the NDLP was rather a limited and modest programme.

US: Clearly the leader in terms of detailed evaluation studies, there is a great deal of evidence from the US about the outcomes of these programmes. There have been cross-state comparisons and comparisons of different programmes within states, including random allocation studies. These tend to show that the programmes have had a positive effect on employment rates, in the context of a strong economy and in combination with other policies to make work pay (as discussed in Chapter Three of this book). A recent Manpower Demonstration Research Corporation (MDRC) study (Freedman et al, 2000) examined the effects of 11 programmes over two years and found that the most successful programme was in Portland, Oregon, where there were significant positive outcomes. The results seem to have been due to a combination of factors: a strong employment orientation to the programme, but also high-quality education, training and job search services; high enforcement; well developed job development and placement services; a relatively less disadvantaged welfare caseload; and a good labour market with a relatively high state minimum wage. It is a combination of factors that make for success, with the 'make work pay' policies playing an important role. On the downside, however, there has been some concern that 'hard to help' clients, who can make up a significant proportion of the caseload, are not well served by mandatory work first programmes and that problems of domestic violence, depression, substance addiction may need to be addressed before work obligations can really be imposed. In addition, three fifths of states use various 'diversion' measures which reduce the numbers entering the welfare system.

Comparing outcomes

Table 10.3 summarises some key points from the evidence about 'outcomes', compared across the countries. We must be wary, of course, of attributing these directly to the programmes. It is also important to note that the economic context in which these programmes were implemented varies, and some were set in a more favourable economic climate than others.

On participation the comparison suggests that while the voluntary schemes may have take-up problems, the compulsory schemes do not necessarily have full participation. In the Netherlands exemptions reduce participation and in the US diversion does the same. On the other hand, although take-up was low among the target group in the UK there have also been a significant number of 'voluntary' starts – people coming forward who are not in the target group or who are in the target group but have not yet been invited for interview. Among caseworkers there seem to be mixed views about the value or otherwise of requiring participation in interviews and in programmes, with the Netherlands and the US apparently at opposite ends of the scale. Even in the US, however, mandatory participation is not necessarily seen as the right approach for all lone parents. The use of sanctions to ensure compliance is high in many states in the US and low in the Netherlands, as might be expected. The extent to which programmes are dealing with a particularly disadvantaged group (that is, with high labour market barriers) also seems to vary across the countries, although in all cases lone parents are seen as facing significant barriers to work.

In terms of outcomes for individuals, all these programmes seem to have a degree of success at improving motivation and confidence and offer some gains in social reintegration[7]. Human capital gains tend to be low, mainly because these programmes rarely offer anything above basic skills and vocational training. Access to further and higher education is limited, perhaps even more so than before such programmes were introduced. There seems to be little provision to help lone parents make significant educational gains. Employment and earnings gains are also

Table 10.3: Labour market programmes for lone parents: comparing 'outcomes'

	Australia	Netherlands	Norway	UK	US
Programme name	JET	No separate title	OFO	NDLP	Various
Participation levels	Take-up c 20-40%	Many exempt	DK	c 20% includes non-target	Some 'diversion'
Caseworker support for some compulsion	Rising	Low	NA	Mixed	High, but qualified
Use of sanctions	NA	Rare	NA	DK	Yes
Disadvantage among client group	Moderate	High	Moderate	Moderate	High
Motivation and confidence gains	High	High	High	High	High
Social reintegration gains	Some	Some	High	Some	Some
Human capital gains	Basic skills	Basic skills	Basic skills	Basic skills	Basic skills
Employment gains	Moderate	Low	DK	Moderate	Moderate
Earnings gains	Moderate	Low	DK	Low	Low
In-work poverty risk (cf to other families)	High but improved	High	Moderate	High	High
Impact on children	DK	DK	DK	DK	Mixed

Note: DK=don't know; NA= not applicable

usually low to moderate, with some impact on exit from benefit but moves into work may be into part-time jobs and be associated with continued benefit receipt. Employment does not necessarily prevent poverty. This is very clear in the US, where the evaluation evidence has looked closely at this, but also in the UK. Evidence on the impact on children is harder to come by. The US evidence suggests that outcomes tend to be broadly neutral for pre-school age children, broadly positive for primary school-age children, but more negative for teenage children, where school performance seems to suffer and where more 'risky behaviour' (for example, drinking, smoking, problem behaviour, poor school attendance) is found (Duncan and Chase-Lansdale, 2001).

Final thoughts

This final section concludes by discussing three main issues arising from this analysis of work-related activity requirements and the implementation of labour market programmes for lone parents.

First, rules regarding requirements to work for lone parents are changing in many countries, and lone parents are now very likely to be expected to seek work once their children reach school or nursery school age. Thus there does seem to be a policy convergence around the idea that it is appropriate to support mothers of pre-school children to provide full-time care, but once children reach school-age then employment obligations should be imposed. However, lone parents with pre-school children may be expected to start thinking about, or preparing for, paid work. Some countries also use a 'stepping stones' model, in which work requirements become more stringent as children get older. One advantage of drawing such a clear line about employment expectations is that it can become possible to treat those on the non-work, or care, side of the line more generously in terms of financial support because there are no incentive issues for them.

However, these changes also raise the general question of whether or not it is 'right' to impose work requirements on lone mothers, and the specific question of whether age of youngest child is the best way of doing this. The general question is very controversial, touching as it does on views about caring, motherhood and the rights of citizens to make their own decisions and choices. In many countries these policy changes have been justified by reference to the changing employment patterns of married mothers. If most married mothers are employed, then the case for excluding lone parents from employment requirements seems to be greatly weakened. And if family-friendly policy measures are in place (childcare, parental leave, flexible working hours, and so on) this also adds to the case for lone mothers to be in employment.

Public opinion across very many countries seems to support the general proposition that mothers of school-age children should work outside the home, but part-time work is supported more often than full-time work, and there is not such strong support when children are pre-school age (Evans, 2000). Using attitude data from the mid-1990s, Evans (2000) finds that, for these five countries (France is not included) around 35% (Australia, UK) to around 50% (Norway, Netherlands, US) agreed that 'women should work when there is a child under school age'. However, over 80% in every country agreed that 'women should work after the youngest child starts school'.

However, there is less information available about attitudes specifically to lone mothers' employment (rather than mothers in general). Anne Skevik, in Chapter Five, reports that a Norwegian survey in 1996 found that one in four people agreed that lone mothers should be expected to work when children are three years old, about one third thought the limit should be when children start school at age six, and about one fifth that the limit should be at age 10. In the UK, a recent study found that 23% agreed that a lone mother with a pre-school child 'has a duty to stay at home and look after the child' and 17% that 'she has duty to work'. About half agreed that lone mothers should be able to choose for themselves whether to go out to work or not. However, if a lone mother's children are of school age, 44% agree she should go out to work, and 4% that she should stay at home. Again about half think she should be able to choose (Hills and Lelkes, 1999). In Australia, Eardley (2000) reports that about 51% agreed that lone mothers should work part time once children go to primary school, about 19% once children are in secondary school and about 13% once children have turned 16 years of age. About 10% thought the lone parent should work when they 'feel ready'. For full-time work, the equivalent proportions were 17% for primary school-age children, 28% for secondary school-age children, 33% for post-16-year-olds, and 16% 'when ready'.

It is difficult to compare these figures as differently worded questions may lead to rather different responses. But they suggest that there is no clear consensus in these countries to support the sorts of work requirements currently being imposed on lone parents. As for lone parents themselves, again the evidence is limited and not necessarily straightforward to interpret. Lone mothers often say they want to take paid work but also that they want to take account of what is in the best interests of their children. Whether or not they perceive those best interests to include paid work varies both across and within countries, by factors such as age, class and race (Duncan and Edwards, 1997b, 1999; see also Chapter Eight of this book). In the UK, many lone parents say they want to work, but often not immediately. In the Netherlands also, many lone parents say they want to work but also that they want to make the decision for themselves.

Making employment for lone mothers conditional on the age of their children is relatively straightforward to administer and it fits with a simple developmental approach to children's capabilities and needs (as children get older they become more independent and have less need of their parents). But, as discussed above, it does not necessarily fit with the views of lone parents themselves, who have more complex views about their children's needs (as do married mothers). And the US evidence quoted above, which suggests that negative outcomes are more likely for teenage children, also raises concerns about increased activity obligations as children get older. There is also some research evidence to suggest that parental conflict and separation can have an impact on children of all ages, not just pre-schoolers. The use of a duration-linked rule (as in France and Norway) may be helpful in enabling lone parents, and their children, to adjust to their situation.

The second main issue that arises from these comparisons is that close attention needs to be paid to the way in which these policies are implemented, including by the 'street-level' bureaucrats, who have much discretion in decision making, and who are acting as gatekeepers for a range of services. We need to consider three main areas: what exemptions are applied, by whom, and what sorts of criteria are used? How is delivery organised and what role do the public, private and voluntary sectors play in this? And what sanctions are imposed and by whom? These countries show there are some common answers to these points, but also substantial diversity in practice. For example, many countries are using or setting up 'one-stop' delivery systems, but with differing degrees of local discretion. The caseworker approach is very common but there is a sharp contrast between Norway, where the 'caseworkers' are lone parents themselves acting in a voluntary capacity, and the US, where they are often private contractors with particular targets to meet. The caseworker model may not be sustainable in practice, especially in compulsory schemes where there are a large number of participants with a wide range of needs. Under such circumstances caseworkers may find they have no choice but to use standard assessments and/or concentrate on the most work-ready individuals.

The way in which compulsion is implemented in practice also requires careful analysis before any conclusions can be drawn about the relative effectiveness of compulsory and voluntary programmes. Compulsion can only be assessed in context and, as I have argued elsewhere:

> Much depends on the nature of the compulsion, the context in which it is operated, and the type of sanctions used. Being required, under threat of loss of benefits, to take any job regardless of individual circumstances, of the pay and condition of that job, and of whether or not adequate child care is available is rather different from being required to seek employment and/or training in a buoyant and well-paid labour market, where child care is readily available and widely used. (Millar, 2000c, p 34)

Nor does compulsion guarantee high levels of participation and caseworkers on the ground can exclude people, even in compulsory programmes. High levels of diversion and exemption produce better statistics but can mean that lone parents are neither getting the help they need to enter work nor an adequate level of support out of work.

The third issue to note is that outcomes in terms of exits into work are relatively modest, especially when the programmes themselves are relatively modest and offer only information and advice. But in the context of a complete package – labour market programmes, in-work benefits and childcare services – good results can be obtained. The most consistent success of the labour market programmes themselves seems to be in improving motivation and confidence. The Norwegian experience suggests that tackling social exclusion at the same time as encouraging labour market participation can make an effective combination. The use of 'exit from welfare/social security into employment' as a measure of success may not be the most useful approach to assessing and developing these programmes. Lone parents face considerable difficulties in keeping jobs, not just in getting them. Issues of retention and progression may need also to be placed more centrally on the policy agenda.

Finally, one potentially important aspect of these policy developments is that lone parents are being brought much more into the mainstream of labour market policies. This potentially means more resources attached to meeting their needs and it may also mean that the category 'lone parent' becomes less important. France has generally treated lone-parent families in much the same way as other one-earner families, and this is also true in countries such as Denmark and Sweden (Lewis, 1997). Australia has moved towards treating lone and married parents in the same way. Using family structure as a marker for particular sorts of policy interventions may become a less important feature of policy in other countries in the future, including the UK.

Notes

[1] These are my interpretations of the information from the national chapters, supplemented by other relevant material. In general, I have not specifically referenced the national chapters but readers should go to these for more complete and contextualised discussions.

[2] New Zealand is another country that has made recent changes to the work requirements for lone parents. Compulsory work-related interviews were introduced in 1997 and in 1999 part-time work tests were introduced for those with a youngest child aged six to 13 (Wilson, M., 2000). Ireland has not made changes to activity conditions for benefit receipt but has opened up labour market programmes to lone parents (McCashin, 1997).

[3] Using the Lødemel and Trickey (2001) definition, "programmes or schemes that require people to work in return for social assistance benefits" (p 6). In their study, which covers six European countries and the US, it is only the US that applies workfare to lone parents. The most common target group for these compulsory work-for-benefits programmes are young unemployed people (or the long-term unemployed).

[4] Here we are considering nursery and primary school together. Those countries that apply activity requirements when children are nursery school age are generally those with well-developed nursery systems, covering a substantial proportion of the age group.

[5] This includes the Departments of Family and Community, of Education, Employment, Training and Youth Affairs, and of Health and Family Services.

[6] This could also have been said of the French 'insertion' approach.

[7] McCashin (1997) also reports that these sorts of gains are found among lone mothers participating in labour market programmes in Ireland.

ELEVEN

Making work pay policies for lone parents

Majella Kilkey and Jonathan Bradshaw

Introduction

The purpose of this chapter is twofold. First, to compare recent developments in making work pay policies for lone parents across the six countries featured in this book. Second, to contextualise those changes by reviewing the international comparative literature on the nature and impact of making work pay policies for lone parents. At one level, making work pay strategies entail the manipulation of the tax/benefit system, in such a way as to widen the differential between in-work and out-of-work incomes in favour of the former. The underlying assumption is, of course, that the higher the potential in-work income is over the out-of-work income, the greater the financial incentive facing lone parents to seek paid work, and in turn, the higher the rate of lone parents' employment (Duncan and Edwards, 1999). The aim of a making work pay strategy, though, may extend beyond ensuring that the differential between in-work and out-of-work incomes is sufficiently large to stimulate lone parents' labour market participation; it may also be concerned with ensuring that in-work incomes per se are sufficiently high so as to protect lone parents from the risk of poverty. In this chapter, we are concerned with making work pay strategies as both a mechanism to increase the rate of lone parents' employment, and as a mechanism for reducing the rate of poverty among lone parents in paid work.

The chapter is divided into five substantive sections. In section one, we collate the information on recent developments in making work pay strategies from each of the national reports, and examine similarities and differences in such strategies across the countries. In order to compare the structure of financial incentives facing lone parents in those countries, it is necessary to draw on comparative data on the tax/benefit package. In section two, therefore, we present data from two sources – the York studies and the Organisation of Economic Co-operation and Development's (OECD's) Benefit Systems and Work Incentives series – on the relationship between the value of in-work and out-of-work incomes for the six countries, as well as other countries. In section three, we draw largely on existing comparative studies to examine the relationship between the structure of financial incentives for lone parents and the employment rate among this group. In section four, we examine the evidence on whether work really does pay to the extent that lone parents are protected from the risk of poverty, also drawing largely on the comparative evidence. A key observation in sections three and four is that there is a good deal of incongruity between the structure of financial incentives facing lone parents, lone parents' employment rates, and their poverty rates. In section five, we explore why this may be the case.

Recent developments in making work pay strategies in the six countries

In general, policy makers have two broad mechanisms at their disposal when designing a making work pay strategy. The one seeks to make work pay by creating a tougher out-of-work benefit regime, while the other seeks to make work pay by creating a financially more generous paid-work environment. In effect, the former is designed to 'push' and the latter to 'pull' lone parents into employment. It is important to note, though, that these mechanisms are not mutually exclusive, and in practice, may be adopted simultaneously.

The push mechanism may have two components:

- restricting lone parents' eligibility for out-of-work benefits – for example, by imposing the obligation to seek work when their children are younger, by imposing time limits on the receipt of benefits, or by imposing sanctions for non-compliance with rules;
- reducing the value of out-of-work benefits – for example, by the abolition of benefits, by direct cuts in the benefit rate, or by indirect cuts via an imposition or increase in taxation or a failure to adequately uprate.

The pull mechanism, meanwhile, may be more varied in form:

- increasing the gross wage rate – for example, via a statutory minimum wage policy;
- reducing the direct tax and social/health insurance contributions burden – for example, by cutting the tax rate or raising the tax threshold;
- increasing the value of in-work benefits;
- increasing the value of disregarded income in the calculation of benefit entitlement;
- decreasing the withdrawal rate of 'portable' income-related/means-tested benefits (for example, social assistance and housing benefit) against earnings;
- increasing the value of childcare assistance, either directly or indirectly;
- improving child support schemes, for example, by guaranteeing payments, increasing compliance or increasing the value of child support;
- introducing one-off back to work bonuses/premiums/advances.

Table 11.1 indicates whether each of the six countries has adopted any of the above policies in recent years (roughly, over the last decade or so). France is the only country that appears to have taken no action on any of the dimensions in the last decade. The last relevant reform was as far back as 1988, when *Allocation de parent isolé* (API) and *Revenu minimum d'insertion* (RMI) first became portable from out of work to in work. In recent years, while various proposals have been mooted, including the integration of API and RMI, and most recently, the introduction of an in-work tax credit *(Prime pour l'emploi)*, nothing has been changed. Indeed, in general, lone parents and their labour supply has not been a policy issue, not least because French lone parents have comparatively high employment rates. While Australia has been somewhat more active than France in recent years in altering the tax and benefit systems in order to make work pay, its efforts have not been significant, and among the changes made, the Child Support scheme has probably been the most important vehicle. In July 2000, however, the Reference Group produced its report on welfare reform, and included were many proposals that would have the effect of increasing incentives to work. At the time of writing, though, none of them has been implemented, although there have been some changes to work requirements.

The other four countries have been much more active, albeit to varying degrees, adopting a dual approach of creating a tougher out-of-work benefit regime, while at the same time introducing positive incentives in favour of paid work. Of the four, developments have been most intensive in the US. The US is the only country both to restrict lone parents' eligibility to out-of-work benefits, and to reduce the value of such benefits. It has also been the second most active country (after the UK) in attempting to improve the financial gains from employment, intervening to increase the gross wage rate, as well as to increase net disposable income. While the UK appears to have been working the most intensively to improve the paid-work environment, it has been the least aggressive in 'pushing' lone parents into paid work. Thus, it is the only country not (at least at the national level) to have taken action to restrict lone parents' eligibility to out-of-work benefits.

Meanwhile the Netherlands and Norway, like the US, have adopted measures which present some lone parents with no choice but to seek paid work. The consequences of restricting non-employed lone parents' eligibility to benefits may differ, though, between Norway on the one hand, and the US and the Netherlands on the other hand. This is the case since, in Norway, lone parents may still have recourse to the benefit of 'last resort' – social assistance – while in the other two, it is eligibility for the benefit of 'last resort' that has been restricted. Compared to both the US and the UK, the Netherlands and Norway demonstrate a rather low level of activity in respect of developing policies to make paid work more attractive to lone parents. Unlike the US and the UK, though, both countries have been concerned with reforming the transitional policy environment. Thus, Norway has decreased the rate at which Transitional Allowance (a portable income-related benefit) is withdrawn against earnings, and the Netherlands has introduced back-to-work premiums.

A key explanation of the difference between the US and the UK on the one hand, and the Netherlands and Norway on the other hand, in the extent of the reforms to make work pay, may be that while the former two countries have adopted an explicit objective to manipulate the tax/benefit system in favour of paid work, the latter two have not. Thus, in the Netherlands, the initiatives to positively support lone parents' employment emerged shortly after the implementation of the *nieuwe Algemene Bijstandswet* (1996) – the legislation which restricted lone parents' right to be exempted from the obligation to seek paid work – apparently in a bid to quell public opposition to that legislation. In respect of Norway, meanwhile, Anne Skevik (in Chapter Five of this book) reports the virtual absence of a concern in the 1998 reforms with financial incentives. Indeed, since Transitional Allowance is both an in-work and an out-of-work benefit, the increase in its rate reported in Table 11.1 cannot be interpreted as an attempt to alter the incentive structure in favour of paid work. Moreover, in 1998 while the rules governing childcare benefit in Norway were also

Table 11.1: Recent developments in making work pay policies[a]

	Push mechanisms		Pull mechanisms							
	1	2	1	2	3	4	5	6	7	8
Australia[b]	x	x	x	x	x	x	✓	x	✓	✓
France	x	x	x	x	x	x	x	x	x	x
Netherlands[c]	✓	x	x	✓	x	✓	x	✓	x	✓
Norway[d]	✓	x	x	x	✓	x	✓	x	x	x
UK[e]	x	✓	✓	✓	✓	✓	x	✓	✓	x
US[f]	✓	✓	✓	✓	✓	✓	x	✓	x	x

Key: Push mechanisms   1 = Restricting eligibility for out-of-work benefits.

                            2 = Reducing the value of out-of-work benefits.

        Pull mechanisms   1 = Increasing the gross wage rate.

                            2 = Decreasing the direct tax/social security contributions burden.

                            3 = Increasing the value of in-work benefits.

                            4 = Increasing the value of disregarded income in calculating benefit entitlement.

                            5 = Decreasing the withdrawal rate of 'portable' income-related/means-tested benefits against earnings.

                            6 = Increasing the value of childcare assistance.

                            7 = Improving child support schemes.

                            8 = Introducing one-off back to work bonuses/premiums/advances.

Notes: [a] We restrict our analysis to the 1990s onwards.

[b] In Australia, changes refer to the period 1990 onwards.

[c] In the Netherlands, changes refer to the period 1996 onwards. It is important to note that there is local discretion in precisely how many of the Dutch reforms are implemented.

[d] In Norway, changes refer to the period 1998 onwards.

[e] In the UK, changes refer to the period 1997 onwards.

[f] In the US, changes refer largely to the period 1990 onwards, although readers should be aware that states have had the opportunity to undertake some of these reforms via 'waivers' since the 1988 Family Support Act. There is also a considerable degree of local discretion in the implementation of many of these reforms.

changed, the rationale was to better 'target' the benefit, rather than to make work pay. The result is that depending on factors such as income and type and cost of childcare used, lone parents may be either financial 'losers' or 'gainers'.

It is worth adding that even in respect of the US and the UK where there is an explicit attempt to make work pay, one should be wary of interpreting all recent developments which might be expected to contribute to that goal in practice as having their origins in such an objective. Thus, for example, the reduction of the value of out-of-work benefits in the UK noted in Table 11.1 refers to the abolition of the Lone Parent Premium in Income Support. This was a reform first proposed by the last Conservative administration (1992-97) in order to abolish the financial advantage that lone parents were believed to have over couples within Income Support scale rates. The proposal was not implemented, however, until the Labour government took office in May 1997. At that stage, the objective of the reform seems to have shifted somewhat: initially, to one of ensuring that the government could meet its manifesto commitment of remaining within the previous administration's spending plans, and subsequently, to one of contributing towards the financing of the emerging 'welfare-to-work' programme for lone parents[1].

Comparative analyses of the value of the tax/benefit package for lone parents in work and out of work

It is difficult to fully compare the nature and impact of making work pay policies for lone parents across these six countries without comparative data on the relationship between the value of the tax/benefit package in work and out of work, and here we must rely on existing comparative analyses. In this section, we draw on two different sources, which have calculated replacement rates for hypothetical or 'model' lone-parent families[2]. The first source is the series of studies coordinated by researchers at the University of York, and in particular, a selection from that series, consisting of Bradshaw et al (1996), Kilkey and Bradshaw (1999) and Bradshaw et al (2000). The second is the OECD's Benefit Systems and Work Incentives series (OECD, 1999). A thorough explication of the methodologies of these sources and an assessment of their strengths and weaknesses are beyond the scope of this chapter, and readers are referred to Eardley (1996) for a full discussion of the York studies, and OECD (1999) for a discussion of its series.

Four limitations, though, are especially pertinent for this analysis, and need to be highlighted. In the first place, the replacement rates derived from both sources are notional or representative, and actual replacement rates are likely to vary around those rates, depending on the actual circumstances of lone-parent families in the countries. Second, due to variations in the assumptions underlying the methodology of each data source, particularly in respect of the model families selected, the elements of the tax/benefit package included, and the treatment of housing and childcare costs, the replacement rates derived are not comparable. Third, due to temporal inconsistencies, neither data source allows us to capture fully the reforms that we are seeking to compare. Finally, with the exception of one of the York studies, the data is static, and we are, therefore, limited in our ability to observe changes in replacement rates over time.

Table 11.2 presents net replacement rates derived from the York studies. They are given for two model lone-parent families: a lone parent with one child aged seven years at half-average earnings, both before and after housing costs; and a lone parent with one pre-school aged child at half-average earnings, before housing costs, but before and after childcare costs. The data are for either 1996 (the European Union [EU] countries) or 1994 (the non-EU countries) and, therefore, refer to the tax/benefit system as it operated prior to the bulk of the reforms in the case of the Netherlands, the UK, Norway and Australia, but after some key reforms in the case of the US.

The data suggests that the group of six countries that this chapter focuses on does not form a distinctive cluster in respect of replacement rates in the broader international context; collectively, they group rather loosely within the range of replacement rates, ranking anywhere between fifth (Norway) and 18th (US) position, depending on the particular model family. Among the six, it is generally in the UK with its comparatively low replacement rates, where lone-parent families face the strongest financial incentive to undertake paid work as opposed to relying fully on social assistance. The one exception is after housing costs for the lone parent with one school-aged child, when as a result of comparatively generous housing assistance in the UK on the one hand, and comparatively poor assistance in the US on the other hand, the incentive to undertake paid work is strongest in the US. The strongest financial disincentive to paid work appears to exist variously in Norway and the US. In the former, replacement rates range from a high of 86% to a low of 73%, and in the US, excluding the after housing costs scenario, they range from 78 to 75%. Incurring childcare costs shifts the structure of incentives in all countries more firmly against paid work. The impact, however, is strongest in France, where replacement rates increase by eight percentage points after childcare costs are taken into account, and weakest in Australia where there is an increase of two percentage points.

Table 11.3 presents net replacement rates derived from the OECD series. They are given for two model lone-parent families and two earnings levels: a lone parent with two children aged six and four, before housing costs, and earning either two thirds average earnings or average earnings; and a lone parent with two pre-school aged children, before housing costs, on average earnings, and before and after childcare costs. The data

Table 11.2: Net replacement rates (Nrrs) derived from 'the York studies' (EU countries, May 1996, non-EU countries, May 1994)

	Lone parent + 1 child aged 7 at half-average earnings[a]		Lone parent + 1 child aged 2 years 11 months at half-average earnings, and before housing costs	
	Before housing costs	After housing costs	Before childcare costs	After childcare costs
	NRR[b] (%)	Rank	NRR[c] (%)	Rank	NRR[d] (%)	Rank	NRR[e, f] (%)	Rank

	NRR[b] (%)	Rank	NRR[c] (%)	Rank	NRR[d] (%)	Rank	NRR[e, f] (%)	Rank
Austria	57	11	46	14	59	11	79	7
Belgium	90	3	84	6	90	2	90	5
Denmark	90	3	91	3	90	2	96	2
Finland	74	7	77	7	73	6	72	12
France	56	13	58	11	57	12	65	14
Germany	73	9	99	2	73	6	78	8
Greece	3	18	-5	16	3	18	70	13
Ireland	51	15	54	13	53	14	54	17
Italy	10	17	9	15	11	17	13	18
Luxembourg	84	5	72	8	83	5	91	4
Netherlands	70	10	65	9	70	10	77	10
Portugal	94	1	90	4	94	1	103	1
Spain	52	14	-31	17	53	14	83	6
Sweden	92	2	128	1	90	2	94	3
UK	46	16	61	10	49	16	56	16
Australia	57	11	57	12	57	12	59	15
Norway	74	7	86	5	73	6	76	11
US	75	6	-91	18	72	9	78	8

Notes:

[a] More precisely, half of the national average male production workers' wages.

[b] Definition of before housing costs replacement rate = $\frac{\text{out-of-work benefit income (A)}}{\text{net disposable in-work income (B)}} \times 100$

where A = social assistance – income tax – social security/health contributions + non-income-related and income-related cash benefits, including advanced child maintenance payments – health costs – school costs. And B = gross earnings – income tax – social security/health contributions + non-income-related and income-related cash benefits, including advanced child maintenance payments – health costs – school costs.

[c] Definition of after housing costs = $\frac{(A)-(C)}{(B)-(C)} \times 100$

where C = housing costs and local taxes – housing benefits.

[d] Definition of before childcare costs = $\frac{(A)}{(B)} \times 100$

[e] Childcare costs are based on the national informants' estimates of the cost for full-time use of the most prevalent form of formal day care available in their respective countries. For details on estimated costs, see Ditch et al (1998, Table 3.11) for the EU countries in 1996, and Bradshaw et al (1996, Table 4.3) for the non-EU countries in 1994.

[f] Definition of after childcare costs = $\frac{(A)}{(B)-(D)} \times 100$

where D = childcare costs – childcare assistance.

Sources: Kilkey and Bradshaw (1999) for 1996 data; Bradshaw et al (1996) for 1994 data

are for 1997, and, therefore, refer to the tax/benefit system as it operated prior to the bulk of the reforms in the case of Norway, Australia and the UK, but after the key reforms in the case of the US and the Netherlands. As with the data derived from the York studies, the OECD data do not suggest that these six countries represent a distinct international grouping in respect of replacement rates. As we might expect, the data indicate that the higher a lone parent's potential earnings rate, the more heavily skewed the structure of financial incentives is in favour of paid work. As with the data in Table 11.2, the OECD data suggest that when a lone parent incurs childcare costs, the balance of financial incentives shifts more strongly in favour of not working. In contrast to the data in Table 11.2, however, that in Table 11.3 indicates that the impact of childcare costs is greatest in Norway, where the replacement rate increases from 74 to 95%. Australia also evinces a substantial increase – from 58 to 70%. The impact of childcare costs is least in the Netherlands, which records only a three-percentage point increase. The rank position of these six countries in respect of replacement rates also differs between the two sources. Thus, it is now in the US, as opposed to the UK, with its comparatively low replacement rates, where lone parents face the strongest financial incentives to enter the labour market. The converse is now found most consistently in the Netherlands, which, with the exception of the childcare case, exhibits the highest replacement rates.

Since the two data sources are not comparable, we do not know whether the differences observed in the replacement rates across the two data sets for the Netherlands and the US (these are the only two countries for which there is temporal consistency between the data and reform of the tax/benefit system) have been caused by the reforms. It may be worth noting, however, that while in the US the variation in replacement rates between the two data sets appears consistent with the objective of making work pay (replacement rates are lower in the later OECD data), this is not the case in the Netherlands. Thus, Dutch replacement rates are higher in the 1997 data set than in the 1996 data set, despite a number of developments designed to offer more support to lone parents in paid work.

It is important to note that there are considerable differences in the replacement rates derived from these two sources. Thus, for example, for the UK the York studies give a replacement rate for one child at average earnings of 46%, whereas the OECD gives a replacement rate of 81% for two children at two thirds average earnings, both before housing costs. Obviously, some of the difference is due to the different income threshold and number of children. We believe, however, that most of the difference is due to the fact that the OECD treats housing subsidies as income in estimating its before housing costs replacement rates, whereas the York studies exclude housing subsidies in their before housing costs replacement rates, but take account of them in their after housing costs replacement rate estimates. We have recalculated the OECD replacement rates excluding housing subsidies from income and this reduces the replacement rates in all countries after net housing costs, but also before housing costs in Denmark, France, Luxembourg, the Netherlands, Spain, Sweden, the UK, Norway and Australia. We were not able to make estimates for some of the other countries. The OECD before housing costs replacement rates excluding housing subsidies from income are shown in brackets in the third column of Table 11.3. They are now closer to the York replacement rates, and, we believe, a better reflection of actual replacement rates.

A recent study by Bradshaw et al (2000) has updated the York data to 1999 for six countries and for one lone-parent family-type in an attempt to capture the most recent developments in the tax/benefit package for lone parents. They also collate data from across the series of York studies in an attempt to analyse changes in the tax/benefit system dynamically. As the authors note, the validity of the dynamic analysis is undermined somewhat by inconsistencies in the methodology across the series, particularly in relation to assumptions about housing costs. As a result, in this analysis we present only the before housing costs data. From our group of six countries, only the UK, Norway and Australia are represented in the study. In Table 11.4 we present the replacement rates derived from that study. The data is for a lone parent with one pre-school aged child and on half-average earnings, and is given before housing after the impact of taxes and benefits, and after the impact of taxes and benefits and childcare costs.

In respect of the UK, we might expect some, although not all, of the recent initiatives to make work pay to be captured in the data for 1999. However, before housing costs and after childcare costs, while replacement rates for this model lone-parent family are lower in 1999 than in 1992 and 1994, they are actually higher in 1999 than in 1996. The explanation for this is that the 1996 results include improvements to Family Credit and the disregard of childcare costs, while the (May) 1999 data includes the abolition of One Parent Benefit and the lone parent premium in Income Support, but not the introduction of Working Families' Tax Credit and the Childcare Tax Credit, which began later in the year. The 1999 data should capture the reforms to Norway's tax/benefit system which

Table 11.3: Net replacement rates (NRRs) derived from the 'OECD Benefit Systems and Work Incentives Series' (all countries, 1997)

	Lone parent + 2 children aged 6 and 4				Lone parent + 2 children aged <5 at average earnings			
	At 66.7% of average earnings[a], before housing costs		At average earnings, before housing costs (and amended OECD rate)		Before childcare costs		After childcare costs	
	NRR[b] (%)	Rank	NRR[c] (%)	Rank	NRR[d] (%)	Rank	NRR[e,f] (%)	Rank
Austria	75	11	70 (na)	2	na	na	na	na
Belgium	85	2	69 (69)	5	na	na	na	na
Denmark	82	6	70 (62)	2	75	3	86	3
Finland	84	3	68 (na)	6	84	1	103	1
France	**60**	**16**	**44 (31)**	**16**	na	na	na	na
Germany	82	6	63 (na)	7	na	na	na	na
Greece	6	19	4 (na)	19	na	na	na	na
Ireland	72	12	61 (61)	10	na	na	na	na
Italy	67	15	51 (51)	14	na	na	na	na
Luxembourg	83	5	58 (53)	13	na	na	na	na
Netherlands	84	3	70 (55)	2	83	2	86	3
Portugal	71	13	51 (51)	14	na	na	na	na
Spain	55	17	41 (39)	17	73	5	77	5
Sweden	100	1	75 (55)	1	na	na	na	na
UK	81	9	63 (38)	7	54	8	61	8
Australia	**69**	**14**	**60 (58)**	**11**	**58**	**7**	**70**	**6**
Japan	81	9	59 (59)	12	63	6	63	7
Norway	82	6	62 (52)	9	74	4	95	2
US	51	18	41 (41)	17	na	na	na	na

Notes: [a] More precisely, 66.7% of the national average male production workers' wages.

[b] Definition of before housing costs = $\frac{\text{out-of-work benefit income (A)}}{\text{net disposable in-work income (B)}} \times 100$

where A = social assistance – income tax – social security/health contributions + family benefits + housing benefits. And B = gross earnings – income tax – social security/health contributions + family benefits + housing benefits.

[c] Amended OECD rate refers to the rate derived following the authors' exclusion of housing subsidies from income in the OECD data (for further details refer to text above).

[d] Definition of before childcare costs = $\frac{(A)}{(B)} \times 100$

[e] Childcare costs are calculated for two children, both in recognised full-time childcare, and for each child are assumed to represent 15% of the gross earnings of an average production worker in each country.

[f] Definition of after childcare costs = $\frac{(A)}{(B)-(C)} \times 100$

where C = childcare costs – childcare assistance.

na = data are not available

Source: OECD (1999, Tables 3.5 and 3.9)

were implemented in 1998. Like the UK, Norway also experienced an increase in replacement rates between 1996 and 1999, but this is as one might expect given that the data are for a lone parent with a child under the age of three. Thus, this lone parent's right to be exempted from the obligation to seek paid work remained intact following the 1998 reforms. Moreover, the subsequent Cash for Childcare initiative, the development of a cash benefit payable to those parents with children under three who do not use state-sponsored childcare, served to increase the out-of-work income for such a lone parent (see Chapter Five of this book). As far as Australia is concerned, the data confirms that there has been very little change in replacement rates over this period.

Comparative analyses of the relationship between replacement rates and employment rates for lone parents

A key purpose of strategies to make work pay in respect of lone parents is to increase the rate of employment among this group. It is difficult to assess fully, however, whether the recent developments in these six countries have succeeded in achieving this. Particularly in the case of Norway and the UK, this is largely because it is still too early. Even with the progress of time, though, establishing a causal relationship between the implementation of initiatives to make work pay and any observed increase

Table 11.4: Net replacement rates (NNRs) over time for a lone parent with one child aged 2 years and 11 months, at half national average male production workers' wages[a]

	After taxes and benefits				After childcare costs			
	1992	1994	1996	1999	1992	1994	1996	1999
Denmark	na	92	90	89	na	100	95	93
Sweden	64	69	91	89	68	75	100	98
UK	47	48	36	41	89	96	55	63
Australia	**56**	**56**	**57**	**58**	**61**	**59**	**61**	**64**
New Zealand	78	74	74	69	95	97	97	92
Norway	72	70	67	84	85	75	72	84

Note: [a] Replacement rates are calculated using the same formulae as in Table 11.2, except that health and educational costs are excluded.

na= data are not available

Source: Bradshaw et al (2000, Table 13)

in the rate of employment among lone parents requires research, which to date appears to have been undertaken only in the US. Thus, there is some evidence from the country reports of Norway, the Netherlands and the UK that the proportion of lone parents in receipt of out-of-work benefits is decreasing and/or that the proportion in employment is increasing in those countries. Only for the US, however, is it reported that the labour market participation rate for lone parents is increasing (by 10 percentage points in the period 1994-99), and that evidence exists to suggest that welfare reform, including initiatives to make work pay, has been responsible for a substantial part of that increase.

The results of previous comparative analyses of the relationship between the structure of financial incentives facing lone parents and their employment rates, suggest that we should be cautious in assuming an association between the two (for example, Whiteford and Bradshaw, 1994; OECD, 1993; Bradshaw et al, 1996; Kilkey and Bradshaw, 1999; Kilkey, 2000). In Figure 11.1, we examine the relationship between employment rates among lone parents (data are for 1996 and are derived from OECD, 1998) and replacement rates for a lone parent with one child aged seven at half-average earnings both before and after housing costs (data is for 1996 and is from Kilkey and Bradshaw, 1999). Due to gaps in both data sources, only three – France, the Netherlands and the UK – of the six

Figure 11.1: Net replacement rates (NRRs) and employment rates in 1996: lone parent with one child aged 7, at half average earnings

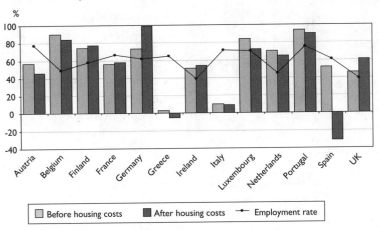

Notes: Employment data are for single adult households with children in 1996.

Sources: NRRs as for Table 11.2; Employment rates (OECD, 1988, Table 1.7)

countries are represented here. These data also point to a good degree of inconsistency between the structure of financial incentives and lone-parents' employment rates. Thus, for example, Greek and Italian lone parents face the strongest financial incentive to undertake paid work (replacement rates are 3 and 5%, and 10 and 9% respectively), but while they have comparatively high rates of employment among lone parents, they do not have the highest. Rather, these are to be found in Austria (77%) and Portugal (75%), which have replacement rates of 57 and 46%, and 94 and 90% respectively, clearly far in excess of those in Greece and Italy.

The data in Figure 11.2 suggests that even when examined dynamically, there is little evidence of a close relationship between changes in replacement rates and changes in lone parents' rates of employment. Thus, among the four countries represented in Figure 11.2, the UK and Norway appear to conform to the expected pattern, both having experienced an increase in the rate of employment among lone parents in the context of

Figure 11.2: Net replacement rates (NRRs) and employment rates over time: lone parent with one child aged 2 years and 11 months, at half average earnings and after childcare costs

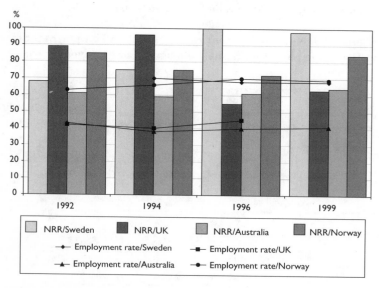

Notes: NRRs as for Table 11.4, after childcare costs.

Source: Bradshaw et al (2000, Tables 8, 13)

falling replacement rates at some point during the 1990s. In Sweden and Australia, however, the pattern is not as expected. Sweden, for example, experienced no change in the rate of lone-parents' employment in the years between 1996 and 1999; a period in which the replacement rate declined. In Australia, meanwhile, during the same time period, lone-parents' employment rate actually increased slightly in the context of an increase in the replacement rate.

Does work really pay?

Increasing the employment rate among lone parents may not be the only goal of making working pay initiatives; they may also be concerned with ensuring that when in employment, lone parents have an income which is sufficient to protect them from the risk of poverty. The country reports reveal that in France neither objective has been of much concern over the last decade, and in Australia during that period, it has been mainly poverty protection that has influenced any changes made. In contrast, an anti-poverty agenda has been less conspicuous in the US and Norway, while both sets of concerns have explicitly motivated the recent policy developments in the UK and the Netherlands[3]. In evaluating recent developments from a poverty reduction perspective, however, there is a high degree of consensus across the country reports of the UK, the Netherlands and the US: in the context of the new tax/benefit regime, lone parents in employment are less likely to be poor (variously defined) than those not in paid work, but a significant proportion of them still experience poverty[4]. Such an evaluation is consistent with the findings of previous comparative research on the poverty reduction capacity of paid work for lone parents (for example, Lewis, 1997b; Bradshaw et al, 1996; Kilkey and Bradshaw, 1999; Kilkey, 2000), and is clearly demonstrated in Table 11.5. The table presents rates of poverty for lone mothers in and out of work derived from the Luxembourg Income Study for the early 1990s, and the poverty rate for children in lone-parent families with no earners and one or more earners from Oxley et al's (2001) study of poverty in selected OECD countries. We see across both data sources that while those with earnings are less likely than those without to experience poverty, in no country does employment provide full protection from the risk of poverty. The rate of poverty among working lone parents and their children, however, varies considerably between countries. It is particularly low in the Nordic countries (where incidentally, the rate of poverty among non-working lone-parent families is also comparatively low), and

Table 11.5: Employment, non-employment and poverty

	% of lone-mother families with income below 50% of median income, early 1990s		% of children in lone-parent families with income below 50% of median income, mid-1990s	
	Lone mother not in paid work	Lone mother in paid work	Lone parent not in paid work	Lone parent in paid work
Austria	58	42	na	na
Belgium	23	3	23	11
Denmark	12	3	34	10
Finland	17	2	10	3
France	**44**	**12**	**45**	**13**
Germany	66	22	62	33
Greece	na	na	37	16
Italy	22	8	79	25
Netherlands	26	3	41	17
Spain	25	17	na	na
Sweden	10	1	24	4
UK	47	9	69	26
Australia	**64**	**20**	**42**	**9**
Norway	17	6	30	5
US	82	35	93	39

Note: na = data are not available

Sources: Columns 1 and 2: data are derived from the Luxembourg Income Study and are published in Kilkey (2000); Columns 2 and 3: Oxley et al (2001)

particularly high in Austria, Germany, the Netherlands, Southern Europe, the UK and the US. Among our six countries, Norway emerges as being the most successful in ensuring that work really does pay.

The data in Table 11.6 suggests that one reason for Norway's relative success in protecting employed lone parents from poverty may be the relatively generous package of social transfers (for example, cash benefits, tax allowances or subsidies for childcare) it gives to those lone parents in paid work. This adds £205 per month in purchasing power parity terms to the earnings from employment of a lone parent in Norway on half-average earnings. In the same vein, the other countries may do less well simply because they give less in the form of social transfers. Indeed, in most countries after childcare costs, the impact of the social transfer package is to reduce net income. Thus, for example, in the UK, the cost of childcare

Table 11.6: Relating the value of the paid work social transfer package to poverty rates

	The social transfer package (after tax, benefits and childcare but before housing costs) paid to a lone parent with 1 child aged <3 and on half-average earnings, 1994		Rank position for poverty rate among lone mothers in paid work, LIS data	Rank position for poverty rate among children in lone-parent families with no earner (Oxley et al, 2001 data)
	Value, ppp£	Rank position	Rank position	Rank position
Austria	−20	4	14	na
Belgium	−120	10	3	6
Denmark	−211	13	3	5
Finland	−93	9	2	1
France	56	3	9	7
Germany	−51	5	12	12
Greece	−58	6	na	8
Italy	−61	7	7	10
Netherlands	−234	14	3	9
Spain	−178	11	10	na
Sweden	−63	8	1	2
UK	−278	15	8	11
Australia	119	2	11	4
Norway	205	1	6	3
US	−183	12	13	13

Note: na = Data are not available

ppp = purchasing power parities

Sources: Column 1: derived from Kilkey (2000); columns 2 and 3: see Table 11.5; column 3: data are derived from the Luxembourg Income Study and are published in Kilkey (2000); column 4: data are derived from Oxley et al (2001)

more than offsets the value of any cash benefits paid to lone parents in employment, resulting in a reduction of income of £278 per month. When viewed within a wider international context, however, there is a far from perfect relationship between the rate of in-work poverty among lone parents and the generosity of the social transfer system. Thus, for example, Denmark, Finland and Sweden all rank much lower in respect of the value of transfers than we would expect given their poverty rates.

Conversely, the relatively generous position of France, Austria and Germany in respect of transfers, is not easy to reconcile with their relatively high rates of poverty.

Placing making work pay strategies in context

The inconsistencies observed in the relationship between the value of the social transfer system and poverty rates, as well as those apparent in the relationship between the structure of financial incentives facing lone parents and their employment rates, are likely to be partly a result of the limitations, alluded to throughout this chapter, in the available data. Thus, despite considerable improvement over the last decade, the techniques for comparing the level and structure of micro welfare state arrangements and economic well-being remain inadequate. Data are also emerging much too slowly to enable us to analyse the most recent policy developments. In this context, the task of relating social policy inputs to outputs and outcomes is a difficult one. The inconsistencies, though, may also have arisen since, as recent developments in most of the countries appear to recognise, making work pay strategies are simply one of the elements that may be required to increase the rate of employment among lone parents and/or their level of economic well-being when in paid work. Changes in the tax/benefit system, therefore, must be analysed alongside the other policy changes observed in the areas of work requirements, labour market programmes, childcare, and family-friendly employment practices.

It may be the case, however, that the social policy environment may be only one, albeit an important one, of the contexts through which opportunities and constraints for lone parents' paid work are structured, and their level of economic well-being determined. The labour market, for example, may be an additional context in which both are structured. The labour market, of course, does not exist in a vacuum, free of the influence of social policies. The structure of the labour market may be influenced at a micro-level by individual policies, such as legislation on sex discrimination, the minimum wage and part-time working, and at a macro-level by the nature of the welfare state itself, for example, whether the provision of care services is collectivised, thereby creating a distinctly female sector of employment. But neither do social policies, and more importantly their outcomes, exist in a vacuum, free of the influence of the labour market. Thus, the effectiveness of policies that might be expected to give lone parents a strong position in the labour market may be undermined if, for example, the lone parents' labour market is characterised by predominantly part-time and low-paid jobs. In introducing and increasing the rate of the minimum wage, the UK and the US respectively have given some consideration to the labour market that they are expecting lone parents to enter. More may, however, need to be done.

It is not simply, though, that there are likely to be other contexts which, in interaction with the social policy sphere, shape lone parents' level of employment and economic well-being. In addition, there are also likely to be factors which mediate the particular impact of those contexts. A particularly important factor may be the characteristics of lone parents in respect of, for example, their route into lone parenthood, their living arrangements, their age, their stage in the childrearing cycle, their number of children, their geographical location, and their ethnicity, especially in respect of its social, economic, political and cultural status. Thus, the degree to which social policies offer resources to lone parents may depend on whether the needs of particular types of lone parents are recognised: for example, policies may attach a higher level of recognition to lone parents with very young children, and offer less support to those with older children. Similarly, geographical location and ethnicity will, for example, structure lone parents' relationship to the labour market. As such, policy needs to become more sensitive to the diversity among the category 'lone parent'.

Conclusion

The purpose of this chapter has been to compare recent developments in making work pay policies for lone parents across six countries, and to contextualise those changes by reviewing the international comparative literature on the nature and impact of making work pay policies. We were concerned with making work pay strategies as both a mechanism to increase the rate of lone parents' employment, and as a mechanism for reducing the rate of poverty among lone parents in paid work. In section one, we examined the similarities and differences in the strategies adopted across the countries to make work pay. We found that while there have been developments in all but France recently which could be interpreted as being part of a making work pay strategy, only in the US and the UK has that objective explicitly motivated the reforms. Not surprisingly, therefore, developments have been more intensive in the US and the UK. The UK, along with Australia and France, however, remain the only countries among these six, not to have restricted lone parents' access to out-of-work benefits.

In order to compare the structure of financial incentives facing lone parents in the countries, we drew on comparative data on the tax/benefit package. Our task, however, was constrained by the lack of sufficiently up to date and dynamic data. The most recent data (for 1999) included only three of our countries – Australia, Norway and the UK, and they suggest that only in Australia are replacement rates similar in 1999 to what they were at the beginning of the decade. In the other two, replacement rates have actually increased in recent years. In the case of Norway, this is in line with the direction of policy reform. In the case of the UK, though, the result is due to the fact that the data refer to a period just a short time before the most significant making work pay initiatives.

Data limitations also constrained our ability to examine the impact of making work pay strategies in respect of employment and poverty rates across the six countries. In relation to employment rates, however, we demonstrated that previous comparative research would suggest the need for a degree of caution when assuming that simply improving the value of in-work incomes relative to those out-of-work will increase lone parents' rate of employment. Similarly, the existing evidence does not suggest that employment per se solves the problem of poverty among lone parents. This indeed, was also supported by evidence in three of the country reports – the UK, the US and the Netherlands – which suggests that while recent developments in making work pay policies seem to have succeeded in lifting some lone parents out of the ranks of the working poor, minorities of employed lone parents remain in poverty. The comparative evidence suggests, moreover, that as with employment rates, the relationship between the value of social transfers and the rate of poverty is not a consistent one. Thus, while there is obviously a need for greater support both to enable lone parents to enter paid work, and to protect them from poverty once there, it would seem that the tax/benefit system should not be the only mechanism for delivering this; rather, a broader package of social policy support, as indeed other chapters in this book indicate some countries are developing, is required, as is action in the other spheres and around the other factors that determine lone parents' resources.

Notes

[1] That the reform, both initially conceived and finally implemented, also entailed the abolition of One Parent Benefit, complicates the interpretation of the reform still further, since One Parent Benefit is effectively an in-work benefit. Furthermore, a subsequent above-inflation uprating of both the Income Support scale rate for a child under 11 years and Child Benefit may have neutralised the financial effect of the reform.

[2] While replacement rates are a widely used tool in comparative research (for example, Bolderson and Mabbett, 1991; Bradshaw et al, 1993, 1996; Eardley et al, 1996; Esping-Andersen, 1990), there are a number of difficulties involved in comparing them across countries. For a full discussion of the issue, readers are referred to Whiteford (1995).

[3] There may, of course, be other objectives underlying developments in the UK and the Netherlands, for example, a desire to reduce expenditure on out-of-work benefits.

[4] From this discussion, we exclude Norway due to a lack of information, and exclude Australia and France since there have not been significant reforms.

TWELVE

Lone mothers, employment and childcare

Hilary Land

A society where being a good parent and a good employee are not in conflict is a prize for us all and one which I believe we can achieve. (Byers Unveils New Approach to Support Working Parents, DTI, Press Release, 7 December 2000)

Stephen Byers, the Secretary of State for Trade and Industry was launching a consultation paper *Work and parents: Competitiveness and choice* (DTI, 2000). He made it very clear that 'parents' includes both fathers *and* mothers. However, it is also clear from reading the paper that any measures to help parents 'to balance work and family life' so that they 'may contribute fully to the competitiveness and productivity of the modern economy' must be based on giving families 'reasonable choices' taking 'the needs of business into account'.

In the past, the 'reasonable' choices facing mothers in the UK were constructed differently. The big increase in economic activity rates, which had occurred among married women in the UK since the Second World War, was almost entirely accounted for by an increase in part-time employment. Very few (5%) of married women had full-time employment while they had a pre-school child. Until 1980, lone mothers irrespective of the age of their child(ren) were *more* likely to be economically active than married mothers in the UK. There was little difference in the level of qualifications of married and lone mothers – neither were well qualified (see Land et al, 2000). Social assistance was there for those without earnings. As the Supplementary Benefit Commission, responsible until 1980 for the means-tested supplementary benefit system (now called Income Support) wrote in their last annual report:

We stress that our support for better working opportunities for lone mothers is not based on the view that they *ought* to be supporting themselves. Many lone parents believe it is better to concentrate their efforts exclusively on the difficult and important task of bringing up children single-handed and they are entitled to do that. Then it is important to raise benefits to a level at which lone parents do not feel compelled to take a job to support their families. Freedom of choice should be the aim. (Supplementary Benefit Commission, 1980, p 12; emphasis in the original)

At this time the UK, along with the Netherlands and Australia, was unusual in allowing lone mothers to remain on benefit until their youngest *left* school (16 years) or in the case of Australia, full-time education. In the other countries discussed in this book, the expectation was that lone mothers would and should return to the labour market when their youngest *started* school, if not earlier. The question of the age of the child at which mothers, whether with or without partners, should return to paid employment has remained controversial.

In the UK by the end of the 1980s the majority of lone mothers were dependent on means-tested benefits. In the context of high levels of public expenditure no longer being politically acceptable, the 'choice' of dependence on state benefits was neither reasonable nor desirable. However, as Jane Lewis discusses in this book, the male breadwinner model was, and is, supported because the presence of an economically dependent wife and child(ren) is believed to be an important stimulus to sustaining male work incentives. It is entirely consistent with this view that attempts were made first to reduce the social security bill by making more absent fathers pay and pay more for their children. Child support systems had been revised in the US and Australia for similar reasons towards the end of the 1980s and the UK studied their systems carefully.

The child support legislation did not solve the 'problem' of rising social security expenditure. Mothers refused to cooperate with the Child Support Agency in naming fathers despite punitive cuts in benefit (for a detailed account of the early years of the Child Support Agency, see Kiernan et al, 1998), so the only other way to reduce the numbers of lone mothers dependent fully on state benefits was to encourage them into the labour market. In 1996 the then Conservative government made it clear that in future lone mothers would be expected to move from welfare to work. This was accompanied by an acknowledgement (but little increased expenditure on services) that lack of childcare was a problem and an announcement that benefits for lone mothers would be cut. It was also argued that lone parents on benefit should not be treated more favourably than couples with children: marriage, not lone parenthood should be favoured. Again the UK looked to the US and Australia for models on which to base their policies. The new Labour government implemented the benefit cuts and vigorously pursued welfare-to-work policies in the form of New Deal programmes for various groups of unemployed claimants, the largest being young people under 25 years of age. However, this was accompanied by a National Childcare Strategy which has resulted in an increased investment in childcare places, the establishment of a minimum wage and a commitment to ending child poverty by supporting poor parents in employment. As Ruth Lister argues in this book, it is clear that the current ideology underpinning the British welfare system is that the social rights embodied in citizenship should in future be acquired by being active in the labour market. In the case of the US, Ann Orloff (Orloff, 1999) has argued that the ending of the Aid to Families with Dependent Children (AFDC) programme and its replacement with the 1996 Personal Responsiblity and Work Opportunity Reconcilliation Act (PRWORA) marked the end of 'maternalism' whereby some women had claims on the state by virtue of their motherhood. This is the direction in which all the countries discussed in this book are going with the growing emphasis on benefits linked only to past or present paid work. However, as Jane Lewis points out in Chapter Eight, there is a crucial distinction between countries which have adopted fully individualised adult-worker models as part of a universal welfare system which recognises care work, as in the case of Scandinavia, and one like the US where subsidies for care are embedded in a residual welfare system and care services are either marketised or have remained within the home.

If lone mothers are to become active citizens in the labour market the experiences of the countries discussed in this book show that there are a number of different ways of addressing the key issues. These concern not only the care of their children but also the ease with which lone mothers are prepared for entry or return to employment. This chapter will explore these issues starting with their education, training and employment experiences prior to becoming a lone mother. The form in which support for childcare takes will be discussed, including access to a free or subsidised service or a cash allowance; the extent to which childcare is seen as a service for all children irrespective of the income, marital or employment status of their parents or only for 'the poor' . This raises the question of whether the main emphasis of the service is on childminding, education or the social, physical and psychological development of the children. The relationship of care services to the school system is important, not only because both systems determine the location, the patterns and availability of care and its cost, which in turn can affect a mother's availability for employment, but also because it may determine the training, level of qualifications and pay of childcare workers, some of whom may be lone mothers. As more mothers with young children become economically active, the demand for formal day care has grown, even in those countries like the UK where dependence on the informal sector has been and remains substantial. Finally, there are the issues concerning the role of employers in providing periods of leave when children are young or ill as well as at the time of birth; the right of return to the same employer and the same position without loss of security, pension rights, and so on, and the right to work shorter hours (DTI, 2000).

The education and employment histories of lone mothers

In the past, discussions of the circumstances of lone mothers have usually examined routes into and out of lone parenthood in terms of their experience of marriage. This is not surprising in countries like the UK with a strong male breadwinner model underpinning tax, social security and wages systems. In his famous report, Beveridge (1942) classified men in terms of their relationship to the labour market and women in terms of their relationship to marriage. Where distinctions were made between different categories of lone mothers, widows have been treated more favourably and entitled to a pension. The widow was the only type of lone mother recognised in the UK's social insurance scheme and following Beveridge's logic, the widow who cohabited or re-married lost her pension but kept it if she took up employment (there was an earnings rule during the 1950s but this was abolished in 1964). In Norway, however, widows were not singled out for special treatment, not least because from the early years of the 20th century the law did not stigmatise the unmarried mother or her children and the basic social insurance system was underpinned by the principles of universality (see Leira, 1993). In France on the other hand, the generous family benefit systems of the post-war years largely ignored all lone mothers, widows included, until the early 1970s (see Lefaucheur and Martin, 1993).

The previous marital history may still be relevant to the standard of living and well-being of the lone mother and her children. If the mother keeps the owner-occupied house, the car and her ex-partner pays child maintenance and shares some childcare, then she will be better off than the never-married lone mother. There is evidence from the US and the UK that non-custodial fathers' involvement in childcare is of growing importance in enabling lone mothers to take up and stay in employment. On current figures only a minority are actually involved in this way. However, it is clear from the data presented in the various chapters in this book that educational and employment histories of lone mothers have a growing impact on their current economic circumstances and their future opportunities. Bradshaw et al (1993) in a study in the early 1990s found that lone mothers were most likely to have post-school qualifications in the US (38%) and Denmark (31%). The UK, Sweden and Australia were in the middle group, with the lowest levels found in France and the Netherlands together with Italy, Spain and Portugal (see Chapter One of this book). However, this sometimes reflected the low level of women's qualifications in general. In the Netherlands there is little difference between lone and married or cohabiting mothers (see Chapter Six of this book), whereas the UK has the largest gap with 21% of lone mothers having post-school qualifications compared with 32% of mothers with partners. This may be because of the few teenage mothers in the Netherlands. It is encouraging to see from Alan Marsh's data (see Chapter Two) that the proportion of lone mothers with *no* qualifications in the UK has declined from 50% in 1989 to nearly 40% in the mid-1990s to 26% in 1999. As Figure 12.1 shows, in the UK there is a very clear correlation between economic activity rates and level of qualification. At degree level not only are economic activity rates high but also there is little to distinguish married from unmarried mothers, or men from women. Marsh draws attention to the lack of marketable qualifications among lone parents, especially those not in employment. "The weaker their attachment to the labour market, the fewer qualifications they have" (see Chapter Two). In his study he found that 16% had never had a paid job and over a third had not been employed for five years. The majority of those who were in employment when they become lone parents were in employment in 1999.

As qualifications are important if lone mothers are to find employment which pays enough to lift them out of poverty, and in the case of the UK, the Netherlands and Norway enables them to work shorter hours while their children are young as mothers with partners choose to do in these countries, then welfare-to-work schemes need to pay attention to the education and training opportunities built into these schemes. Of these

Figure 12.1: Employment by levels of highest education attainment

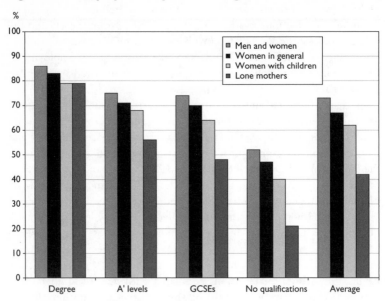

Source: NOMIS database Select Committee on Education and Empoyment (Seventh Report, 1998, para 17)

three countries the UK's New Deal programmes would seem to be the most concerned to get lone mothers into paid employment but with the least amount of support for education and training. In Australia, those lone mothers who had participated in Jobs, Education and Training (JET) programmes had average earnings one third higher than the average for non-participants (see Chapter Four of this book).

The New Deal for Lone Parents (NDLP) introduced in July 1997 was a prototype that built on the previous Conservative government's eight pilot projects, and extended the scheme to all Income Support claimants who were lone parents in 1998. In contrast to the New Deal for Young People (NDYP) there was no option of a year's full-time education and training and only very limited support for those wanting or needing education and training before taking up employment (see Land, 1999 for details). Though lone parents are not expected to participate until their youngest child has reached school age (five years in the UK), *all* benefit claimants of working age, including lone parents and disabled people are *required* to attend an annual interview at a job centre with a personal job adviser. In the first year of the NDLP, only 6% of the 93,690 lone parents who attended an initial interview had taken up education or training opportunities whilst on NDLP (DfEE, 1999). After two years the figure was 9% (DfEE, 2000), less than half the proportion on the NDYP.

The NDLP only supports training up to National Vocational Qualifications (NVQs) level 2 (exceptionally level 3), which is comparable to the standard school leaving qualification at aged 16. Those who wish to gain a higher qualification can study at colleges of further education (FE) while drawing benefit and the fees will be waived. However, childcare support in FE, although better funded than it was, is uneven and there are big differences in levels of provision between urban and rural areas and big cities and smaller towns. It does not meet all lone parents' needs. As a result, those lone mothers who succeed and go into higher education (HE) start in debt (see Callender and Kemp, 2000) and are faced with even more patchy childcare provision. However, the government in September 2001 is introducing a new means-tested childcare grant for mature students in HE, along the lines of the childcare credit in the Working Families' Tax Credit (WFTC) (see below). It is not confined to lone parents because those student parents whose partner has modest earnings and is claiming the WFTC cannot claim the additional childcare credit, which is only available to two *earner* couples. Since the introduction of fees and student loans the proportion of full-time student parents in England and Wales has fallen from 8% in 1995 to 5% (Callender and Kemp, 2000). In the Netherlands and Norway student parents have access to publicly funded childcare and in many municipalities they have priority in the allocation of places. It is interesting to note that although many grandparents in France provide little childcare for lone mothers, they do provide significant financial support to their daughters following divorce (see Olier and Herpin, 1999, p 303). In the UK grandparents are an important source of childcare and assistance in kind. They are less likely to give financial help to their lone-mother daughters even when they are students. Compared with the parents of any other group of students, lone parents are the poorest of all students in England and Wales and have the largest debt (see Callender and Kempson, 1996; Callender and Kemp, 2000).

Childcare provision

Tax relief and credits

Childcare is provided in many different settings and the form, complexity and extent of subsidies from the state vary (see Table 12.1). The tax system may be used to reduce the cost of supporting or paying the carer and this may take the form of a tax relief or allowance (which reduces a taxpayers' taxable income and therefore is worth more to those who pay tax at the higher rates) or a tax credit (which reduces the amount of tax payable which is more equitable across income groups, especially if the credit is paid in cash to those whose tax bill is too low to take full advantage of the credit). Tax relief for paid childcare has been available in the US since the 1970s but could not be used for care provided by relatives. France introduced a form of tax relief for carers employed in the home more recently in 1986, but made it conditional on the carer receiving payment of at least the minimum wage and guaranteed protection of

Table 12.1: Institutional differentiation of childcare and corresponding forms of state subsidy

Institution providing childcare	Paid	Unpaid
Family	Mothers, fathers	Mother
Form of subsidy	Maternity pay	Tax relief to husband
	Paid parental leave[a]	
Household	Au pair girls, nannies, domestic helpers	– –
Form of subsidy	Tax relief	
Social networks	–	Relatives, friends, neighbours
Form of subsidy	–	None
Informal labour market	Grandmothers, un-registered childminders, friends	–
Form of subsidy	Tax relief or credit, allowances associated with welfare-to-work programme	–
State sponsored and private market services	Professional childcare workers, registered child minders	Volunteers
Form of subsidy	Subsidised places[a] both capital and revenue[b], allowance to parent, tax relief or tax credit	None

[a] Employers may contribute to the cost of these forms of care.
[b] Includes places in public and private sector.

Source: This table is developed from Leira (1989, p 45, Figure 2.1)

their pension rights (see Fagnani, 1998; Chapter Seven of this book). The nearest the UK has come to providing tax relief for childcare was the Housekeeper's Allowance for lone parents (initially for widowers) introduced in 1918 and the Additional Personal Allowance (APA) for lone parents and equivalent to the generous Married Couple's Allowance (MCA) since the mid 1970s (for the history of these allowances see Land, 1983). The Housekeeper's Allowance was abolished in 1990 and the APA, together with the MCA, was phased out completely in 2000. No evidence of the use of paid care was needed to claim the APA, but the housekeeper had to be maintained by the taxpayer. In the UK the report of the Millennium Childcare Commission published early in 2001 (an independent body chaired by Harriet Harman, the first New Labour's Secretary of State for Social Security who lost her post following the uproar against the cuts to lone parents' benefits), there are proposals for introducing tax relief for childcare.

There is support for childcare in the various welfare-to-work programmes for without it any compulsion to participate either in the programme or in employment would be impossible. In the US this may take the form of a directly sponsored place or reimbursement of receipted childcare expenses if the carer is a registered or licensed childminder, which may include relatives who meet certain basic standards concerning their premises, lack of criminal conviction, and so on. In Illinois, for example, two thirds of mothers receiving childcare subsidies used informal types of care, with 41% using relatives and 25% using in-home care (see Chapter Three of this book). The Australian scheme also pays subsidies directly to the childcare provider in the formal sector. The UK system is more complex. The childcare tax credit, administered by the Inland Revenue, is not really a credit. It is a cash benefit which currently may be paid directly to the caring parent or via the employer in the earning parent's wage packet. It pays up to 70% (subject to a ceiling) of the cost of formal childcare (nursery, registered childminder or approved out of school scheme). Care provided in the child's own home even if paid (for example, a nanny) is excluded, along with any care provided by a friend, relative or neighbour, irrespective of evidence of payment unless they are a registered childminder. It was announced in the 2001 Budget that inclusion of formal care employed in the child's home was under consideration. In 1998 over half of mothers with a pre-school child relied on a relative (usually a grandmother) or friend to provide care. For those working part time, dependence on informal care was even higher (ONS, 2000; LaValle et al, 2000). In August 2000, about 12% (124,000) of families receiving the WFTC were getting this credit. Nine out of 10 were lone parents (that is, 20% of all lone parents on WFTC), which is not surprising because the majority of couples in receipt of WFTC are dependent only on one earner and therefore do not qualify. (For a couple to claim, *both* must be in employment at least 16 hours a week.) In other words the WFTC is mostly supporting lone parents on the one hand and the single breadwinner family on the other. However, it is important to note that one of the largest categories (10%) of WFTC recipients are in childcare or health occupations (Inland Revenue, 2000, Table 5.2). Childminders are very likely to be eligible for WFTC because unlike in France, Australia or Norway, where they are likely to be employees of the local authority and must be paid at least a minimum wage, they are all self-employed and only a third of the fees they receive are treated by the Inland Revenue as income. They are only allowed to care for three children under eight years of age at a time and on average they charge £100 a week per child (*The Guardian*, 4 February 2001).

Childcare services: their location and coverage

In the US and the UK most of the increase in day nursery places occurred in the private sector (see Figure 12.2 for the UK). The local authority and not-for-profit sector has declined in the UK (see Figure 12.3). In Australia there has been more investment in creating places in the public or not-for-profit sectors. In this respect Australia is more similar to France and Norway. As a result of the National Childcare Strategy in the UK by the end of 2000, 427,000 children were being helped by the provision of new places in nurseries, after-school and holiday schemes. This means there is a place for one in seven children under eight years of age, compared with one in nine when the Labour government came into office in 1997. There are plans to create a total of 1.6 million new places by 2004 including out-of-school hours care for 865,000 children funded in part by national lottery money. Alongside this expansion in day care must be added the expansion of nursery *education* places. At the end of 2000, the Secretary of State for Education and Employment announced there was universal provision for all four-year-olds whose parents want a place (half day) and the government aims to be able to offer all parents of three-year-olds a place if they wish by 2004. Many of these places will not be in nursery schools but in the voluntary sector, playgroups, private nurseries and with a few selected childminders. Many of these locations will be providing

Figure 12.2: Day nursery provided (1990-2000)

Source: DfEE Statistical return 2000 – Daycare

Figure 12.3: Places in day nurseries, with childminders and in playgroups or pre-schools (1990-2000)

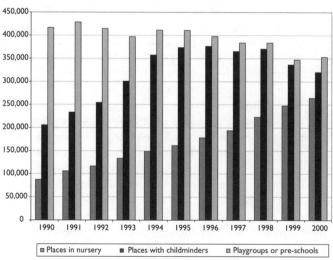

Note: From 1992, figures for childminders are affected by the extension of registration to places for children aged 5-7 years old.
Source: DfEE Statistical return 2000 – Daycare

'wrap-round' care *and* education. The care must be paid for but the education will be free.

The bulk of the increase in state funding for day care in the UK has so far been used to *create* new places. However, "the DfEE expects that virtually all new provision will be sustainable within one to three years through parental fees and employer contributions. However, in some areas of multiple deprivation there may be a need for ongoing subsidy of some types of provision" (Day Care Trust and DfEE, 1999). The Chancellor of the Exchequer in a speech to the National Council for One Parent Families promised that "there should be a childcare place in areas of need for every lone parent entering employment by 2004" (Home Office Press Release, 144/00). Is the government anticipating more compulsion on lone parents to move from welfare-to-work after 2004? There is a proliferation of funds and schemes targeted at poorer areas, and one of the significant features is that local government is not necessarily in the lead in either controlling the money or managing the programmes. This is different from the role of local government in Norway, France and the Netherlands, which has much more discretion and control over funds. In the US and Australia, policies at the level of the state are key determinants of the level and type of provision available in each state.

The geographical distribution of childcare places, as well as the type of provision available, is an important issue in other ways. Nursery provision is found more often in big cities, and childminders in rural areas and small towns (see Fagnani, 1998; DfEE, 2000). Different strategies have been adopted to reduce the impact of these inequalities. One of the arguments for introducing the childcare allowance in Norway in 1998 was to compensate parents who did not have access to publicly funded day care in their locality. However, the allowance itself has attracted criticism on the grounds that more affluent parents will use the allowance to subsidise private care in the home and the principle of state payments being made for *not* using a public service seems strange (Leira, 1998a). Waerness, however, argues that middle-class Norwegian mothers are very committed to approved state day care services while working-class mothers will prefer to use the allowance to stay at home themselves (Waerness, 1998). The allowance is unlikely therefore to undermine public provision. In the case of France, where part-time employment among mothers is less common, Fagnani argues that increased support for private family-based childcare arrangements "are increasingly preferred: largely because they are more convenient for active, dual-earner couples with very demanding jobs" (Fagnani, 1998, p 149). This may threaten the viability of publicly provided institutional care, which depends in part on the full fees that the more affluent parents can afford to pay, although so far their commitment to the educational and social values of collective care seems to be constraining the withdrawal of their children from these services. In the UK, although informal care or care in the child's home attracts no direct financial support it is still widely used, not only because there is no alternative for many parents but because it is a positive choice. With no tradition of collective day care in the UK, only a minority of parents have either experienced such care as a child or have used it for their own children.

A recent national study in the UK found that three quarters of parents who worked or studied outside the home said their current childcare arrangements were not ideal and the figure for poorer households and lone parents was even higher (La Valle et al, 2000). In 'an ideal world' of affordable and accessible childcare nearly one in five parents said they would prefer to work only when their children were in school and *most* would prefer an informal carer, that is a relative or friend. There was also evidence from this study that there was more dissatisfaction with the quality of childcare for four- to 11-year-olds than for pre-school children (primary school children typically have six hour school days including lunch breaks and so on). However, the educational and social aspects of nursery and after-school care was valued.

The objectives and quality of childcare

All of the countries studied in this book are developing welfare policies, include childcare provision, to promote and support lone mothers in making the transition into employment and then sustaining them in that employment. An important part of the context in which these policies are developed are the general attitudes towards mothers with young children being in employment at all. Another is the attitudes of lone mothers themselves. From the evidence in this book it is clear and unsurprising that lone mothers tend to share the prevailing attitudes towards mothers' employment in general. Lone mothers compare their experiences of motherhood and employment both with other mothers and with their own experiences before they became a lone parent, although Kilkey and Bradshaw warn against assuming that the attitudes of lone mothers towards employment are determined in a simple way (Chapter Eleven of this book). In the US and France there is no doubt that welfare policies are promoting the model of the employed mother and this model assumes that full-time employment is the 'reasonable choice'. In the case of the US this should commence when the child is a few months old, but in France as well as in Sweden there is support for mothers to stay at home until the child is three years old if the mother has more than one child. It is interesting to note that when in France mothers with two children rather than three or more became eligible for the *Allocation parentale d'education* (APE) in 1994, employment rates among lone mothers with two children and the youngest under three years fell from 69% in 1994 to 53% in 1997 (Fagnani, 1998, p 62; Chapter Seven of this book). Three years old is a key age in Norway and France and is becoming one in the UK (see above) with respect to access to subsidised early years provision.

In Norway, the Netherlands, Australia and the UK the model of the mother with young children being in full-time employment is not well established. This is particularly so in the case of the mother with pre-school children. There is evidence from attitude surveys in the UK and in the Netherlands (see Chapter Six of this book) that there is no clear consensus. The preferred pattern, particularly in the UK and the Netherlands, is one that combines shorter hours of employment with responsibilities for young children. The most recent evidence from the new WFTC in the UK, eligibility for which is a minimum of 16 hours employment, but with a premium for those employed at least 30 hours, shows that the majority (60%) of the half million lone mothers claiming it are employed for less than 30 hours (the average is 26 hours). This is also the case for female-headed couple households (perhaps because in addition to some childcare responsibilities the mother has some caring responsibilities for a sick or disabled partner). In contrast, over 80% of the traditional male breadwinners as well as three quarters of lone fathers, were employed more than 30 hours a week (Inland Revenue, 2000, Table 6.2).

Childcare work and workers

Historically day care services in the public sector have been developed to meet a number of different objectives. The origins of some have been closely allied to health and welfare provision and emphasis placed on minding and keeping safe. Such services have included children of lone mothers who needed to work or whose parents or environment have been judged inadequate or even dangerous in some way. Other services have developed in conjunction with the main education system and have therefore included objectives concerning the children's social, psychological and educational development. The dominant theories and philosophies of child development underpinning the various day care services were and still are different (see Penn, 2000 for example). One clear trend in many countries in recent years has been an increased emphasis on the educational aspects of childcare. In 1998 responsibility for day care shifted to the Ministry of Education from the Ministry of Health and Social Affairs in Sweden. A similar shift has occurred in the UK and from September 2001 the inspectorate of the Department for Education and Employment will be responsible for all pre-school and early years provision including childminders. In France, during the early 1980s more emphasis was placed on the psychological and social development of children.

> The term '*garde*' (keep) was gradually replaced by '*accueil*' (welcome) in childcare vocabulary because the latter corresponds to the idea of '*eveil*' (psychological and physical development) and education of young children. (Martin et al, 1998, p 144)

However, over the same period, as unemployment, and in the UK, US and Australia, child poverty, became more pressing, the development and expansion of day care was caught up with other priorities. In France during the 1990s employment policies were given priority over early childhood policies. "These must be placed in a context where all social policies notably family policy are now overshadowed by employment policy considerations" (Martin et al, 1998, p 148). In the UK, US and Australia emphasis on welfare-to-work programmes for lone mothers has stimulated an expansion of day care provision with varying levels of public or professional control over the quality of services on offer, depending in part on where the expansion has been located – in the informal sector, the private market or the public sector. At the same time the growth of the service sector in all the countries in this book and particularly the flow of educated mothers into the health, welfare and other professions located in the public and private sectors, has also increased the demand for day care in the home and in early years services. In their analysis of the interface between family policy measures and women's labour market patterns in five European Union (EU) countries, including France and the UK, which they acknowledge "is extremely complex and difficult to interpret", Almquist and Boje conclude:

> Provision of child care by the welfare state thus increases the rate of female employment in two ways. Firstly, women get employment by

caring for the children within institutions or as a family day carer, and secondly those families who have their children cared for in institutions or by family day carers are free to take up regular employment. (Almquist and Boje, 1999, p 286)

Lone mothers on welfare are potential childcare workers. The level of qualifications and training necessary to take up employment in the expanding childcare sector as well as the level of pay on offer is therefore very important, not only in terms of the quality of service being provided to the children but in terms of the well-being of the workers themselves. In the US most formal day care services are found in the private market where training and pay levels are very low. In the UK nursery teachers are trained for four years post-18 to postgraduate level. Nursery nurses and nannies take two year vocational training, starting at age 16, which is equivalent to NVQ level 3. Childminders are not required to train but mainly at the instigation of the National Child Minders Association there is now a course at level 3 which new childminders are now recommended to take. (However, it is not interchangeable with, or a substitute for, any other qualification.) Nursery teachers are paid twice as much as nursery nurses who in turn are paid twice as much as untrained day care workers who are found in the bottom 10% of the earnings distribution. Minimum wage legislation has helped to lift their pay (prior to the legislation half of all childcare workers were earning less than half the minimum wage, Select Committee on Education and Employment, 2000, para 27), but many private nurseries employ young women in their late teens and early twenties who until they are 22 are only entitled to 85% of the minimum wage. The majority of day care workers are currently untrained and the government is aiming to provide training to NVQ level 2. A quarter of the expansion in day care places between 2001 and 2004 is expected to come from an increase in childminders. The shift towards greater emphasis on the educational aspects of childcare might have been expected to increase the professionalisation of day care. However, pressures arising from employment patterns associated with the 'flexible' labour market together with the political belief that public expenditure must be constrained if not cut, has meant that family-based care is being favoured over institutional childcare, even in a country like France where the public commitment to collective day care with qualified staff has been much more firmly established and for longer than in any of the countries included in this book (see Fagnani, 1998; Martin et al, 1998, p 154-5).

Combining employment and parenthood

One of the most important issues for all mothers is the length of their working day and week. In the UK and US there is no discussion of, or active policies for, reducing the working week as there is in France (to 35 hours for all) or in the Netherlands (to 32 hours for parents). The UK has the highest average weekly hours for full-time employees in the EU (see Table 12.2). The 'long hours' culture in the UK means, as in the US, that hours of employment have been increasing over the past 20 years, reversing the trend towards shorter hours over the previous three decades (see Table 12.3). This, together with the need for both parents to take paid work, albeit often part-time for the mother, means that families in the UK and US are having to work longer hours to earn 'a family wage'. That puts lone parents, particularly if they have few or no qualifications, at a very real disadvantage, unless the benefit system can make up the difference. In this respect the WFTC, which replaces the less generous Family Credit, is an important development in the UK, as are the tax credit schemes in the US. Over half of the WFTC recipients are lone parents as discussed above and in the US they are 70% of Earned Income Tax Credit (EITC) recipients (see Chapter Three of this book).

Table 12.2: Average hours usually worked per week by full-time employees (1998)

	Male	Female
UK	45.7	40.7
France	40.3	38.7
Netherlands	39.2	38.5

Source: ONS (2000, p 74)

Table 12.3: The average length of the working day in 1982 and 1992 (Britain)

	Full-time workers		Part-time workers	
Hours spent work and travel	Male	Female	Male	Female
1982	45.3	40.7	20.7	22.4
1995	53	48	28	26

Source: CSO (1982, p 147) and CSO (1995, p 216)

In Australia both lone and partnered fathers work longer hours than mothers and those working full-time work longer hours than the average employee (Chapter Four of this book, Table 4.3). Fathers, and increasingly mothers, are working longer hours when they have young children in the UK. Frequent shift changes and the obligation to work overtime, often with short notice, bear hard on parents. Flexible employment is desired by many mothers, with or without partners, but on their own not their employers' terms (for example, see DTI, 2000). As a result of the EU Part-Time Working Directives, the rights of part-time employees have been considerably strengthened. This is not the case in the US. Shift work accounts for a significant proportion of those working evenings and nights in the UK. Both in the US and the UK women with young children are much more likely to work unsociable hours than those without. Those with partners rely on them to care for their children but lone mothers have to rely heavily on relatives and friends because formal day care is not available. In any case many would not wish to leave their children at these times with anyone other than relatives or friends (see La Valle at al, 2000).

The combination of employment and the care of young children can be made easier if parents can take leave in connection with their caring responsibilities starting with maternity leave around the time of birth and parental leave while the child(ren) are young or during periods of sickness or disability. Maternity and parental leave are now rights in EU countries, but there are big variations both in the length of leave and the level at which it is paid, if at all. In Australia and the US there is only a right to unpaid leave (see Table 12.4). In the UK, US and Australia neither mothers nor fathers have a right to return to work part-time after a period of maternity or parental leave. This contrasts with the Scandinavian countries where at any point of time there is a significant proportion of mothers 'on leave' from employment. For example, if such mothers of pre-school children are excluded from those counted as economically active, their economic activity rates for 1995 falls from 73 to 61% (Nyberg, 2001, p 3, Table 1).

For lone parents whose own health is poor or who have children with health problems it is even more important that they have rights to leave not just when the children are very young, as well as rights to work shorter hours. As Alan Marsh's study shows, the incidence of ill health and disability among lone parents *and* their children in the UK is high, and some of this may be accounted for by the experience of long-term poverty and the consequences of domestic violence in an earlier

Table 12.4: Parental leave by country

Country	Paid	Amount	Duration	Who can take it?	Right to reduced hours
France	From the second child	Flat rate paid by state	Until younger child is 3 years, 4 years if child is ill or disabled	Both parents	Can be used to work half-time
Netherlands	–	–	6 months until child is 8	Both parents	Can reduce working hours for up to six months until child is 8 years
Norway	Yes	Proportion of earnings (40% for 42 weeks or 80% for 52 weeks)	52 weeks – 4 weeks must be taken by father, 3 weeks before parturition and 6 weeks immediately after must be taken by the mother	Both parents	Can use some parental leave to reduce working hours until child is in school (aged 6)
UK	No	–	12 weeks in total until child is 5 years	Both parents	No entitlement to reduce hours
		100% earnings for 6 weeks, flat rate for 12 weeks (from 2003 paid for 26 weeks)	Maternity leave 40 weeks	Mother only	

Notes: Australia: no universal entitlement to paid parental leave. Unpaid leave can be taken by one parent or shared. US: no universal entitlement to paid parental leave. Right to 12 weeks' unpaid leave for medical or family reasons.

Source: DTI (2000); Olier and Herpin (1999)

relationship (see Chapter Two of this book). Neither welfare-to-work programmes or employers have taken their needs fully into account, and in this respect it is encouraging that it was announced in the 2001 Budget that the childcare needs of families with child(ren) with health problems is to be considered.

The location of employment in relation to home is also important. In the UK the decline in social housing over the past 20 years as local authorities sold off their better housing stock, has meant that those who rely on social housing have great difficulty *choosing* to live near employment or near family and friends. Lone parents in the UK and the US are heavily dependent on social housing. This coupled with inadequate and expensive transport puts many jobs literally out of reach. Journey times are now considerably longer and when added to the longer hours of work mean that both full- and part-time workers are spending more time away from home. Indeed for full-time workers it is adding the equivalent of an extra day each week.

The location of school in relation to home and the need to escort children to school, places considerable constraints on the timing and location of the lone mother's employment. Countries which place a higher priority on safe and inexpensive travel for young and old make the daily lives of all parents and children easier. Meanwhile some only manage by running a car and it is interesting to note that a study of US welfare reforms in 1999 found that excluding the value of a vehicle from asset limits was one of eight measures which increased the employment rate of lone mothers (see Chapter Three of this book).

The care of children goes far beyond the provision of nurseries, after-school clubs, holiday play schemes and professionally trained childminders, nursery and play workers. The acknowledgement of the needs of children when planning housing, transport and the location of schools and community services (including day care) is also required. The United Nations convention on the Rights of the Child requires all countries that have ratified the convention to take children's needs into account in these areas of policy, as well as in the provision of services and benefits directly affecting the welfare of children and their families. Norway was one of the first countries to develop the machinery of government which makes this both possible and necessary.

Conclusion

Despite the growing trend of mothers to take up paid employment when their children are young and the increased provision of formal childcare in all the countries included in this book, the 'reasonable choices' are framed differently both by and for lone mothers and are much harder in some countries than others. Where the world of employment takes account of children, at least by giving all mothers (and fathers) the right to paid leave and shorter hours of work, supported by the social security system, it is easier for lone mothers to contemplate moving from welfare to work. The 'right to time to care' (Knijn and Kremer, 1997) is a key issue in the reconceptualisation of the meaning of social citizenship in the context of restructured welfare states in which all citizens are expected to be active in the labour market. Another key question is how far children and their care are seen to be the private responsibility of parents or one shared with the wider society. At one extreme is the UK where the government is currently refusing to ban registered childminders from smacking the children in their charge on the grounds that a failure to leave the decision to parents "would be a denial of parents' rights" (House of Commons Oral Answers, 11 January 2001, col 1233). The education of children has been accepted as a public responsibility, but the care of children and *their* rights as future citizens are still less firmly established in public policies in some countries than in others. The question "in what ways can care be transformed from being a private virtue into becoming a public concern?" (Leira, 1989, p 43) remains.

THIRTEEN

Supporting employment: emerging policy and practice

Karen Rowlingson and Jane Millar

Governments in most developed countries have recently been grappling with the question of how to increase the proportion of lone parents in paid work. This book has focused on six countries in detail and has also considered some of the broader thematic issues underlying policy in this field. This chapter highlights some of the key issues to emerge from the experience of other countries and explores some of the wider issues that are raised by this comparative cross-national analysis of this subject.

Policy lessons from other countries

In comparison with most other developed countries, the UK has a low rate of employment among lone parents. Policy makers want to know how this can be increased. At the same time, however, policy makers are also trying to eradicate child poverty. Children in lone-parent families are at a high risk of poverty in the UK, and stay poor for long periods. But these two policy goals are not necessarily both served by the same policy measures and indeed may sometimes be in conflict with each other. The example of the US shows clearly that increased employment is no guarantee for escaping poverty. And so the real question is how to increase employment rates for lone parents while also eradicating child poverty.

Potentially there is a lot we might learn from other countries as most developed countries are also trying to encourage lone parents to take up and stay in paid work. They are approaching this in various different ways, with different levels of effort, and targeting different types of lone parent. In some cases, they are not targeting lone parents at all, but trying to encourage all those of working age who are currently 'economically inactive' to engage with the labour market.

Different ways of increasing employment participation

The different ways in which countries attempt to increase employment rates among lone parents were analysed here under three main headings:

- making work possible through activation policies;
- making work pay through financial support for employment;
- making work feasible through support for childcare and parental leave.

Policies that aim to make work possible are often referred to as 'activation' policies but this word can mean many different things. Activation policies can aim to merely inform and advise lone parents of work (a key feature of UK activation policies), or to offer education and training at a basic level (a key feature of the Australian model), or to increase social skills and self-confidence (a key feature of the Norwegian model). These different approaches can be tailored to different types of lone parent or to different stages in the movement from 'inactivity' to employment. Those who have been out of the labour market for some time might need help with self-confidence before receiving advice and information and then education or training. Others might only need information. Those with limited skills might need further education or training. Activation includes both work preparation activities and job seeking activities, or some combination of the two. It may also include 'workfare' approaches that require participation in work.

Making work pay policies aim to make lone parents (and other benefit recipients) better off in paid work than if they were solely in receipt of benefits. These measures can include both 'sticks' (keeping out-of-work benefits low) and 'carrots' (increasing the financial return from employment). In most of the countries discussed throughout this book there has been an increasing emphasis on the latter. Again these can include a range of different policies, including direct wage regulation, wage subsidies, tax and national insurance rebates or holidays, and tax credits. They can also include benefits that are not necessarily conceptualised as primarily make work pay measures, such as generous family allowances. They can include provisions to offset the costs of working – childcare credits or allowances for travel costs, and so on. They can be paid in different ways and over different time periods.

There is thus much variation in practice, but an important common element of these policies is that they reflect a movement away from a simple model that contrasts benefits/dependency on the one hand with wages/independence on the other. Instead of seeking to move lone parents completely off benefits, current policy in many countries increasingly emphasises the goal of helping lone parents to combine (part-time) work and (supplementary) state support, through one or more of the sort of 'make work pay' measures listed above. There is therefore no longer such a sharp dichotomy between lone parents who are mothers and lone parents who are workers; lone parents are increasingly both mothers *and* workers. There is, however, a wide range of cross-national variation in the extent to which wages are being supplemented by additional direct state support. The data are somewhat limited on this and so it is difficult to make exact comparisons. Norway seems to have a high proportion of those employed receiving benefit support, and this may be a key factor in the lower levels of in-work poverty found there. In the Netherlands there seems to be less chance to combine wages with other financial support and this makes part-time work difficult in practice. In the US the Earned Income Tax Credit (EITC) and the Food Stamp programme provide supplements to wages in theory but there can be take-up problems in practice. In France, lone parents receive about a quarter of their income from benefits, this includes non-working lone parents but, as we have seen, these are in the minority in France. In Australia and the UK, employed lone parents divide more or less equally between those combining work and benefits and those relying mainly upon earnings.

These sort of making work pay polices are very much focused on the immediate needs of lone parents in the labour market. However, training and education policies can also be seen as a form of longer-term make work pay measures. The goal of these measures is to increase the earnings potential of lone parents, so that they can earn higher wages and have less need of wage supplementation. Such an approach may also reduce the danger that ongoing wage supplementation over long periods simply depresses wages and creates an in-work poverty trap for lone parents. The extent to which different countries invest in education and training for lone parents also varies quite widely and it seems that training is more often seen as part of activation (getting lone parents into work) than as part of making work pay (getting lone parents into better jobs). The focus thus tends to be on low level, basic qualifications rather than on higher, more skilled work.

The third leg of policy to support employment involves measures to reconcile work and care, or paid work and unpaid work. Lone parents can be given help to make them active and can be given financial help to make work pay, but if they cannot find suitable childcare then work will not be feasible. The childcare issue is not simply one of affordability. If it were, then generous support through benefits, tax credits or direct subsidies would be enough. It is also an issue of availability, suitability and flexibility. In the UK, financial support for childcare through the Working Families' Tax Credit (WFTC) has increased substantially in recent years but lone parents (along with other mothers) seem reluctant to use the formal sources of childcare that qualify for such support. Lack of availability is part of the picture but it also seems that mothers prefer to use close relatives rather than engage in buying care from a more formal source. This is probably partly because close relatives can be more flexible in terms of hours and so on, but there also seems to be some reluctance to turn 'care' into a commodity, by buying it. Formal day care appears to be seen more positively in some countries, such as Norway, where it is seen as a positive social and educational experience for children. In the US, formal day care has become essential for many parents even though the quality appears to be highly variable.

The relative importance and relative success of these three different types of measures is obviously of interest to policy makers. But disentangling them is very difficult, if not impossible, and weighing these measures up against factors such as the state of the economy and labour market demand complicates the picture still further. Most countries are combining these various measures, to a greater or lesser degree. And this may be essential in seeking to achieve the dual goals of increased employment and reduced poverty. Combinations of different measures provide the most powerful and the most flexible package, with the total effect greater than the sum of the parts.

Different levels of effort

The different degrees to which countries are tackling the goal of increased employment can be seen in two ways: the degree of compulsion which is attached to labour market programmes and the amount of money being spent on policies in this field (for example, on training programmes, childcare services, and so on).

Compulsion is a complex and emotive topic. In the UK, it has been almost taboo to consider compelling lone parents to become more active in the labour market. But compulsion can be applied in a number of different areas and in a number of different ways. In the US, lone parents are compelled to be economically active to qualify for benefits. The sanctions applied to non-compliance are severe and include no benefit paid at all. In the UK, lone parents will soon be compelled to attend an interview about work but they will not be compelled to seek work or take work. The sanction against non-compliance to attend interviews in the UK comes into effect after three failures to respond and consists of a benefit reduction. The extent to which compulsion is actually applied in practice is also variable. Street-level bureaucrats sometimes have discretion over who is to be compelled, and what they are compelled to do. This is clear in the example of the Netherlands where large proportions of lone parents have been exempted from work requirements.

This all leads to the central importance of implementation. Policies that look good on paper may be unsuccessful in practice. Once again, the Netherlands is a good example of how discretion at the local level can undermine national level policy goals. But this example is not only a reflection of the importance of discretion, but also a reflection of the importance of aligning policy to socio-cultural views – of the general public, of lone parents and of street-level bureaucrats. If policy is out of tune with one or more of these groups, it is much less likely to be successful.

The 'stick' of compulsion may be accompanied by the 'carrot' of extra resources. In Norway, for example, lone parents have recently been expected to become economically active far earlier (in terms of the age of their children) than they were before. In return for this, lone parents with children under the age of three are given more generous benefits and lone parents with children over three are given more services and financial support to take paid work. Similarly in France, lone parents with pre-school age children are given generous support to stay at home, but those with children above this age are expected to be in employment. It is as if there is a deal between the government and the people that both sides have signed up to and which both accept as fair. In the US, a stricter workfare regime has been accompanied by increased spending in other areas and, although we have not examined the costs of these programmes in detail, it is clear that welfare-to-work policies are not a cheap option. Paying people to stay full time on benefits is often less costly than providing adequate hours of good quality childcare and supplementing wages. Education and training is also an expensive option, with high short-term costs that may not be recouped for some years.

Targeting different types of lone parent

These different policy tools are applied with different levels of compulsion/ support in different countries. They are also applied to different types of lone parent. The main way that this is achieved is by focusing on the age of the lone parent's youngest child. Many states in the US expect economic activity from lone parents when their youngest child is a matter of months old. Other countries tend to cluster around the age at which children go to school or nursery. Even following the introduction of compulsory work-focused interviews, the UK is at the other end of the spectrum from the US, since the UK has no requirement for lone parents to seek work before their youngest child leaves full-time secondary education. The age of the youngest child is one means of separating lone parents into groups with different activity requirements but it is not necessarily the only way of doing this. France and Norway have duration-linked rules so that when women separate from a partner they have some entitlement to benefit even if their children are school age. Marital status may also be used to determine activity requirements, with different expectations applied to widows, who are in many countries entitled to national insurance benefit support where earnings rules are often more generous than in social assistance.

Broader issues

So far, this chapter has reviewed some of the more specific measures in terms of the types of approach being used in different countries. We now turn to a consideration of some of the broader issues that need to be taken into account by policy makers when developing policies in this field.

The first issue here has already been mentioned: the role of socio-cultural views. Policies will not succeed in increasing employment rates if various constituencies within nations do not share the same policy goals. For example, if lone parents are adamant that their main role is to care for their children, then they will not cooperate fully with policies that threaten this role. If officials who implement policies similarly believe that lone parents should be looking after their children rather than working, policies have even less chance of succeeding. This is the clear lesson of the Netherlands. The US has a strong work ethic culture and mothers are generally expected to work. This is partly why policies in the US appear to have been relatively successful – they go with the grain of expectations. Norway also has a strong gender-neutral work ethic culture and so the increasing work requirements for lone parents do not generally seem to have been controversial. In France employment for lone parents is not even a policy issue and there is no debate over whether or not employment should be the norm. The UK has a more gendered work ethic culture, with the male breadwinner/female housewife model only slowly breaking down. Policies that challenge this culture too strongly will find it difficult to achieve results.

Cultural norms and individual identities are linked to prevailing conceptions of citizenship. During the 1950s, when a breadwinner/housewife model broadly reflected people's expectations, aspirations and actual behaviour, responsible citizens were expected to engage with the labour market (if they were men) and stay at home when they had children to care for (if they were women). Today, expectations, aspirations and behaviour have all changed, particularly among women. Reflecting this, policy attention and citizenship rights increasingly focus on the formal, public sphere of the labour market rather than the informal, private sphere of care in the home. Little attention is paid to unpaid care work and yet it is essential for the well-being of millions of children and adults who need care. Notions of citizenship are increasingly tied to the obligation to work but the obligation to care also needs to be considered. The strong focus on paid work as citizenship makes it more difficult to recognise, value and support care work.

So far in this chapter it has almost been taken for granted that UK policy should be aimed at encouraging lone parents to take up paid work. But is this the case? The evidence suggests that lone parents in paid work in the UK experience less financial hardship than those not in paid work. Nor is there any hard evidence to show that children suffer if their mothers work. Lone mothers value paid work not just for income but also because it brings them into contact with other people and wider society. So employment could help lone parents improve their living standards and their social integration. But this is a complex area. As argued above, paid work is no guarantee of avoiding poverty and some children might, at some points, need more attention and care than can be provided by a working lone parent. The time costs of combining paid work and care can be very high. A balance is needed. Until very recently, lone parents in the UK were given very little support or encouragement to return to work. Arguably more is needed and current policies intended to help lone parents into paid work can be seen as redressing this. But we should be careful about expecting more of lone mothers than of married mothers – not least because any one woman might move in and out of these two groups. A general expectation of employment also means that lone parents are no longer in the position of determining what they feel is in the best interests of their children. A blanket decision that paid work is always the best option may therefore not be the answer. Furthermore, our knowledge about the nature and impact of employment on the welfare of lone parents and their children is very limited. We do not know much about how people cope, whether they are better off, whether they are able to hold onto jobs and improve their situation over time. Much of the evidence we do have shows that maintaining employment can be difficult and many employed lone parents are struggling financially. So it is still something of a leap of faith to promote employment-based policies for UK lone parents, if we are also concerned about their living standards and quality of life.

Another broad issue is the nature of labour demand. Most policies to increase the employment rates of lone parents concentrate on supply-side measures. They focus on the individual lone parent rather than consider the level and geography of demand for labour. However, lone parents tend to be concentrated in areas of low-labour demand and this makes it difficult for them to find paid work. Policies that aim to stimulate demand in particular areas would help increase participation rates. The relative success of US policies in increasing employment rates among lone parents has partly been seen as a result of the booming economy in the late 1990s. As the prospect of economic recession looms ever closer it will be interesting to see how employment rates are affected. But perhaps the word 'interest' is far too detached – there will be much concern for the fate of families of lone parents who lose their paid jobs.

So far, this book has focused on the lone parent herself. But policy in the UK at least has also been driven by an increasing focus on children. What is best for children? We know little about this because until recently there has been very little research about, and with, children. We need to know more from lone parents, and direct from children themselves, about the experience of living in a working lone-parent family as opposed to a non-working lone-parent family. How do children feel about their mothers working? Do they see the benefits in terms of increased resources and status? Are they proud of their mothers and do they wish to emulate them? Or do they feel they see too little of their mothers and wish they had more time with them? And how do working lone parents feel about employment?

One last group to consider is the non-resident father. Non-resident fathers can, in theory, play a very constructive role in the lives of lone parents and their children. Governments have generally concentrated on their role in relation to financial child support but fathers can also provide other care and support. This can be beneficial to both mothers and their children. In particular, it could help mothers to get and stay in paid work. How can policies be developed to encourage and enable good fathering? Such policies would be important in their own right as well as, perhaps, increasing employment rates of lone parents.

Finally, as we pointed out in the Introduction, these changes in policy and practice have been, and are, directly affecting the lives of millions of women and children across many countries. Lone parents and their children have generally not been well served by public policy. In most countries they are among the poorest families and few countries have been willing to set state benefits high enough to keep lone parents out of poverty. Paid employment may prove to be a better option. Or lone parents may simply enter the ranks of the working poor, and their children will continue to live in hardship and also have reduced parental time and care. Lone mothers and their children are most likely to avoid poverty in countries with high levels of gender and class/income equality. Policies to support, encourage or compel lone parents into employment cannot be divorced from this wider context.

References

Aarts, L. and Velema, W. (2000) *Markt in wording*, Den Haag: Ministerie van Sociale Zaken en Werkgelegenheid.

ABS (Australian Bureau of Statistics) (1997) *Family characteristics*, catalogue no 4442.0, Canberra.

ABS (1998) *Family and labour market patterns over time*, Research in progress 1/98, Survey of Employment and Unemployment Patterns, mimeo, Canberra.

ABS (various years) *Labour force status and other characteristics of families*, catalogue no 6224.0, Canberra.

Adams, G. and Schulman, K. (1998) *Illinois: Child care challenges*, Washington, DC: Children's Defense Fund.

Akker, P. van den, de Graaff, W. and Kersten, A. (1998) *De Regeling kinderopvang Alleenstaande Ouders Geëvalueerd*, Den Haag: Ministerie van Sociale Zaken en Werkgelegenheid.

Allen, I. and Bourke-Dowling, S. (1999) *Teenage mothers*, London: Policy Studies Institute.

Almquist, A. and Boje, T. (1999) 'Who cares, who pays and how is care for children provided? Comparing family life and work in different European welfare systems', in MIRE, *Comparing social welfare systems in Nordic countries and France*, vol 4, Copenhagen Conference, Paris: MIRE.

Anderson, E. (1993) *Value in ethics and economics*, Cambridge, MA: Harvard University Press.

Avenel, M. (2001) 'Les enfants de moins de 6 ans et leurs familles en France métropolitaine', *Etudes et résultats*, no 97, Paris: Ministère de l'Emploi et de la Solidarité, DREES.

Avenel, M. and Algava, E. (2001) 'Les bénéficiaires de l'API', *Etudes et résultats*, Paris: Ministère de l'Emploi et de la Solidarité, DREES.

Avort, A. van den, Cuijvers, P. and de Hoog, C. (1996) *Het Nederlandse Gezinsleven aan het einde van de twintigste eeuw*, Den Haag: Nederlandse Gezinsraad.

Bainbridge, J., Meyers, M. and Waldfogel, J. (2000) 'Child care reform and the employment of single mothers', Paper presented at the Association for Public Policy Analysis and Management Conference, Seattle, Washington, 2 November.

Bardsley, M. (1999) 'Project megapoles', *Health in Europe's capitals*, London: Directorate of Public Health East London and the City Health Authority.

Beishon, S., Modood, T. and Virdee, S. (1998) *Ethnic minority families*, London: Policy Studies Institute.

Belorgey, J.M. (ed) (2000) *Minima sociaux, revenus d'activité, précarité*, Paris: La Documentation Française.

Berkel, R., van and Brand, A. (1999) 'Onbenutte kwaliteiten in Rotterdam', in S. Grotenhuis and J. van der Zwaard (eds) *Met de nbeste bedoelingen: Professionele interventies in het gezin*, Maarsen/Den Haag: Elsevier/De Tijdstroom/Nederlandse Gezinsraad, pp 39-52.

Berlin, G.L. (2000) *Encouraging work, reducing poverty: The impact of work incentive programs*, New York, NY: Manpower Demonstration Research Corporation.

Berthoud, R. (2000) 'Family formation in multi-cultural Britain: three patterns of diversity', Paper 2000-34, Working Papers of the Institute for Social and Economic Research, Colchester: University of Essex.

Beveridge, W. (1942) *Social insurance and allied services* (Beveridge Report), Cmd 6404, London: HMSO.

Blair, T. (2000) House of Commons *Hansard*, 16 March, col 257W.

Blank, H. and Poersch, N.O. (2000) *State developments in child care and early education 1999*, Washington, DC: Children's Defense Fund.

Bolderson, H. and Mabbett, D. (1991) *Social policy and social security in Australia, Britain and the USA*, Aldershot: Avebury.

Bradshaw, J. and Millar, J. (1991) *Lone parent families in the UK*, London: HMSO.

Bradshaw, J., Terum, L.I. and Skevik, A. (2000) 'Lone parenthood in the 1990s: new challenges, new responses?', Paper presented at the Year 2000 International Research Conference on Social Security, 'Social Security in the Global Village', Helsinki, 25-27 September.

Bradshaw, J., Ditch, J., Holmes, H. and Whiteford, P. (1993) *Support for children: A comparison of arrangements in fifteen countries*, DSS Research Report No 21, London: HMSO.

Bradshaw, J., Stimson, C., Skinner, C. and Williams, J. (1999) *Absent fathers?*, London: Routledge.

Bradshaw, J., Kennedy, S., Kilkey, M., Hutton, S., Corden, A., Eardley, T., Holmes, H. and Neale, J. (1996) *The employment of lone parents: A comparison of policy in twenty countries*, London: Family Policy Studies Centre.

Bruning, G. and Plantega, J. (1999) 'Parental leave and equal opportunities', *Journal of European Social Policy*, vol 9, no 3, pp 195-209.

Bryson, A. and Marsh, A. (1996) *Leaving family credit*, London: The Stationery Office.

Bryson, A., Ford, R. and White, M. (1997) *Making work pay: Lone mothers, employment and well-being*, York: Joseph Rowntree Foundation.

Bubeck, D. (1995) *Care, gender and justice*, Oxford: Clarendon.

Burtless, G. (2000) *Can the labor market absorb three million welfare recipients?*, mimeo, Brookings Institute.

Callender, C. and Kemp, M. (2000) *Changing student finances: Income, expenditure and the take up of student loans among full and part-time higher education students in 1998/9*, RR213, London: DfEE.

Callender, C. and Kempson, E. (1996) *Student finances*, London: Policy Studies Institute.

Centraal Bureau voor Statistiek (1998) *Bijstandsstatistieken*.

Chambaz, C. (2000) 'Les familles monoparentales en Europe: des réalités multiples', *Etudes et résultats*, no 66, Paris: Ministère de l'Emploi et de la Solidarité, DREES.

Chaupin, S. and Guillot, O. (1998) 'Au sortir de l'allocation de parent isolé', *Recherches et Prévisions*, no 50-1, pp 17-26.

Cohen, G., Forbes, J. and Garraway, M. (1995) 'Interpreting self reported limiting long term illness', *British Medical Journal*, vol 311, no 7007, pp 722-4.

Coleman, D. and Chandola, T. (1999) 'Britain's place in Europe's population', in S. McRae (ed) *Changing Britain: Families and households in the 1990s*, Oxford: Oxford University Press, pp 37-67.

Coleman, J.S. (1993) 'The rational reconstruction of society', *American Sociological Review*, vol 58, pp 1-15.

Coleman, J.S. (1995) 'Rights and interests: raising the next generation', *American Sociological Review*, vol 60, pp 782-3.

Commissie Toekomstscenario's Herverdeling Onbetaalde Zorgarbeid (1995) *Onbetaalde Zorg Gelijk Verdeeld*, Den Haag:VUGA.

Coote,A. (1981) 'The AES: a new starting point', *New Socialist*, November/ December, pp 4-7.

Crompton, R. (ed) (1999) *Restructuring of gender relations and employment: The decline of the male breadwinner*, Oxford: Oxford University Press.

CSO (Central Statistical Office) (1982) *Social Trends 12*, London: HMSO.

CSO (1995) *Social Trends 25*, London HMSO.

Daly, M. (2000) *The gender division of welfare*, Cambridge: Cambridge University Press.

Daly, M. and Lewis, J. (2000) 'The concept of social care and the analysis of contemporary welfare states', *British Journal of Sociology*, vol 51, no 2, pp 281-98.

Danziger, S.H. (ed) (1999) *Economic conditions and welfare reform*, Kalamazoo, MI: Upjohn Institute for Employment Research.

Danziger, S.H., Heflin, C., Corcoran, M. and Oltmans, E. (2001) *Does it pay to move from welfare to work?*, University of Michigan working paper (www.ssw.umich.edu/poverty/pubs.html).

Danziger, S.K. and Seefeldt, K.S. (2000) 'Ending welfare through work first: manager and client views', *Families in Society*, vol 81, no 6, pp 593-604.

Danziger, S.K., Corcoran, M., Danziger, S., Heflin, C., Kalil,A., Levine, J., Rosen, D., Seefeldt, K., Siefert, K. and Tolman, R. (2000) 'Barriers to the employment of welfare recipients', in R. Cherry and W. Rodgers (eds) *Prosperity for all? The economic boom and African Americans*, New York, NY: Russell Sage Foundation.

Daycare Trust and DfEE (Department for Education and Employment) (1999) *Focus on funding for childcare 2000-2001*, no 8, London: Daycare Trust.

De Vaus, D. and Wolcott, H. (eds) (1997) *Australian family profiles: Social and demographic patterns*, Melbourne: Australian Institute of Family Studies.

Deacon, A. (1998) 'The green paper on welfare reform: a case for enlightened self-interest?', *Political Quarterly*, vol 69, no 3, pp 306-11.

Dench, G. (1994) *The frog, the prince and the problem of men*, London: Neanderthal Books.

Dennis, N. and Erdos, G. (1992) *Families without fatherhood*, London: Institute for Economic Affairs.

Department of Family and Community Services (FACS) (1999) *Annual report 1997/98*, Canberra: Australian Government Publishing Service.

DEWRSB (Department of Employment, Workplace Relations and Small Businesses) (1998) *Work and family: State of play 1998 – Executive summary*, Canberra (www.dewrsb.gov.au/workplaceRelations/workAndFamily/state_1998.htm).

Dex, S. (1988) *Women's attitudes towards work*, London: Macmillan.

DfEE (Department for Education and Employment) (2000) *Statistics of education: Children's day care facilities, at 31 March*, England: National Statistics.

DfEE (2001a) *Towards full employment in a modern society*, Cm 5084, London: The Stationery Office.

DfEE (2001b) *Statistical first release: New Deal for Lone Parents statistics, to October 2000*, London: DfEE.

Ditch, J., Barnes, H., Bradshaw, J. and Kilkey, M. (1998) *A synthesis of national family policies in 1996*, York: The European Observatory on National Family Policies, Commission of the European Communities.

Dorsett, R. and Marsh, A. (1998) *The health trap: Poverty, lone parents and smoking*, London: Policy Studies Institute.

Drenth, A. van, Knijn, T. and Lewis, J. (1999) 'Sources of income for lone mother families: policy changes in Britain and the Netherlands and the experiences of divorced women', *Journal of Social Policy*, vol 28, no 4, pp 619-42.

Drøpping, J.A., Hvinden, B. and Vik, K. (1999) 'Activation policies in the Nordic countries', in M. Kautto, M. Heikkilä, B. Hvinden, S. Marklund and N. Ploug (eds) *Nordic social policy: Changing welfare states*, London: Routledge, pp 133-58.

DSS (Department of Social Security) (1996) *Social security statistics 1996*, London: The Stationery Office.

DSS (1998) *New ambitions for our country: A new contract for welfare*, Cm 3805, London: The Stationery Office.

DSS, DoH (Department of Health) and Family Services, Department of Employment, Education, Training and Youth Affairs, Department of Finance and Administration (1997) *JET, the jobs education and training program: Evaluation report*, Canberra: Australian Government Publishing Service.

DTI (Department of Trade and Industry) (2000) *Work and parents: Competitiveness and choice*, Cm 5005 London: The Stationery Office.

Duncan, G. and Chase-Lansdale, L. (2000) 'Welfare reform and child well-being', in R.M. Blank and R. Haskins (eds) *The new world of welfare*, Washington, DC: Bookings Institute Press.

Duncan, S. and Edwards, R. (1997a) 'Single mothers in Britain: unsupported workers or mothers?', in S. Duncan and R. Edwards (eds) *Single mothers in an international context: Mothers or workers?*, London: UCL Press, pp 45-79.

Duncan, S. and Edwards, R. (eds) (1997b) *Single mothers in international context*, London: UCL Press.

Duncan, S. and Edwards, R. (1999) *Lone mothers, paid work and gendered moral rationalities*, Basingstoke: Macmillan.

Eardley, T. (1996) 'Lessons from a study of social assistance schemes in OECD countries', in L. Hantrais and S. Mangen (eds) *Cross-national research methods in the social sciences*, London: Pinter, pp 51-62.

Eardley, T. (2000) 'Sole parents and welfare dependency', *Social Policy Research Centre Newsletter*, no 76, Sydney: University of New South Wales.

Eardley, T., Bradshaw, J., Ditch, J., Gough, I. and Whiteford, P. (1996) *Social assistance schemes in OECD countries: synthesis report*, DSS Research Report, no 46, London: The Stationery Office.

Ellingsæter, A. (1999) 'Dual breadwinners between state and market', in R. Crompton (ed) *Restructuring gender relations and employment: The decline of the male breadwinner*, Oxford: Oxford University Press, pp 40-59.

Elshtain, J.B. (1981) *Public man and private woman*, Oxford: Blackwell.

Engbersen, G. and van der Veen, R. (1987) *Moderne armoede; over leven op het sociaal minimum*, Leiden/Antwerpen: Stenfert Kroese.

Engbersen, G., Vrooman, J.C. and Snel, E. (eds) (1997) *Arm Nederland. De Kwetsbaren. Tweede Jaarraport Armoede en Sociale Uitsluiting*, Amsterdam: Amsterdam University Press.

Engelen, M., Bunt, S. and Samson, L. (1999) *Activersingsinstrumenten in de bijstand*, Den Haag: Ministerie van Sociale Zaken en Werkgelegenheid.

Enjolras, B., Laville, J.L., Fraisse, L. and Trickey, H. (2001) 'Between subsiduarity and social assistance – the French republican route to activation', in I. Lødemel and H. Trickey (eds) *'An offer you can't refuse': Workfare in international perspective*, Bristol: The Policy Press, pp 41-70.

Esping-Andersen, G. (1990) *The three worlds of welfare capitalism*, Cambridge: Polity Press.

Esping-Andersen, G. (2001) 'Challenge to the welfare state in the 21st century. Ageing societies, knowledge based economies and the sustainability of European welfare states', Paper presented to the conference 'Comparer les Systemes de Protection Sociale en Europe', Ministère de l'Emploi et de la Solidarité, Paris, 8-9 June.

Evans, M.D.R. (2000) 'Women's participation in the labour force: ideals and behaviour', *Australian Social Monitor*, Melbourne: Melbourne Institute of Applied Economic and Social Research.

Fagnani, J. (1998) 'Recent changes in family policy in France: political trade-off and economic constraints', in E. Drew, R. Emerch and E. Mahon (eds) *Women, work and the family in Europe*, London: Routledge, pp 58-65.

Fein, D. and Wang, L. (1999) *Carrying and using the stick: Financial sanctions in Delaware's a better chance program*, Boston, MA: Abt Associates Inc.

Field, F. and Piachaud, D. (1971) 'The poverty trap', *New Statesman*, 3 December.

Finlayson, L. and Marsh, A. (1998) *Lone parents on the margins of work*, DSS Research Report no 80, Leeds: Corporate Document Services.

Finlayson, L., Ford, R., Marsh, A., McKay, S. and Mukherjee, A. (2000) *The British lone parent cohort, 1991 to 1998*, DSS Research Report no 80, Leeds: Corporate Document Services.

Ford, J., Quilgars, D. and Rugg, J. (1998a) *Creating jobs? The employment potential of domiciliary care*, Bristol/York: The Policy Press/Joseph Rowntree Foundation.

Ford, R. (1996) *Childcare in the balance: How lone parents make decisions about work*, London: Policy Studies Institute.

Ford, R., Marsh, A. and Finlayson, L. (1998b) *What happens to lone parents: A cohort study 1991-1995*, Research Report no 77, London: The Stationery Office.

Ford, R., Marsh, A. and McKay, S. (1995) *Changes in lone parenthood*, DSS Research Report no 40, London: HMSO.

Forskrift 1998-10-00 no 60: vedlegg nummer 1 til ftrl kap 15, st nad til enslig mor eller far – retningslinjer for oppf lgingsordningen/ brukermedvirkning for enslig mor eller far, Oslo: the National Insurance.

Fragonard, B. (ed) (1993) *Cohésion sociale et prévention de l'exclusion*, Rapport de la Commission présidée par Fragonard, B., dans le cadre de la préparation du 11ème Plan, Paris: La Documentation Française.

Freedman, S., Friedlander, D., Hamilton, G., Rock, J., Mitchell, M., Nudelman, J., Schweder, A. and Storto, L. (2000) *National evaluation of welfare-to-work strategies: Evaluating alternative welfare-to-work approaches: Two-year impacts for eleven programs*, New York, NY: Manpower Demonstration Research Corporation.

Fukuyama, F. (1999) *The great disruption*, London: Profile Books.

Fuller, B. and Kagan, S.L. (2000) *Remember the children: Mothers balance work and child care under welfare reform*, Berkeley, CA: University of California at Berkeley Graduate School of Education.

Galinsky, E., Howes, C., Kontos, S. and Shinn, M. (1994) *The study of children in family and relative care*, New York, NY: Families and Work Institute.

Gallagher, J., Gallagher, M., Perese, K., Schreiber, S. and Watson, K. (1998) *One year after federal welfare reform: A description of state Temporary Assistance for Needy Families (TANF) decisions as of October 1997, assessing the new federalism*, Occasional Paper no 6, Washington, DC: Urban Institute Press.

Galston, W.A. (1991) *Liberal purposes: Goods, virtues and diversity in the liberal state*, Cambridge: Cambridge University Press.

Garfinkel, I. and McLanahan, S. (1986) *Single mothers and their children: A new American dilemma*, Washington, DC: Urban Institute Press.

Giddens, A. (1992) *The transformation of intimacy: Sexuality, love and eroticism in modern societies*, Cambridge: Polity Press.

Gilligan, C. (1982) *In a different voice*, Cambridge, MA: Harvard University Press.

Glennerster, H. (1999) 'A third way?', in H. Dean and R. Woods (eds) *Social Policy Review 11*, London: Social Policy Association, pp 28-44.

Gregson, N. and Lowe, M. (1994) 'Waged domestic labour and the renegotiation of the domestic division of labour with dual career households', *Sociology*, vol 28, no 1, pp 55-78.

Hakim, C. (1996) *Key issues in women's work: Female heterogeneity and the polarisation of women's employment*, London: Athlone.

Hales, J., Lessof, C., Roth, W., Gloyer, M., Shaw, A., Millar, J., Barnes, M., Elias, P., Hasluck, C., McKnight, A. and Green, A. (2000) *Evaluation of the New Deal for Lone Parents: Early lessons from the phase one prototype: synthesis report*, DSS Research Report no 108, Leeds: Corporate Document Services.

Han, W. and Waldfogel, J. (2001) 'Child care costs and women's employment: a comparison of single and married mothers with pre-school-aged children', *Social Science Quarterly*, vol 82, no 3, pp 552-68.

Harding, A. and Szukalska, A. (1999) *Trends in child poverty in Australia: 1982 to 1995-96*, Discussion Paper no 42, Canberra: National Centre for Social and Economic Modelling, University of Canberra.

Harding, A. and Szukalska, A. (2000) 'Making a difference: the impact of government policy on child poverty in Australia, 1982 to 1997-98', Paper prepared for the 26th General Conference of the International Association for Research in Income and Wealth, Cracow, Poland, 27 August-2 September.

Harkness, S., Machin, S. and Waldfogel, J. (1996) 'Women's pay and family incomes in Britain, 1979-1991', in J. Hills (ed) *New inequalities: The changing distribution of income and wealth in the UK*, Cambridge: Cambridge University Press, pp 158-80.

Haskey, J. (1998) 'One-parent families and their dependent children', in R. Ford and J. Millar (eds) *Private lives and public responses*, London: Policy Studies Institute, pp 22-41.

Hatland, A. (1992) *Til dem som trenger det mest? Økonomisk behovsprøving i norsk sosialpolitikk*, Oslo: Oslo University Press.

Helburn, S. (ed) (1995) *Cost, quality, and child outcomes in child care centers: Technical report*, Denver, CO: Department of Economics, Center for Research in Economic and Social Policy, University of Colorado at Denver.

Hernes, H. (1987) *Welfare state and woman power: Essays in state feminism*, Oslo: Oslo University Press.

Hills, J. and Lelkes, O. (1999) 'Social security, selective universalism and patchwork redistribution', in R. Jowell, J. Curtice, A. Park and K. Thomson (eds) *British social attitudes, the 16th report: Who shares new Labour values?*, Aldershot: Ashgate, pp 1-22.

Himmelweit, S. (1995) 'The discovery of "unpaid work": the social consequences of the expansion of "work"', *Feminist Economics*, vol 1, no 2, pp 1-19.

HM Treasury (2000a) *Tackling poverty and making work pay: Tax Credits for the 21st century*, London: HM Treasury.

HM Treasury (2000b) *Pre-Budget report*, London: HM Treasury.

Hoff, S.J.M., Dronkers, J. and Vrooman, J.C. (1997) 'Arme ouders en het welzijn van kinderen', in G. Engbersen, J.C. Vrooman and E. Snel (eds) *Arm Nederland. De Kwetsbaren. Tweede Jaarraport Armoede en Sociale Uitsluiting*, Amsterdam: Amsterdam University Press, pp 123-42.

Holtermann, S. and Clarke, K. (1992) *Parents, employment and childcare*, Manchester: Equal Opportunities Commission.

Holtermann, S., Brannen, J., Moss, P. and Owen, C. (1999) *Lone parents and the labour market: Results from the 1997 Labour Force Survey and review of research*, Sheffield: Employment Service Report 23.

Home Office (1998) *Supporting families*, London: The Stationery Office.

Hooghiemstra, E. and Knijn, T. (1997) 'Onder moeders paraplu: alleenstaande ouders op de armoedegrens', in G. Engbersen, J.Vrooman and E. Snel (eds) *Arm Nederland. De Kwetsbaren. Tweede Jaarrapport Armoede en Sociale Uitsluiting*, Amsterdam: Amsterdam University Press, pp 103-21.

Hooghiemstra, E. and Niphuis-Nell, M. (1995) *Sociale Atlas van de Vrouw. Deel 3: Allochtone Vrouwen*, Rijswijk: Sociaal en Cultureel Planbureau.

House of Commons Select Committee on Education and Employment (2001) *First report 2000-01, early years*, London: The Stationery Office.

Hvinden, B. (1999) 'Activation: a Nordic perspective', in *Linking welfare and work*, Dublin: European Foundation for the Improvement of Living and Working Conditions.

Illinois DHS (Department of Human Services) (2000a) *Affordable child care* (brochure), available from www.state.il.us/agency/dhs.

Illinois DHS (2000b) *Child care* (brochure), available from www.state.il.us/agency/dhs.

Ingelhart, R. (1977) *The silent revolution: Changing values and political styles among Western publics*, Princeton, NJ: Princeton University Press.

Ingelhart, R. (1990) *Culture shift in advanced industrial society*, Princeton, NJ: Princeton University Press.

Ingles, D. (1997) *Low income traps for working families*, Centre for Economic Policy Research, Discussion Paper No 363, Canberra: Australian National University.

Inland Revenue (2000) *Working Families' Tax Credit, quarterly enquiry UK, August 2000*, London: ONS.

INSEE (Institute National de la Statistique et des Études Économiques) (1994) *Les familles monoparentales. Contours et caractères*, Paris: Institut National de la Statistique et des Études Économiques.

Jensen, A. and Clausen, S. (1999) 'Samboerskap som foreldreskap', Appendix to NOU 1999:25, *Samboerne og samfunnet*.

Johnson, A. and Meckstroth, A. (1998) *Ancillary services to support welfare to work*, Princeton, NJ: Mathematica Policy Research, Inc.

Join-Lambert, M.-T. (ed) (1998) *Chômage: Mesures d'urgence et minima sociaux*, Paris: La Documentation Française.

Jordan, A. (1980) *Research questions on income security for sole parents*, Research Paper no 6, Development Division, Canberra: Department of Social Security.

Jordan, A. (1994) 'Labour market programs and social security payments', *Social Security Journal*, December, pp 60-78.

Julnes, G. and Halter, A. (1999) *When families leave welfare behind: Illinois families in transition, first survey findings*, Institute for Public Affairs, University of Illinois at Springfield and School of Social Work, University of Illinois at Urbana-Champaign.

Katz, M. (1996) *In the shadow of the poorhouse: A social history of welfare in America*, New York, NY: Basic Books.

Kiernan, K., Land, H. and Lewis, J. (1998) *Lone motherhood in twentieth century Britain*, Oxford: Clarendon Press.

Kilkey, M. (2000) *Lone mothers between paid work and care: The policy regime in twenty countries*, Aldershot: Ashgate.

Kilkey, M. and Bradshaw, J. (1999) 'Lone mothers, economic well-being and policies', in D. Sainsbury (ed) *Gender and welfare state regimes*, Oxford: Oxford University Press, pp 147-84.

Kjeldstad, R. (1998) *Enslige forsørgere: Forsørgelse og levekår før og etter overgang til en ny livsfase*, Sosiale og konomiske studier 100, Statistisk Sentralbyrå.

Kjeldstad, R. and Rønsen, M. (2000) 'I gode og onde dager – enslige forsørgere på et arbeidsmarked i endring', Paper presented at the Social Security Seminar, 30 November-1 December, Oslo: Statistics Norway.

Knijn, T. (1994) 'Fish without bikes. Revision of the Dutch welfare state and its consequences for the (in)dependence of single mothers', *Social Politics*, vol 1, no 1, pp 183-207.

Knijn, T. and Kremer, M. (1997) 'Gender and the caring dimension of welfare states: toward inclusive citizenship', *Social Politics*, vol 4, no 2, pp 328-61.

Knijn, T. and van Wel, F. (1999) *Zorgen voor de Kost*, Utrecht: SWP Uitgeverij.

Knijn, T., Lewis, J. and Gerhard, U. (2001: forthcoming) 'Contract and contractualisation', in B. Hobson, J. Lewis and B. Siim (eds) *Key concepts in gender and social politics in Europe*, Aldershot: Edward Elgar.

Knox,V., Miller, C. and Gennetian, L. (2000) *Reforming welfare and rewarding work: A summary of the final report on the Minnesota family investment program*, New York, NY: Manpower Demonstration Research Corporation.

Koren, C. (1997) *Trygd og omsorgsarbeid*, Norwegian Social Research report no 17, Oslo: Norwegian Social Research.

La Valle, I., Finch, S., Nove, A. and Lewin, C. (2000) *Parent's demand for childcare*, Research Brief no 176, London: DfEE.

Lagarenne, C. and Legendre, N. (2000) 'Les travailleurs pauvres en France: facteurs individuels et familiaux', *Economie et Statistique*, no 335, 2000-5, Paris: Institut National de la Statistique et des Etudes Economiques.

Land, H. (1983) 'Who still cares for the family?', in J. Lewis (ed) *Women's welfare, women rights*, London: Croom Helm, pp 64-85.

Land, H. (1999) 'New Labour, new families?', in H. Dean (ed) *Social Policy Review 11*, London: Social Policy Association, pp 127-44.

Land, H. and Lewis, J. (1998) 'Gender, care and the changing role of the state in the UK', in J. Lewis (ed) *Gender, care and welfare state restructuring in Europe*, Aldershot: Ashgate, pp 51-84.

Land, H. and Rose, H. (1985) 'Compulsory altruism for some or an altruistic society for all?', in P. Bean, J. Ferris and D. Whynes (eds) *In defence of welfare*, London: Tavistock, pp 74-98.

Land, H., Martin, B. and Spencer, S. (2000) *Forty five years of plugging the gaps in women's education: From daughters to mothers*, Bristol: School for Policy Studies, University of Bristol.

Le Corre, V. (2000) *Les modes de garde at l'accueil des jeunes enfants*, Paris: Document de travail no 1, Direction d la recherche, des études, de l'évaluation et de la statistique (DREES), Ministère de l'Emploi et de la Solidarité.

Lefaucheur, N. and Martin, C. (1993) 'Lone parent families in France: situation and research', in J. Hudson and B. Galaway (eds) *Single parent families: Perspectives on research and policy*, Toronto, New York: Thompson Educational Publishing, pp 31-50.

Lefaucheur, N. and Martin, C. (1997) 'Single mothers in France: supported mothers and workers', in S. Duncan and R. Edwards (eds) *Single mothers in an international context: Mothers or workers?*, London: UCL Press, pp 217-40.

Leira, A. (1989) *Models of motherhood*, Report 89:7, Oslo: Institut for Samfunnsforskning.

Leira, A. (1992) *Welfare state and working mothers: The Scandinavian experience*, Cambridge: Cambridge University Press.

Leira, A. (1993) 'The "woman-friendly" welfare state? The case of Norway and Sweden', in J. Lewis (ed) *Women and social policies in Europe*, Aldershot: Ashgate, pp 49-71.

Leira, A. (1998a) 'Perspectives: caring as social right: cash for childcare and daddy leave', *Social Politics*, vol 5, no 3, pp 362-78.

Leira, A. (1998b) 'The modernisation of motherhood', in E. Drew, R. Emerch and E. Mahon (eds) *Women, work and the family in Europe*, London: Routledge, pp 159-69.

Levitas, R. (1998) *The inclusive society? Social exclusion and new Labour*, Basingstoke: Macmillan.

Lewis, J. (ed) (1997a) *Lone mothers in European welfare regimes: Shifting policy logics*, London: Jessica Kingsley Publishers.

Lewis, J. (1997b) 'Introduction', in J. Lewis (ed) *Lone mothers in European welfare regimes: Shifting policy logics*, London: Jessica Kingsley Publishers, pp 1-20.

Lewis, J. (1998) 'The problem of lone-mother families in twentieth-century Britain', *Journal of Social Welfare and Family Law*, vol 20, no 3, pp 251-83.

Lewis, J. and Astrom, G. (1992) 'Equality, difference and state welfare: labour market and family policies in Sweden', *Feminist Studies*, vol 18, no 1, pp 59-87.

Lewis, J. and Glennerster, H. (1996) *Implementing the new community care*, Buckingham: Open Univeristy Press.

Lister, R. (1997) *Citizenship: Feminist perspectives*, London: Macmillan.

Lister, R. (2000a) 'Strategies for social inclusion: promoting social cohesion or social justice', in P. Askonas and A. Stewart (eds) *Social inclusion: Possibilities and tensions*, Basingstoke: Macmillan, pp 37-54.

Lister, R. (2000b) 'To Rio via the third way: New Labour's "welfare" reform agenda', *Renewal*, vol 8, no 4, pp 9-20.

Lister, R. (2001: forthcoming) 'Towards a new welfare settlement?', in C. Hays (ed) *British politics today*, Cambridge: Polity Press.

Lødemel, I. (1997) *The welfare paradox: Income maintenance and personal social services in Norway and Britain, 1945-1966*, Oslo: Scandinavian University Press.

Lødemel, I. and Trickey, H. (2001) *'An offer you can't refuse': Workfare in international perspective*, Bristol: The Policy Press.

McCashin, T. (1997) *Employment aspects of young lone motherhood in Ireland*, Dublin: National Youth Federation and Treoir.

McHugh, M. and Millar, J. (1997) 'Single mothers in Australia: supporting lone mothers to take work', in S. Duncan and R. Edwards (eds) *Single mothers in international context*, London: UCL Press, pp 149-78.

McKernan, S., Lerman, R., Pindus, N. and Valente, J. (2000) 'The relationship between metropolitan and non-metropolitan locations, changing welfare policies, and the employment of single mothers', Revised version of paper presented at the Joint Center for Poverty Research Conference on Rural Dimensions of Welfare Reform, Washington, DC, 4-5 May.

Maloy, K., Pavetti, L., Shin, P., Darnell, J. and Scarpulla-Nolan, L. (1998) *Description and assessment of state approaches to diversion programs and activities under welfare reform: An interim report of the findings of the first phase of the research*, Washington DC: Assistant Secretary for Planning and Evaluation, Administration for Children and Families, US Department of Health and Human Services.

Mandos, E. and Werf, C. van der (1997) *Alleenstaande Ouders in de Bijstand*, Den Haag: Ministerie van Sociale Zaken en Werkgelegenheid.

Marsh, A.M. and McKay, S. (1993) *Families, work and benefits*, London: Policy Studies Institute.

Marsh, A.M. and McKay, S. (1994) *Poor smokers*, London: Policy Studies Institute.

Marsh, A.M., Ford, R. and Finlayson, L. (1997) *Lone parents, work and benefits*, London: Policy Studies Institute.

Marsh, A.M., McKay, S., Smith, A. and Stephenson, A. (2001) *Low-income families in Britain: Work, welfare and social security in 1999*, DSS Research Report no 138, Leeds: Corporate Document Services.

Martin, C. (1997) *L'après divorce*, Rennes: Presses Universitaires de Rennes.

Martin C., Math, A. and Renaudat, E. (1998) 'Caring for very young children and dependent elderly people in France: towards a commodification of social care?', in J. Lewis (ed) *Gender, social care and welfare state restructuring in Europe*, Aldershot: Ashgate, pp 139-74.

Mason, K. and Kuhlthau, K. (1992) 'The perceived impact of child care costs on women's labor supply and fertility', *Demography*, vol 29, pp 523-43.

Mead, L. (1986) *Beyond entitlement: The social obligations of citizenship*, New York, NY: Free Press.

Mead, L. (1996) *Are welfare employment programs effective?*, Discussion Paper no 1096-96, Wisconsin: University of Wisconsin, Madison.

Meyer, D. (2001) 'Benefits for children in the US', in K. Battle and M. Mendelson (eds) *Benefits for children: A four country study*, Canada: Caledon Institute, pp 257-311.

Meyers, M.K. (1993) 'Child care in JOBS employment and training program: what difference does quality make?', *Journal of Marriage and the Family*, vol 55, pp 767-83, August.

Meyers, M.K. and Heintze, T. (1999) 'The performance of the child care subsidy system?', *Social Service Review*, vol 73, no 1, pp 37-64.

Millar, J. (1996) 'Mothers, workers, wives: policy approaches to supporting lone mothers in comparative perspective', in E. Bortolia Silva (ed) *Good enough mothering*, London: Routledge, pp 97-113.

Millar, J. (2000a) 'Changing obligations and expectations: lone parenthood and social policy', in T. Boje and A. Leira (eds) *Gender, welfare state and market*, London: Routledge, pp 226-41.

Millar, J. (2000b) *Keeping track of welfare reform*, York: York Publishing Services for Joseph Rowntree Foundation.

Millar, J. (2000c) 'Lone parents and the New Deal', *Policy Studies*, vol 21, no 4, pp 333-45.

Millar, J. and Warman, A. (1996) *Family obligations in Europe*, London: Family Policy Studies Centre.

Millar, J. and Whiteford, P. (1993) 'Child support in lone-parent families: policies in Australia and the UK', *Policy & Politics*, vol 21, no 1, pp 59-72.

Millikowsky, H. (1968) *Lof der Onaangepastheid*, Meppel: Boom.

Ministerie van Sociale Zaken en Werkgelegenheid (1997) *Kansen op Combineren. Arbeid, Zorg en Economische Zelfstandigheid*, Den Haag: Ministerie van Sociale Zaken en Werkgelegenheid.

Ministerie van Sociale Zaken en Werkgelegenheid (1999a) *Op weg naar een nieuw evenwicht tussen arbeid en zorg*, Den Haag: Ministerie van Sociale Zaken en Wergelegenheid.

Ministerie van Sociale Zaken en Werkgelegenheid (1999b) *Jaarboek Emancipatie '99. Wie zorgt in de 21ᵉ eeuw?*, Den Haag: VUGA.

Ministerie van Sociale Zaken en Werkgelegenheid (2000) *Lijnen naar de Toekomst. Evaluatie Algemene bijstandswet 1996-1999*, Den Haag: Ministerie van Sociale Zaken en Werkgelegenheid.

Morgan, P. (1995) *Farewell to the family*, London: Institute for Economic Affairs.

Muffels, R., Dirven, H.-J. and Fourage, D. (1995) *Armoede, Bestaansonzekerheid en Relatieve Deprivatie: Rapport 1995*, Tilburg: Tilburg University Press.

National Child Minding Association (2000) 'Smoking and smacking: children deserve better' (www.ncma.org.uk).

National Governors' Association (NGA) Center for Best Practices (1999) *Round two summary of selected elements of state programs for temporary assistance for needy families*, Washington, DC: NGA.

Nelson, J.A. (1999) 'Of markets and martyrs: is it OK to pay well for care?', *Feminist Economics*, vol 4, no 1, pp 43-59.

Newman, J. (2000) *Jet Program a demand driven success*, FACS Press Release, 15 July (www.facs.gov.au).

NICHD Early Child Care Research Network (1999) 'Child outcomes when child-care center classes meet recommended standards for quality', *American Journal of Public Health*, vol 89, pp 1072-7.

NICHD Early Child Care Research Network (2000) 'The relation of child care to cognitive and language development: results from the NICHD study of early child care', *Child Development*, vol 71, no 4, pp 960-80.

Niphuis-Nell, M. (1997) 'Eenoudergezinnen, stiefgezinnen en niet-verzorgende ouders', in M. Niphuis-Nell (ed) *Sociale Atlas van de Vrouw. Deel 4: Veranderingen in de primaire leefsfeer*, Rijswijk: Sociaal en Cultureel Planbureau, pp 85-114.

Noack, T. and Keilman, N. (1993) 'Familie og husholdning', in *Sosialt Utsyn*, Statistisk Sentralbyrå, Oslo: SSD.

Noddings, N. (1984) *Caring: A feminine approach to ethics and moral education*, Berkeley, CA: University of California Press.

NOS C43 1993: Levekårsundersøkelsen.

NOU 1975:18, Stønad til enslige forsørgere m.v.

Novak, M. and Cogan, J. (1987) *The new consensus on family and welfare: A community of self-reliance*, Milwaukee, WI: American Enterprise Institute.

Nyberg, A. (2001) 'Economic power, work and gender', Paper presented at CAVA International Seminar, 1 January, University of Leeds.

Observatoire national de la pauvreté et de l'exclusion sociale (2000) *Les travaux de l'Observatoire de la pauvreté et de l'exclusion sociale*, Paris: La Documentation Française.

OECD (1993) *Breadwinners or childrearers: The dilemma for lone mothers*, Paris: OECD.

OECD (1996) *Economic outlook, Historical statistics*, Paris: OECD.

OECD (1998) *Employment outlook*, Paris: OECD.

OECD (1999) *Benefit systems and work incentives*, Paris: OECD.

Olier, L. and Hespin, N. (1999) 'One-parent families: assisted but more vulnerable', Collection MIRE, vol 4, *Comparing social welfare systems in Nordic countries and France*, Paris: MIRE.

ONS (Office for National Statistics) (1997) *Labour Force Survey Quarterly Bulletin*, no 20, June.

ONS (1998) *Living in Britain: Results from the 1996 GHS*, London: The Stationery Office.

ONS (1999) *Labour Force Survey 1998*, London: The Stationery Office.

ONS (2000) *HMSO Social Trends 2000*, London: The Stationery Office.

Oppenheimer, V. (1994) 'Women's rising employment and the future of the family in industrialised societies', *Population and Development Review*, vol 20, no 2, pp 293-42.

Orloff, A. (1999) 'Ending the entitlements of poor mothers, expanding the claims of poor employers parents: gender, race and US social policy in an era of retrenchment', Working Paper 99/3, European Forum on *Recasting the welfare state*, Robert Schuman Centre, European University Institute.

Ot prp no 4 (1979-80) Om endringer i lov av 17 juni 1966 nr 12 om folketrygd mv.

Oxley, H., Thai-Thanh, D., Förster, M. and Pellizzari, M. (2001) 'Income inequalities and poverty among children and households with children in selected OECD countries: trends and determinants', in K. Vleminckx and T. Smeeding (eds) *Child well-being, child poverty and child policy in modern nations*, Bristol: The Policy Press.

Pateman, C. (1988) 'The patriarchal welfare state', in A. Gutman (ed) *Democracy and the welfare state*, Princeton, NJ: Princeton University Press, pp 231-60.

Pavetti, D. (2000) 'Welfare policy in transition: redefining the social contract for poor citizen families with children and immigrants', Paper presented at Conference on Understanding Poverty, Madison, Wisconsin, May.

Pearse, V. (2000) 'Parents participation and planning – the parenting payment intervention pilot', Paper given at the 7th Australian Institute of Family Studies Conference, Sydney, July.

Penn, H. (2000) 'Policy and practice in childcare and nursery education', *Journal of Social Policy*, vol 29, no 1, pp 37-54.

Phillips, M. (1997) *The sex change state*, London: Social Market Foundation.

Piecyk, J.B., Collins, A. and Lee Kreader, J. (1999) *Patterns and growth of child care voucher use by families connected to cash assistance in Illinois and Maryland*, mimeo, National Center for Children in Poverty.

Plantenga, J. (1999) *Alleenstaande moeders en de systematiek van de verzorgingsstaat*, Utrecht: Economisch Instituut.

Popay, J. and Jones, G. (1991) 'Patterns of health and illness amongst lone-parent families', in M. Hardy and G. Crow (eds) *Lone parenthood: Coping with constraints and making opportunities*, Hemel Hempstead: Harvester Wheatsheaf, pp 66-87.

Popenoe, D. (1993) 'American family decline, 1960-1990: a review and appraisal', *Journal of Marriage and the Family*, vol 55, no 3, pp 527-55.

Portonnier, J.C. (1998) *Glossaire bilingue de la protection sociale – social protection: a bilingual glossary, Volume 1 Les termes Français/French terms*, Paris: Mission recherche (MIRE), Ministère de l'Emploi et de la Solidarité.

Ramsburg, D. and Montanelli, D.S. (2000) *1999 Report on Illinois child care*, Springfield, IL: Illinois Department of Human Services.

Raymond, J. (1987) 'Bringing up children alone: policies for sole parents', *Social Security Review Issues*, Paper no 3, Canberra: Australian Government Publishing Services.

Reference Group on Welfare Reform (2001) *Participation support for a more equitable society*, Canberra: Australian Government Publishing Service.

Rowlingson, K. and McKay, S. (1998) *The growth of lone parenthood: Diversity and dynamics*, London: Policy Studies Institute.

Rowlingson, K. and McKay, S. (2001: forthcoming) *Lone parent families: Gender, class and state*, London: Pearson Education.

RTV (1996a) *Evaluering av nettverksprosjektene for enslige forsørgere – 'På vei fra passivitet til selvforsørging'*, Utredningsavdelingen Rikstrygdeverket, rapport 8/96.

RTV (1996b) *Evaluering av nettverksprosjektene for enslige forsørgere – 'Tiltak og virkning'*, Utredningsavdelingen Rikstrygdeverket, rapport 10/96.

Rubery, J., Smith, M. and Fagan, C. (1998) 'National working-time regimes and equal opportunities', *Feminist Economics*, vol 4, no 1, pp 71-101.

Sainsbury, D. (1999) 'Gender and social-democratic welfare states', in D. Sainsbury (ed) *Gender and welfare state regimes*, Oxford: Oxford University Press, pp 75-114.

Select Committee on Education and Employment (2000) *Early years: First report 2000-01*, London: The Stationery Office.

Sevenhuijsen, S. (1998) *Citizenship and the ethics of care*, London: Routledge.

Shaver, S. (1990) *Gender, social policy regimes and the welfare state*, Discussion Paper no 26, Sydney: Social Policy Research Centre, University of New South Wales.

Siim, B. (1987) 'The Scandinavian welfare states – towards sexual equality or a new kind of male domination?', *Acta Sociologica*, vol 30, nos 3-4, pp 255-70.

Skevik, A. (1996) *Holdninger til enslige forsørgere*, INAS-notat 1996:4.

Skevik, A. (1998) *Children's right, father's duty, mother's responsibility: Policies and attitudes towards lone parents*, NOVA-skrift 1998:2.

Skevik, A. (1999) 'Mothers, carers, wives and workers: lone mothers in Norwegian social policy', in MIRE, *Comparing social welfare systems in Nordic countries and France*, vol 4, Copenhagen Conference, Paris: MIRE.

Skevik, A. (2001) *Family ideology and social policy: policies toward lone parents in Norway and the UK*, Oslo: NOVA (Norwegian Social Research).

Skrede, K. (1999) 'Shaping gender equality – the role of the state: Norwegian experiences, present polices and future challenges', in MIRE, *Comparing social welfare systems in Nordic countries and France*, vol 4, Copenhagen Conference, Paris: MIRE.

Social Exclusion Unit (1999) *Teenage pregnancy*, Cm 4342, London: The Stationery Office.

Social Security Select Committee (2000) *The contributory principle*, London: The Stationery Office.

Song, M. and Edwards, R. (1997) 'Comment: raising questions about perspectives on black lone motherhood', *Journal of Social Policy*, vol 26, no 2, pp 233-44.

St prp no 1 1993-94: *Statsbudsjettet for budsjetterminen 1994*.

Staatscourant 43 (1996) *Regeling Kinderopvang en buitenschoolse opvang alleenstaande ouders 1996*, Den Haag: Directie Bijstandszaken.

State Policy Documentation Project (1999) *Child care provision after leaving cash assistance* (www.spdp.org).

St meld (Stortingsmelding) no 35 1994-95: Velferdsmeldingen.

Stolk, B. van and Wouters, C. (1983) *Vrouwen in Tweestrijd*, Deventer: Van Loghum Slaterus.

Sullerot, E. (1984) *Pour le meilleur et sans le pire*, Paris: Fayard.

Supplementary Benefit Commission (1980) *Report of the Supplementary Benefit Commission for the year ended 1979*, Cmnd 8033, London: HMSO.

Syltevik, L. (1996) 'Fra relasjonelt til individualisert alenemoderskap. En studie av alenemødre som mødre, lønnsarbeidere og klienter i velferdsstaten', Doctorate thesis submitted at the University of Bergen.

Tapinos, G. (1996) *Europe mediterraneenne et changements demographiques: existe-t-il une specificite des pays de sud?*, Turin: Fondazione Giovanni Agnelli.

Terum, L.I. (1993) *Stønad, samliv og sjølforsørging*, INAS-rapport 93:1.

Thair, T. and Risdon, A. (1999) 'Women in the labour market. Results from the spring 1998 LFS', *Labour Market Trends* (March), pp 103-27.

Thélot, C. and Villac, M. (1998) *Politique familiale. Bilan et perspectives*, Paris: La Documentation Française.

Thomson, K. (1994) 'Working mothers: choice or circumstance?', in R. Jowell, J. Curtice, A. Park, L. Booth and D. Ahrendt with K. Thomson, *British Social Attitudes: The twelth report*, London: Sage Publications, pp 61-90.

TK (Tweede Kamer) zitting 1992-1993, 22545, nr 9, Den Haag.

TK zitting 1993-1994, 22545, nr 17, Den Haag.

Tronto, J.C. (1993) *Moral boundaries: A political argument for an ethic of care*, London: Routledge.

Turok, I. and Edge, N. (1999) *The jobs gap in Britain's cities: Employment loss and labour market consequences*, Bristol/York: The Policy Press/Joseph Rowntree Foundation.

Ungerson, C. (1999) 'The production and consumption of long-term care: does gender still matter?', Paper for a conference on 'Beyond the health care state', EUI, Florence, February.

US Bureau of the Census (1999) *Statistical abstract of the United States 1999*, Washington, DC: US Government Printing Office.

US Bureau of the Census (2000) *Poverty in the United States 1999*, Washington, DC: US Government Printing Office, pp 60-210.

US Department of Health and Human Services (2000) *Change in welfare caseloads since enactment of new welfare law: Total TANF recipients by state*, Washington, DC: US Department of Health and Human Services.

US Department of Health and Human Services, Child Care Bureau (1999) *Access to child care for low-income working families*, Washington, DC: US Department of Health and Human Services.

US General Accounting Office (2000) *Welfare reform: State sanction policies and number of families affected*, GAO/HEHS-00-44, Washington, DC: US Government Printing Office.

US House of Representatives, Committee on Ways and Means (1996) *1996 Green book: Background material and data on programs within the jurisdiction of the committee on ways and means*, Washington, DC: US Government Printing Office.

US House of Representatives, Committee on Ways and Means (1998) *1998 Green book: Background material and data on programs within the jurisdiction of the committee on ways and means* (www.waysandmeans.house.gov/publica.htm).

Vanstone, A. and Abbott, T. (2001) *Australians working together – helping people to move forward. Budget Statement*, Canberra: Australian Government Publishing Services.

Waerness, K. (1998) 'The changing "welfare mix" in childcare and the care for the frail elderly in Norway', in J. Lewis (ed) *Gender, social care and welfare state restructuring in Europe*, Aldershot: Avebury, pp 207-28.

Walby, S. (1997) *Gender transformations*, London: Routledge.

Ward, C., Dale, A. and Joshi, H. (1996) 'Income dependency within couples', in L. Morris and E.S. Lyon (eds) *Gender relations in public and private*, Basingstoke: Macmillan, pp 95-120.

Webster, E. and Harding, G. (2000) *Outsourcing public employment services: The Australian experience*, Melbourne Institute Working Paper no 4, March, Melbourne: University of Melbourne.

Wel, F. van (1992) 'De ongehuwde moeder in de media van de jaren zestig', *Jeugd en Samenleving*, vol 7, no 8, pp 430-44.

Wel, F. van and Knijn, T. (2000) *Alleenstaande ouders over zorgen en werken*, Den Haag: Ministerie van Sociale zaken en Werkgelegenheid.

Weuring, R. (1996) *Alleenstaand Moederschap: een Zelfstandig Bestaansrecht?*, Utrecht: Universiteit van Utrecht (masterthesis).

White, S. (2000) 'Social rights and the social contract – political theory and the new welfare politics', *British Journal of Political Science*, vol 30, pp 507-32.

Whiteford, P. (1995) 'The use of replacement ratios in international comparisons of benefit systems', *International Social Security Review*, vol 48, no 2, pp 3-28.

Whiteford, P. (1997) 'From welfare to work? The JET Programme for lone parents in Australia', Paper given at the Social Policy Association Annual Conference, University of Lincoln, July.

Whiteford, P. (2000) *The Australian system of social protection – an overview*, Policy Research Paper no 1, Canberra: Department of Family and Community Services.

Whiteford, P. and Bradshaw, J. (1994) 'Benefits and incentives for lone parents: a comparative analysis', *International Social Security Review*, vol 47, nos 3-4, pp 69-89.

Wiemann, B. (1988) 'Opkomst en neergang van de ongehuwde moederzorg in Nederland (1880-1985)', *Amsterdams Sociologisch Tijdschrift*, vol 15, no 2, pp 337-68.

Wilson, M. (2000) 'The policy response to the employment task force and changing patterns of domestic purposes benefit receipt: a cohort analysis', *Social Policy Journal of New Zealand*, vol 14, pp 78-103.

Wilson, S. (2000) 'Welfare to work policies in Australia and the welfare reform process', Paper given at the Year 2000 International Research Conference on Social Security, International Social Security Association, Helsinki, September.

Wilson, W.J. (1987) *The truly disadvantaged*, Chicago, IL: Chicago University Press.

Wistow, G., Knapp, M., Hardy, B., Forder, J., Kendall, J. and Manning, R. (1996) *Social care markets: Progress and prospects*, Buckingham: Open University Press.

Wolfe, A. (1989) *Whose keeper? Social science and moral obligation*, Berkeley, CA: University of California Press.

Women's Unit (1999) *Women's individual income 1996/7*, London: Cabinet Office.

Yearbook of Social Security Statistics (*Trygdestatistisk årbok*) (various years) Oslo: the National Insurance.

Young, I.M. (1995) 'Mothers, citizenship and independence: a critique of pure family values', *Ethics*, vol 105, pp 535-56.

Zwaard, J. van der (1998) *Met Hulp van Vriendinnen*, Utrecht: Uitgeverij SWP.

Index

net replacement rates (NRRs) 216-25, 230
New Deal for Lone Parents (UK) 14, 29, 196-7, 238-9
evaluation 202-3
New Labour
child poverty measures xv-xvi, xviii-xix
welfare reform project xv-xx
welfare-to-work policy xvi-xvii, 11-36, 154-5
Norway 87-105
'activation' principle 87-8, 92, 95, 97-9, 102-5, 193-4, 202
attitudes towards care work 160-1, 246
attitudes towards employment 101-2, 246
benefits and work 92-5, 97-9, 196
making work pay policies 214-15, 217, 219, 220, 222, 223, 224-5, 226, 230, 257
childcare
access to 244
benefits 92-3, 95-6, 103-4
for student parents 239
demographic patterns 88-91, 172
employment patterns 91, 92-97, 104, 222, 223, 224-5
employment as right 100-1
focus on paid work 4-5
'help to self-help' movement 97, 99-100
inclusive approach to lone mothers 236
OFO scheme 97-9, 102-3, 104, 196
evaluation 202
poverty rates 91
Survey of Level Living 90-1, 94, 96-7, 101-2
welfare reform 95-7, 102-3, 191, 193-4
number of children 175-7
see also demographic patterns
nursery workers in UK 248

O

obligation to work 161-3
see also active welfare state; welfare-to-work programmes
OECD Benefit Systems and Work Incentives series 216-25
OFO scheme (Norway) 97-9, 102-3, 104, 196, 202
ONE experiment (UK) 14, 35
'one-stop' delivery systems 198, 208
Oppfølgingsordningen for enslige forsørgere (OFO) 97-9, 102-3, 104, 196
evaluation 202

P

paid work
at centre of policy 1, 2, 4-5, 153-6, 189-210, 256-7
care and obligation to work 161-3, 261-2
see also employment; welfare-to-work programmes
parental leave 82-3, 250, 251
Parenting Payment Intervention Pilot (Australia) 201
Parenting Payments (Australia) 4, 65-6, 67, 84, 191
part-time work
Australia 83
France 139, 157-8
gender comparison 157-9
Netherlands 114-15, 123, 193
paternity leave 82-3, 250, 251
pensioner benefits in Australia 80, 81
Personal Responsibility and Work Opportunity Reconciliation Act (1996)(US) 4, 40, 48-9, 57, 235
policy context in UK xv-xx, 30-4, 154-6, 255-9
poverty protection 225-8, 230
poverty rates 6
Australia 67-8
France 142, 145
and making work pay policies 225-8
Netherlands 109, 110, 121-2

DEMOGRAPHY LIBRARY
POPULATION STUDIES CTR.
UNIV. OF PENNSYLVANIA
403 MCNEIL/6298